Kurds, Arabs and Britons

KURDS, ARABS and BRITONS
The Memoir of Wallace Lyon in Iraq 1918–44

EDITED AND WITH AN INTRODUCTION
BY D. K. FIELDHOUSE

I.B.Tauris *Publishers*
LONDON • NEW YORK

Acknowledgement of souces for maps and pictures, with thanks.

The maps were drawn from the following originals:

Maps 1 and 2: C. M. Andrew and A. S. Kanya-Forstner, *France Overseas* (Thames and Hudson, London 1981;

Map 3: J. Marlowe, *Late Victorian* (Cresset Press, London, 1967);

Map 4: C. J. Edmonds, *Kurds, Turks and Arabs* (Oxford University Press, London, 1957).

Illustrations:

Jacket Illustration is from A. M. Hamilton, *Road Through Kurdistan* (Faber and Faber, London, 1937);

from the Middle East Centre archive, Oxford:
 Illustrations 2, 7, 9, the Vyvyan Holt Collection
 Illustrations 8, 11, 12, 15, the Edmonds Collection
 Illustrations 14, 16 the Freya Stark Collection

from C. J. Edmonds, *Kurds, Turks and Arabs*, Illustration 6;

from J. Marlowe, *Late Victorian*, Illustrations 2, 5;

the other Illustrations are from the W. A. Lyon Papers.

Published in 2002 by I.B.Tauris & Co Ltd,
6 Salem Road, London W2 4BU
175 Fifth Avenue, New York NY 10010
www.ibtauris.com

In the United States of America and in Canada distributed by
St. Martin's Press, 175 Fifth Avenue, New York NY 10010

Copyright © D. K. Fieldhouse, 2002

The right of D. K. Fieldhouse to be identified as the author of this work has been asserted by him in accordance with the Copyright, Designs and Patents Act, 1988.

All rights reserved. Except for brief quotations in a review, this book, or any part thereof, may not be reproduced, stored in or introduced into a retrieval system, or transmitted, in any form or by any means, electronic, mechanical, photocopying, recording or otherwise, without the prior written permission of the publisher.

ISBN 1 86064 613 1

A full CIP record for this book is available from the British Library
A full CIP record for this book is available from the Library of Congress

Library of Congress catalog card: available

Set in Monotype Garamond by Ewan Smith, London
Printed and bound in Great Britain by MPG Books Ltd, Bodmin

Contents

List of Illustrations	vi
Preface	vii
Acknowledgements	x
A Note on Spelling	xi
Maps	xiv–xviii

Introduction: The Background, Iraq 1918–44 — 1

1. Iraq as a British Dependency 1918–44 / 1 2. The Iraqi State 1918–44 / 22
3. The Kurds and British Over-rule / 33 4. Wallace Lyon's Career / 48

'Buyurun Bakinez': A Memoir by Wallace Lyon — 59

1	Mosul, Dohuk and the 1920 Rising, 1918–20	61
2	Arbil: The 'Election' of King Faisal, 1921	84
3	Arbil and Kirkuk: Tribal Risings and the Campaign against the Turks, 1922	107
4	Sir Henry Dobbs, 1923–24	129
5	The Visit of King Faisal and the League of Nations Commission, 1924–25	141
6	Bringing Sulaimani under Iraqi Rule, 1925–26	154
7	Sulaimani: Shaikh Mahmud and Local Society, 1926–29	164
8	Kirkuk: People and Locusts, 1929–30	170
9	Mosul: The Frontier Commission and the End of the Mandate, 1930–32	178
10	Baghdad: Land Settlement in Kut and Kirkuk, 1932–33	194
11	Kirkuk: The Army Coup and Revolution, 1934–41	202
12	Political Adviser to the Indian Army in Iraq and the End of Service, 1941–44	219
	Select Bibliography: Iraq 1914–44	229
	Index	231

Illustrations

1. Lieut. Col. W. A. Lyon in uniform, c. 1939.
2. W. A. Lyon, Capt. C. E. Littledale and Sir Henry Dobbs, the High Commissioner in a characteristically informal pose, mid-1920s.
3. Sir Arnold Wilson, 1921, from a portrait by Eric Kennington, after he had left Baghdad.
4. Sir F. Humphreys, the High Commissioner, Vyvyan Holt, the Oriental Secretary and others, in 1932, just before the end of the mandate.
5. The Cairo Conference, March,1921, which decided the future of Iraq. Front row: Sir Herbert Samuel, Winston Churchill, Sir Percy Cox. Second row: Sir Arnold Wilson, Gertrude Bell, Jafar al-Askari, T. E. Lawrence.
6. The Mosul Commission, 1925, which settled the future of Mosul.
7. The Mardin Frontier Conference, 1930, described by Lyon.
8. Miss Gertrude Bell and others, c. 1921. She was a dominant influence on Baghdad policy 1918-21 as Oriental Secretary and eventually became an enthusiastic proponent of Faisal as king.
9. Sir K. Cornwallis, the Ambassador, Lord Mountbatten, the Regent Abd al-Illah, and Nuri as-Said, prime minister, in 1941, after the end of the Rashid Ali crisis.
10. King Faisal visiting the Patriarch at Khoun Khyat in 1926, as part of his strategy of assuring non-Muslims of his favour.
11. Mahmud Pasha, chief of the Jaf, and Babakr-i Selim Agha, chief of the Pizhdar, who supported the government loyally throughout the critical period before 1925.
12. The Lady Adila Khan of Halabja, widow of Usman Pasha Jaf, brother of Mahmud Pasha, and another strong supporter of the government.
13. Shaikh 'Mulla' Mustafa Barzani, 1923: a leading Kurdish nationalist and rival of Mahmud Bazanji, who features in Lyon's account as a great warrior.
14. Kurds drinking coffee in a typical Kurdish tent.
15. An RAF plane over the Gara Sind, 1924: typifying the dangers pilots faced when 'pacifying' Kurdish rebels in the early 1920s as part of Churchill's scheme to police Iraq from the air.
16. Shaikh Mahmud Barzinja in exile in 1942, taken by Freya Stark, who sympathized with him.

Preface

Wallace Lyon was an administrator in Iraq from the end of the war with the Ottoman empire in 1918 until near the end of the Second World War. After service in France he had been an officer with the 52nd Sikh Frontier Force which was sent to Iraq in 1917 as part of the British and Indian force that was to complete the conquest of Mesopotamia in 1918. Thus he happened to be in Mesopotamia late in 1918 when the Civil Administration was urgently looking for civil administrators. He was sent to Kurdistan where he spent most of the next twenty-six years. In this he was exceptional. The great majority of British non-technical officials were gradually replaced by Iraqis after 1921, when the Iraqi state and monarchy were set up, culminating in 1932, when Iraq became a sovereign state. Lyon survived this second cut by being appointed Land Settlement Officer. After the attempted revolution of 1941 he rejoined the Indian Army and was appointed a Political Adviser with the British Army, 'Paiforce', remaining until the end of 1944. He then resigned from the Indian Army and entered the Consular Service, serving until 1949 and his final retirement as Consul in Harar.

After retirement he wrote his memoirs. This, as is explained in 'A Note on Spelling', was done secretively and was completed in 1964. It was not intended for immediate publication, mainly because many of those mentioned in it were still alive; though he told his daughter, Sheila Lyon, for whom it was written, that he hoped that I, as her husband, would eventually edit and publish it. He did not give it a title, simply putting 'Buyurun Bakinez' (roughly translated as 'take a look inside') on the cover. Hence the title of this book is mine, a deliberate echo of the title of C. J. Edmonds's *Kurds, Turks and Arabs*. Lyon died in 1977; and by the end of the century it is unlikely that many if any of those mentioned in the memoir are still alive. The time therefore seems ripe for publishing an edited version.

The case for doing so is that, although there is a very large literature on what may be called the high politics of the creation and organization of Iraq during this first quarter-century, and a good deal on the Kurds as an ethnic group and political problem, there is very little on how the British actually ran or manipulated the Kurdish region of northern Iraq during the period of the Mandate to 1932, or thereafter while Britain had extensive treaty rights there. There are only three comparable personal memoirs on Kurdistan in this period of which I am aware: W. R. Hay's *Two Years in Kurdistan. Experiences of a Political Officer 1918–1920* (London, 1921); Edmonds's *Kurds, Turks and Arabs* (London, 1957); and A. M. Hamilton's *Road through Kurdistan: The Narrative of an Engineer in Iraq* (London, 1937). Hay left Iraq in October 1920 to work in the Indian Political Department, so his account covers only the critical first two years after the end of the First World War. Lyon is not mentioned in his account, though they must have known each other. Edmonds was a close colleague and friend of Lyon from 1922 and there is much synergy between their accounts. But Edmonds left Kurdistan in 1925 to become Assistant Adviser to the Ministry of Interior until 1933, then briefly Adviser to the Ministry for Foreign Affairs, and finally, from 1935 to 1945, Adviser to the Ministry of Interior. Edmonds thus moved from the Kurdish area to the central government in Baghdad in the mid-1920s and never wrote in detail about his later experiences, though there is a great deal in his unpublished papers about the problems of Kurdistan after 1925. Finally Hamilton, a New Zealander, was a road engineer in the Ruwandiz region from 1928 to 1932. His book is mainly about building the road through the Ruwandiz gorge, but also contains much material on people and events in Kurdistan which intermesh with Lyon's narrative for those four years.

By contrast with these men, Lyon stayed almost continuously in Kurdistan until 1944, and this gives his memoir its special value. It provides a detailed and lively account of the life and work of a Briton who had to deal with the problems of a mixed Arab, Turkish and Kurdish population, and in particular with the feuds of the Kurdish shaikhs in the mountains. In the early years, until 1926, these were complicated by Turkish irredentism and perpetually by the existence of a largely open Persian frontier. His account plays down the dangers and emphasizes the excitement and the interest of the job. It therefore fills a substantial gap in the history of the evolution of modern Iraq and, in particular, of Kurdistan and throws much light on the origins of later and contemporary Kurdish problems. Lyon became a devoted supporter of the interests of the Kurds and in the end decided to retire largely because of the continuing refusal of Arab politicians to fulfil promises made to the Kurds or to give them a fair share in the increasing wealth generated by petroleum. After retirement he remained in contact with Kurdish leaders and strongly supported their claims for greater autonomy.

In editing the memoir I have cut out virtually all the material relating to Lyon's private life and family, both before and after 1918, indicating briefly in parenthesis when he went on leave, married and so on, but summarizing his earlier and later life at the end of the Introduction. I have also, regretfully, had to shorten the rest of the text very substantially to make it possible to publish at reasonable length. In particular I have excised much interesting material on sporting activities and many anecdotes. Other adjustments to the text are indicated in the 'Note on Spelling'. In the Introduction I have attempted to do two things: to put Lyon's regional narrative into the broader context of Iraqi history, and so to make his text largely self-explanatory; and at the same time to provide my own interpretation of that very controversial subject from the standpoint of a general imperial historian rather than that of a specialist or expert in Iraqi or Middle Eastern history, which I am not. To do this rigorously I would have needed to spend a long period of basic research in the archives, including the Public Record Office and various other MS collections of Lyon's contemporaries. I have not done so, partly because I was not prepared to devote several more years to the project, and partly because I am not writing my own account and would have used such information mainly to footnote Lyon's text. I did, however, work through some of the more relevant material in the Edmonds Papers in the Middle East Archive at St Antony's College, Oxford, which provided collaborative evidence on the period before and after 1925 and which, as mentioned in the 'Note on Spelling', enabled me to standardize Lyon's somewhat variable spelling of names, places and titles. For the rest I have relied on the wide range of published material and on the advice of friends and colleagues.

D. K. Fieldhouse
Jesus College, Cambridge
March 2000

Acknowledgements

I received valuable help and advice from Clare Brown, Archivist at the Middle East Centre, St Antony's College, Oxford, on both primary sources and photographs. I am grateful also to Professor W. Roger Louis of the University of Texas at Austin for reading the MS and making helpful comments; to Anna Flood, who copied the original memoir on to disks; to the History Department and the Faculty of Asian Studies, Australian National University, for providing excellent facilities to me as a Visiting Fellow in 1999 and 2000; and to Janet Law who copy-edited the final version. My wife Sheila was able to fill in a number of gaps from her father's conversations. Jesus College, Cambridge, met the cost of transcribing the memoir.

A Note on Spelling

In editing Lyon's memoirs I faced a number of technical decisions. The most important was how to reproduce his text. This was written after his final retirement (from Ethiopia) in 1949 and was finished by 1964. He did so secretively (because, for whatever reason, his wife did not approve of his doing it), from memory, and without access to standard reference works or even his own papers. These, including the letters he wrote regularly to his parents and later his wife, would have been extremely helpful to me. None has survived, apart from a small folder of limited value, which I have referred to as 'Lyon Papers'. The longhand script was then typed by a secretary who was evidently not familiar with the place or period. The result is that the spelling of names of people, places and institutions in the typescript (the longhand version does not survive) is both internally inconsistent and also often different from that used by most of his contemporaries (which differed widely) and in his own reports etcetera of the period, as well as by later historians. Thus, the text usually has 'sheikh', though his reports concerning the Mosul Commission of 1925 have the then usual 'shaikh' (by contrast with the later 'shaykh'); and he appears later (though not consistently) to have altered 'Leiva' (for district) in the typescript to the more usual 'liwa'. I decided that, since the importance of the book lies in the light it throws on the relations between the Kurds, Arabs and British officials during this crucial first quarter-century of Iraqi history, it was more important that the printed version should be compatible with other works of the same period and the names readily recognizable than that it should slavishly follow the typescript. I therefore took the book published by C. J. Edmonds in 1957, *Kurds, Turks and Arabs*, together with Edmonds's papers in the Middle East Centre of St Antony's College, Oxford, as the standard for spelling. Edmonds, who was a close friend and colleague of Lyon from 1922 to 1944, wrote his book with full access to his own diaries and papers, retaining contemporary usage. Where I could not match a name or term in his work I used *Iraq, 1900–1950. A Political Economic and Social History* by S. H. Longrigg (another contemporary and colleague), Sir A. T. Wilson's *Mesopotamia 1917–1920: A Clash of*

Loyalties, and other contemporary works. In this way I have aimed to provide both internal consistency and compatibility with other related studies. Where I was unable to find an equivalent spelling in these or other sources, I have left the original.

I have taken further liberties with the original typescript. It was deficient in dates and some relevant details, and I have in some cases inserted these in square brackets. The punctuation was somewhat haphazard, and either Lyon or his typist was over-exuberant in the use of the upper case and exclamation marks. I have therefore done some copy-editing to tidy it up, adopting modern conventions, and translated a few archaic slang words. My alterations and substitutions in the text (but not altered spellings or punctuation) are indicated by square brackets, the extensive excisions by the conventional full points. Lyon did not use any diacritical marks; neither have I, either in the text or my own additional material. I am confident that Lyon would have approved of these changes; he did not write for publication nor regard this as a sacred text. A copy of the original MS is deposited in the Archive of the Middle East Centre, St Antony's College, Oxford, for comparison.

The following lists show the original spelling of a number of places, people, tribes and official titles, as they appear in the original typescript in the left-hand column and their replacements in the right.

Places

Acra	Aqra
Ainsifni	Ayn Sifni
Alton Keupri	Altun Kopru
Amadia	Amadiya
Asker	Askar
Azizeyah	Aziziya
Babagurga	Baba Gurgur
Baradost	Baradust
Bazian	Bazyan
Beirout (etc)	Beirut
Bira Kupra	Bira Kapra
Chemechemal	Chamchemal
Ctesipon	Ctesiphon
Deir al Zor	Deir ez-Zor
Dihala	Diyala
Diwania	Diwaniya
Duwin Qaleh	Duwin Qala
Ghazir	Khazir
Goweir	Quweir (ferry over the Great Zab)
Habbanieh (etc)	Habbaniyah

A Note on Spelling · xiii

Haibes Sultan	Haiba Sultan
Hakiari	Hakari
Halebja	Halabja
Hasstch	Hassech
Howega	Hawija
Jabel Hanrin	Jabal Hamrin
Kanikin	Khanaqin
Kerind	Karind
Kerman Shah	Kermanshah
Khailani	Khalhani
Koisanjak	Koi Sanjaq
Kushnao	Khoshnaw
Kut Alamara	Kut-al-Amara
Mergasur	Margasur
Pizhder	Pizhdar
Rania	Ranya
Rowanduz	Ruwandiz
Sangao	Sangaw
Serkhuma	Sarkhuma
Shahjbazher	Shar Bazher
Shaklawa	Shaqlawa
Shergat	Sharqat
Simel	Simayl
Spillik	Spilik
Sulaimania	Sulaimani
Tel Afar	Tal Afar
Telkeif	Tall Kayf

Names of People and Tribes

Abdulillah	Abd al-Ilah
Ahmed Barzani	Ahmad Barzani
Ahmed Osman	Ahmad Usman
Ali Ridah	Ali Rida al-Askari
Babeker	Babakr
Bedouin	Beduin
Bekr Sidqi	Bakr Sidqi
Berzinja	Barzinja
Euzdemir	Oz Demir [Ali Shefiq]
Feisul	Faisal
Fettah Pasha	Fattah Pasha
Hashimite	Hashemite
Herki	Harki
Hikmat Suleiman	Hikmat Sulayman
Hussein Beg	Husain Beg Nastchizada
Hussein (Husayn), Sharif	Husain
Ismael Agha (Simko)	Ismail Agha

xiv · Kurds, Arabs and Britons

Jaffar Pasha	Jafar al-Askari
Jebbur (Jibbur)	Jibbur
Jemil Agha	Jemal Agha
Jemil Madfai	Jamil al-Midfai
Kerim Fetteh Beg	Kerim-i Fattah Beg
Kirdars	Qirdars
Marshiman	Marshimun
Michaeli	Mikaeli
Mirani Abdulqadir	Mirani Abdul Qadir Beg
Muzabim-Al-Pachachi	Muzahim al-Pachachi
Naftchis	Naftchizadas
Nuri el Said	Nuri as-Said
Pizider	Pizhdar
Reshid Ali	Rashid Ali al-Gaylani
Riza Shah	Reza Shah
Roghzadi	Ruthzadi
Sayed Ahmed Khaniqa	Saiyid-i Ahmad Khanaqah
Sayed Taha	Saiyid Taha
Sayed Talib	Saiyid Talib
Tahsin Askeri	Tahsin al-Askari
Turkhani	Takhani
Umar Nedmi	Umar Nazmi Beg
Yacobis	Yaqubizadas
Yezides	Yezidis
Zerari	Zarari

Terms and Titles

Emir	Amir
Fetwa	fatwah
Leiva	liwa
Levies/levies	Levies
Mutasarrif	mutasarrif
Quimagam	qaimmaqam
Reemeedhan	Ramadan
Sanjak	sanjaq
Serai	serai
Sheikh	Shaikh
Suni	Sunni
Valiet	wilayat

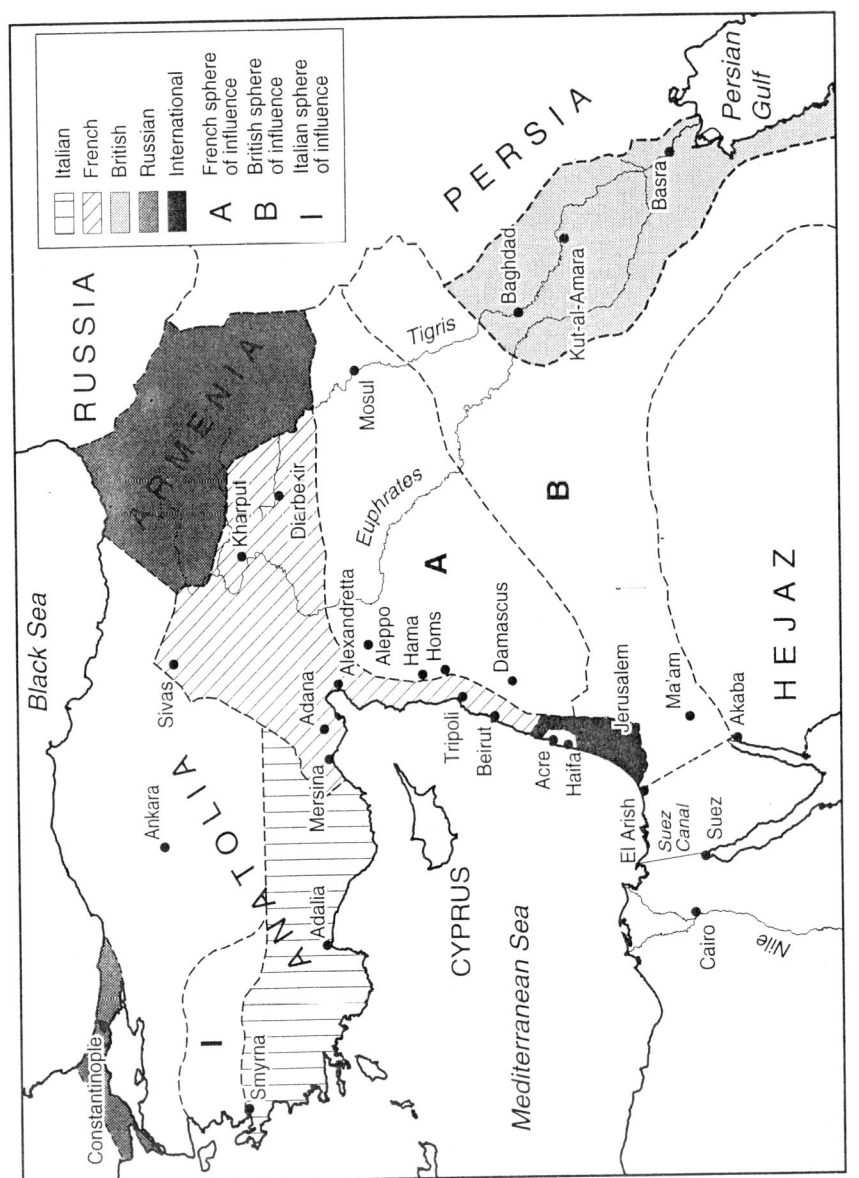

Map 1 The Sykes–Picot Agreement, 1916

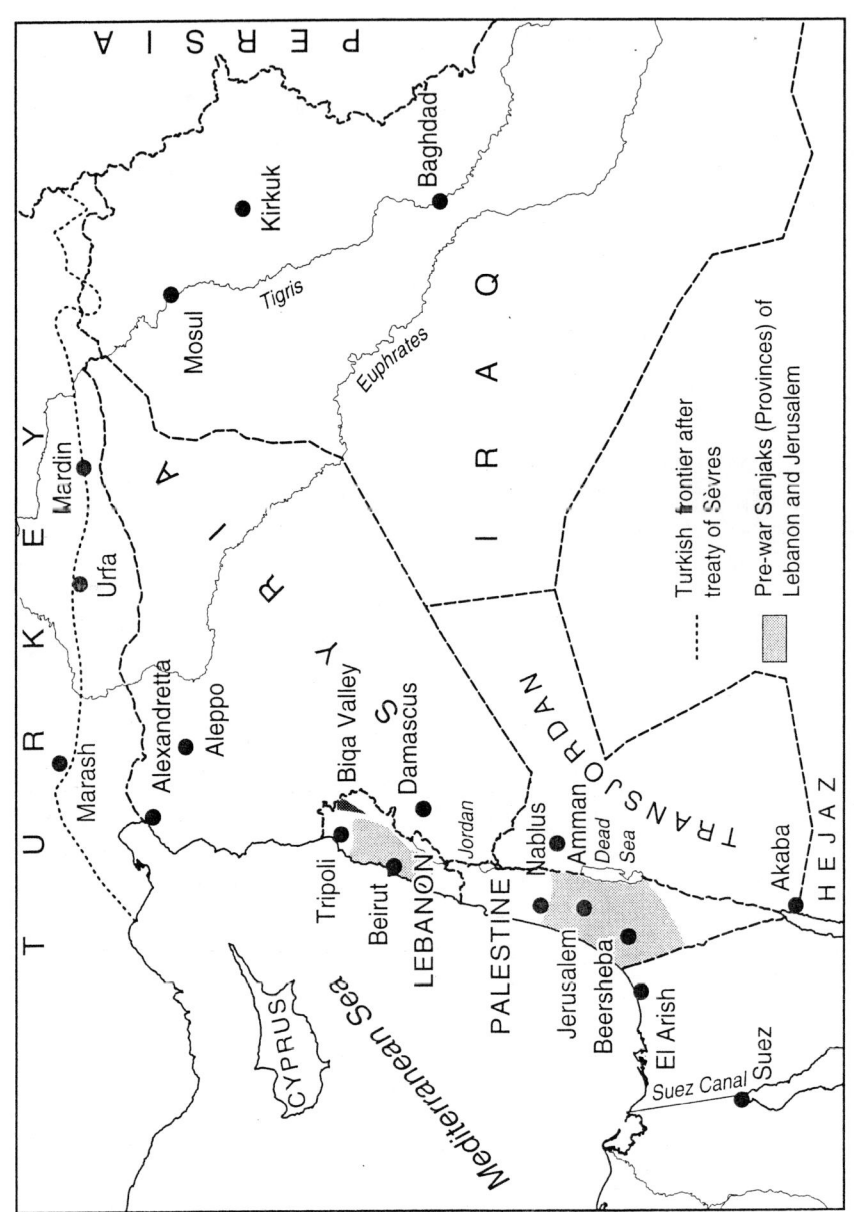

Map 2 The Middle East Mandates, 1922

Map 3 Iraq, 1926

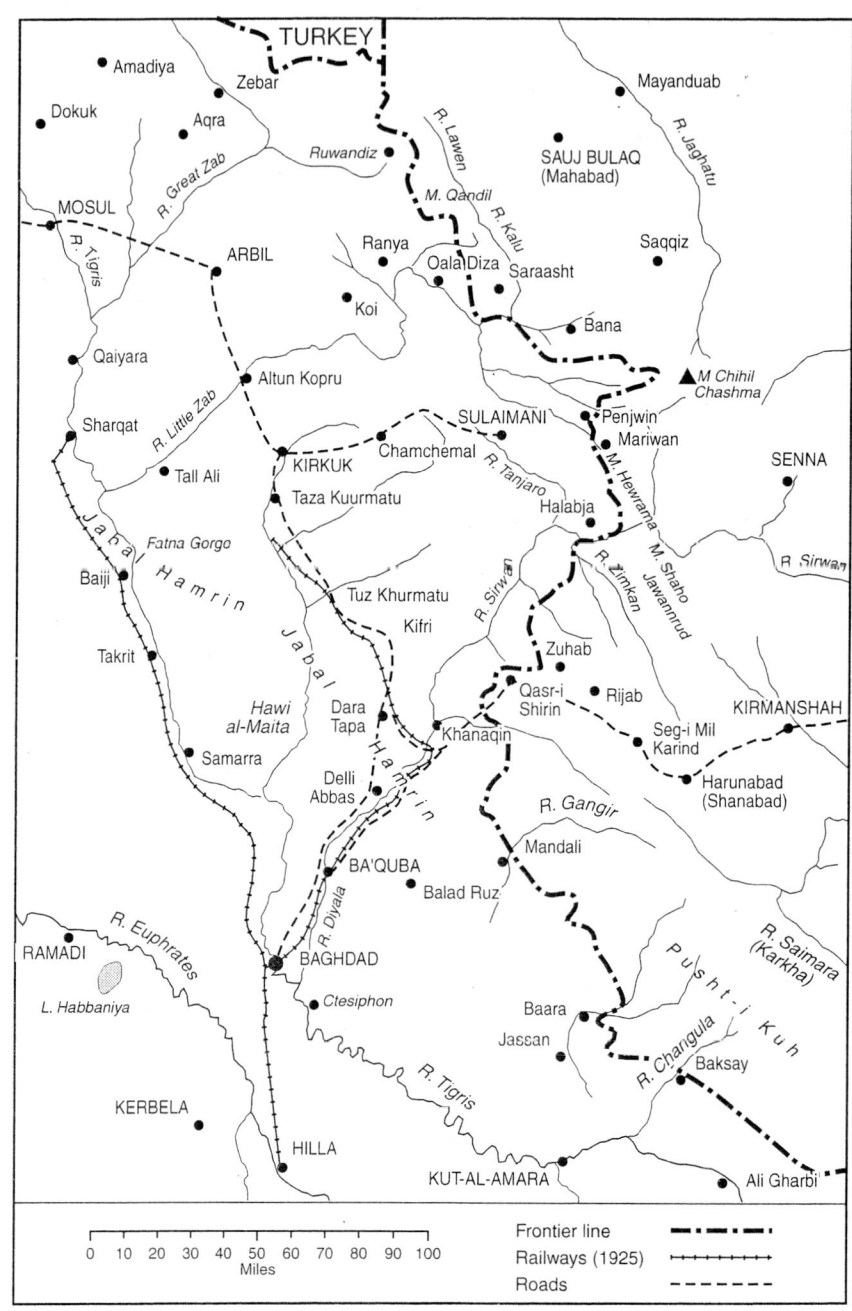

Map 4 Part of the Iraqi-Persian boundary

INTRODUCTION

The Background: Iraq 1918–44

1. Iraq as a British Dependency 1918–44

The fundamental fact of Iraqi history until the Revolution of 1958 was the ambiguity of the British position there. During this period Britain's formal position in what had previously been loosely called Mesopotamia went through three phases. Initially, from the first landing of Indian troops in Basra in November 1914 to 1920, this was a military occupation: there was no civil state and no long-term strategy. From 1920 to 1932 Britain acted as Mandatory under the League of Nations to the newly created state of Iraq, British powers being defined by the treaty drawn up in 1922 but only finally ratified by the Iraqi parliament in 1924. Finally, from 1932, when Iraq became a sovereign state and the Mandate was ended, the British position depended entirely on the treaty that was renegotiated in 1930 to last for twenty-five years, though this could be revised after 1950.

These changes reflected the peculiarity of the British position. Seen in the wider context of British and European overseas expansion, Iraq was exceptional in that its occupation was never expected to lead to permanent alien rule. There were earlier precedents. It can be argued that initially the many protectorates declared in parts of Africa in the later nineteenth century were regarded as transient: they were not formally annexed as colonies because their future was uncertain, and it was assumed that alien control was to be supervisory rather than intensive. Similar principles operated in places such as the Malay States, which were protected states, not British dependencies. But over time the concept of a protectorate or protected state hardened into quasi-colonial rule; and by 1918 neither Britain nor other European protecting states conceived of giving up their control. In all but name and juridical status these places had become colonies.

In fact, the closest parallel to the post-1918 position of Iraq was that of Egypt since 1882. Britain had occupied Egypt on the somewhat specious grounds of the instability of the Khedival regime and its effects on

European interests. But the occupation was stated to be temporary: the Khedive remained the nominal ruler under notional Ottoman suzerainty, and all senior public offices were held by 'Egyptians', though many of them were in fact Turks, Circassians, Albanians and so on from other parts of the Ottoman empire. Moreover, Britain accepted the continued paramountcy of the Porte in Istanbul. British officials in Egypt were technically advisers to their local ministers, though in practice their advice had to be accepted. It was only in 1914, when war was declared on the Ottomans, that Britain declared a protectorate over Egypt; and thereafter it was an open question whether Egypt would remain part of the British empire indefinitely.

There were many similarities between the initial occupation of Egypt and that of Mesopotamia in and after 1914. Before 1914 the British had no intention of annexing any part of Mesopotamia, or indeed other parts of the surviving Ottoman empire in the Middle East. Since the early nineteenth century it had been a basic premise of British foreign policy that the Ottoman empire in the Straits and to the south should be protected against the Russians or other predators, mainly to safeguard the British route to India and the East. This strategy had been called into question by the growing influence of Germany in Istanbul before 1914 and more particularly the threat posed by the projected Berlin to Baghdad railway if it was extended south to Basra and the Gulf. But before 1914 British strategy was to negotiate on the Basra railway question in order to internationalize the southern section; and in this it had been largely successful by 1914.[1] Thus, there was no long-term British intention of occupying Basra or any other part of Mesopotamia. As late as early October 1914 Lord Hardinge, Viceroy and Governor-General of India, in whose sphere of influence the Gulf lay, together with Sir Percy Cox, Secretary to the Foreign Department of the Indian government, were against sending an Indian force to the Gulf for fear both of pushing the Turks into war and also alienating the Indian Muslim population.

Hence the evolution of British control over Mesopotamia from 1914 was primarily the accident of war. The Indian Expeditionary Force (IEF) sent to the Gulf early in October 1914 was intended to secure the safety of the Abadan oil refinery and pipeline in Persia, along with Kuwait and Mohammera as quasi-British protectorates, against possible Turkish attack. It was only with the formal declaration of war on 5 November (after the Turks had attacked Russian Black Sea forts) that the IEF occupied Basra. Even so, British intentions remained entirely unclear for six years, until the acceptance of the League of Nations Mandate in 1920. During the war the safety of Basra and the Abadan oil refinery seemed to demand defence in depth against the Turks holding the rest of Mesopotamia. This necessarily involved the occupation of Baghdad; but the IEF was not authorized to attempt this until April 1915, and this led to military defeat at Ctesiphon in November, the retreat to Kut-al-Amara, and the surrender of April 1916. It was not until the end of 1916 that the push to Baghdad was resumed, partly at least to relieve Turkish pressure on Russia; and the city was not taken until August 1917. Thereafter it was necessary to continue the campaign against strong Turkish forces in Mosul wilayat, and this continued until after the Armistice of Mudros with Turkey on 30 October 1918 with the military occupation of Mosul City on 7 November. Since this occurred after the armistice, the Turks continued to claim until 1926 that Mosul was theirs.

At no time before the end of 1918, therefore, were the British clear about their future position in Mesopotamia. Indeed, their indecision had hampered the military occupation because it was impossible to assure the local population that the region would not be returned to the Ottomans. Their collaboration was therefore for the most part conditional and uncertain. The fact was that the future of Mesopotamia was of little direct importance to the British government: its treatment was conditioned by complex international considerations and negotiations.[2] Broadly, two parallel and to some extent interacting forces were eventually to determine the future of Mesopotamia.

The first was the diplomacy that reflected the territorial ambitions of all the Allies once war had begun with the Ottomans. By early in 1915 claims were being staked. Russia wanted Istanbul and the Straits and possibly parts of eastern Anatolia. The French from the start demanded control of Syria, which was then understood to include the wilayats of Aleppo and Syria, Lebanon, Beirut and the sanjaq of Jerusalem. France was a minor trading partner of these areas but was a major investor there and had long regarded itself as the protector of Christian interests. Britain had no specific claims but was certain to wish to dominate the Persian Gulf and to keep possible rivals away from Basra, and would expect rewards to balance those of France. When they entered the war both Italy and Greece expected territory in western Anatolia. For the future of Iraq, the most important of these competing claims were those of Britain and France.

Their negotiations began late in 1915 after the so-called de Bunsen Interdepartmental Committee in Britain had spent several months drawing up scenarios for the future of the Middle East. The negotiations were carried out on the British side by Sir Mark Sykes, then an assistant to Maurice (later Lord) Hankey, Secretary to the Committee of Imperial Defence, later the First Secretary of the Cabinet. Sykes had worked with Kitchener when British High Commissioner in Cairo. He was a francophile and also a believer in the need for the Arab subjects of the Ottomans to govern themselves. On the French side the negotiator was François Georges-Picot (always known as Picot), a professional in the French Foreign Affairs Ministry. They discussed the issues during the winter of 1915–16, even visiting Petrograd in March 1916 to obtain Russian agreement. The result was the famous Sykes–Picot Agreement which was given its final form in letters exchanged between London and Paris.

The Agreement was never implemented in full; its main significance was that it was later said to be inconsistent with commitments being made simultaneously with the Sharif of Mecca. In essence the Agreement was for a broad division of Syria and Mesopotamia into two spheres of interest running west to east. France would dominate north of a line roughly from Damascus to Mosul (it was assumed that Russia would have the north-eastern part of Mesopotamia), Britain all areas south of a line from Gaza to Kirkuk. The Jerusalem sanjaq, due to its special religious significance, would come under a different international regime. Within their allocated sphere the French would have direct control over the coastal region of Syria, but the four main inland cities, including Damascus, would be under some unspecified Arab regime, though with French influence. Britain would control Haifa and Acre to provide direct access to the sea and had gained French acceptance of their control of the Mesopotamian wilayats of Baghdad and Basra, and so security for the route to India. They also extracted guarantees for their prospective oil interest in the Mosul region.

While this old-fashioned (because reminiscent of late nineteenth-century partitions) territorial distribution was being negotiated, a parallel set of proposals had been evolved in Cairo and commitments made which were later alleged to be inconsistent with Sykes–Picot. These stemmed from pre-1914 schemes hatched by Kitchener as Consul General in Cairo who retained the earlier British dream of controlling the whole route from the Mediterranean to India.[3] His idea was that Husain, the Sharif of Mecca, guardian of the Muslim holy cities of Mecca and Medina, might be induced to throw off Ottoman rule and become the ruler of a maritime state ruled by his Hashemite family but under British protection. Husain, for his part, appointed by Istanbul only in 1908, was ambitious and feared that he might be replaced by Istanbul, which had the right of appointment to the Sharifate. He also had ambitions to replace the Sultan as Caliph. Before 1914 Kitchener had been approached by some influential Arabs including the Amir Abdullah, a son of the Sharif, about whether Britain would support Arab ambitions for greater freedom from Ottoman rule. Kitchener had been evasive; but in November 1914, once Britain was at war with Turkey, Kitchener sent messages to Abdullah which suggested strong British support for an Arab movement and the possibility of the Caliphate being transferred to Mecca or Medina.

This was the genesis of what became the 1916 Arab Revolt in the Hejaz, and also of the myth that the British had promised to create an Arab kingdom covering most of Syria and Mesopotamia. From the British standpoint there were obvious potential advantages in an Arab resistance movement to distract Turkish forces from other fronts, notably the Dardanelles, and British support for this would please the substantial number of Arab nationalists in Cairo. A complex correspondence took place from 1914 to 1915 between British officials in Cairo, led by Sir Henry McMahon (acting High Commissioner) and Khartoum (Governor-General Sir Reginald Wingate) on the one side and on the other Abdullah and other Arab leaders. An Arab Bureau was set up in Cairo by Sykes in November 1915, staffed by a group of expert Arabists led by Dr D. G. Hogarth and (Sir) Ronald Storrs and eventually including T. E. Lawrence and Gertrude Bell. Meantime, on 24 October 1915, McMahon, in the face of disasters in Gallipoli and a reported loss of confidence by the Sharif, had made the first apparently firm commitment to Husain. He stated that, subject to three reservations, Britain was 'prepared to recognize and support the independence of the Arabs' within the wide limits Husain had demanded. There were three major excluded areas: the coastal districts to the west of the four main Syrian 'districts' of Damascus, Homs, Hama and Aleppo; districts covered by existing British commitments (effectively the Persian Gulf area of Arabia); and regions in which the interests of France made it impossible for Britain to act alone.

On the face of it this appeared to promise British support for an independent Arab kingdom covering virtually all inland Syria, much of northern Mesopotamia, and southern Arabia. Since the eventual pattern of post-1919 territories was strikingly different it was then and later widely asserted that the British had played a double game. Hence the later claim by Lawrence and others that the British had stimulated an heroic Arab rising, which started in September 1916 and ended with the conquest of Damascus in 1918, but had then reneged on their commitments to the Arabs. In fact, it is clear that this over-dramatized the situation. Although Sykes–Picot was officially 'secret' until it was published by the post-revolutionary Soviet government in 1917, the negotiations were known to Husain and his son, the Amir Faisal, from the start. They may not have liked the result but they acquiesced. Kedourie among others has therefore claimed that the Sharif's later disappointments were unreasonable. He had been misled by Kitchener's suggestion of the Caliphate and was pushed on by a number of Arabs, many of them from Mesopotamia, who had deserted from Ottoman appointments in the army and administration and who had gambled their lives and careers on inheriting senior positions in a vast Arab kingdom. In Kedourie's view, Sykes–Picot, far from being a dishonourable rejection of commitments to Arab nationalism, was 'the last responsible attempt on the part of Europe to cope with the dissolution of the Ottoman Empire, and to prevent the dissolution from bringing disaster'.[4]

Neither the Sykes–Picot Agreement nor the promises made to Husain survived into the post-war settlement of the Middle East. But they had important consequences for the future of Iraq. Territorially the 1916 project was replaced by the allocation in 1920, at the San Remo Conference, of League of Nations Mandates for Syria (including both the Mediterranean and inland regions) to France and of the whole of 'Palestine' (as the old sanjaq of Jerusalem was now called) and Mesopotamia to Britain. Mandates (a new concept) were protectorates in all but name, which seemed to imply quasi-colonial control. But in June 1918 the British government promised, in the so-called 'Declaration to the Seven' (Syrian nationalists), that the British government would recognize 'the complete and sovereign independence' of inhabitants of territories liberated from the Ottomans by the Arabs. Then on 8 November 1918 the British and French governments issued a joint Declaration promising 'national governments as administrators deriving their authority from the initiative and free choice of indigenous populations'. These specious promises were made in the context of the apparent success of the Arab army under Amir Faisal which, after a long campaign in the Hejaz, later romanticized by Lawrence in *The Seven Pillars of Wisdom* and other publications, was finally permitted by General Allenby, after his defeat of the Turks in Palestine and Syria, to be the first to enter Damascus. This appeared to conform to the criterion of the British Declaration of June 1918; and on that assumption Faisal and his army, led mostly by Iraqi-born ex-Ottoman officers, was able to set up a 'national' regime in inland Syria, strongly supported by the secret Iraqi society in Aleppo, Al Ahd al-Iraqi. Among their leaders were Jafar al-Askari, the Military Governor of Aleppo, and Ali Jawdat al-Ayyubi, both to be leading political figures in Iraq.

One root of most later developments in Iraq lay in the fact that this dream of an independent Arab kingdom of Syria was destroyed by the French in July 1920 when they ejected Faisal from Damascus. From the occupation of Damascus by British/Australian troops and, symbolically, by the Hejaz army under Faisal, late in 1918, until then it had seemed possible that Faisal would be king of an independent Syrian state east of the French coastal region and including the four main Syrian towns defined in the Sykes–Picot Agreement. This quasi-state was in fact dominated by two groups: the Syrian secret society al-Fatat, which dated from pre-1914 days, and Faisal's Northern Army, mostly officered by Iraqis, many of them members of the Iraqi secret society Al Ahd al-Iraqi. In 1919–20 those who dominated the Syrian government aimed at exploiting British military weakness in northern Iraq by sending military expeditions east towards Mosul, in effect following the model of Sykes–Picot to expand the 'Syrian' kingdom.[5] They had considerable early success, taking Deir ez-Zor in December 1919 and then Tal Afar (a mere 20 miles west of Mosul) in June 1920, where two British officers, Lieutenant Stuart and Major Barlow, and two British soldiers were murdered. The Syrian force then attempted to press on to Mosul, but were defeated by a British force and retreated to Deir ez-Zor. In any case, the following month the French ejected Faisal from Damascus and the dream of an Arab empire based on Syria was over. Faisal, and some of his entourage of mainly ex-Ottoman officers and administrators, went into exile, while many others remained unemployed and dissatisfied in Syria. The British felt some obligation towards both Faisal and his officers. Some, such as Lawrence, believed that Britain had reneged on its commitments to the Hashemite family and, in effect, owed Faisal, and possibly also his brother Abdullah, a kingdom. Others recognized that until the Iraqi officers were repatriated and given employment their friends in Baghdad and elsewhere would constitute a continuing threat to British control. This was one major source of the creation in 1921 of an Iraqi kingdom under Faisal, coupled with that of the entirely artificial kingdom of Trans-Jordan under Abdullah.

The other main root of later developments was the crisis within Mesopotamia in 1919–20. From the end of 1918 until 1921 the internal situation remained dangerously unstable. Government consisted of a military administration under Arnold Wilson as Acting Civil Commissioner during the absence in Persia of Sir Percy Cox, the Civil Commissioner. In Baghdad the central government was set up along broadly British Indian lines, with five major departments under British secretaries (many of them from the Indian Civil Service or the Indian Army) and subordinate departments. Regional government consisted (initially) of sixteen divisions (liwas) into which the three wilayats of Ottoman Mesopotamia had been divided, subdivided into districts (qadhas) and sub-districts (nahiyas). Divisions were run by Political Officers (POs) with two Assistant Political Officers (APOs). To operate this system Wilson had had to recruit from whatever talent he could find. Many were taken from the occupying army, which was mainly the Indian Army: these included Wallace Lyon, who was recruited as an APO at the end of 1918. Others came from the group of Arabists who had been in Mesopotamia during the war in various capacities and had considerable local expert knowledge, or were recruited from Arabic-speaking territories under British control, notably the Sudan. It is important that few could be offered long-term contracts because the future of the country was uncertain: most were on one- or three-year contracts. According to S. H. Longrigg, who was one of those appointed as a PO, most of these officers were imbued with 'energy, personal integrity and good intentions'. But they had the same limitations as their contemporaries in India. They were seen as infidels by most Muslims, particularly the Shia majority, and by many Sunnis, who regretted no longer being under the Caliphate. Although the great majority of indigenous officials were necessarily retained, they now found themselves in relatively subordinate positions and Wilson had made little effort to use educated, especially ex-Sharifian, officers. They also found that the new officials were 'pitiless to long-familiar laxities'. There were other widely-felt grievances. The military occupied many houses, particularly those of notables. Taxation was more burdensome because more efficiently collected. Inflation rates were high. Post-war retrenchment resulted in the dropping of a number of infrastructural projects and there was a general sense of unrealized expectations.[6]

These were predictable consequences of a post-war situation in a newly occupied country. The special feature of Mesopotamia was that its future was entirely uncertain until 1921. It was not until the San Remo Conference of April 1920 that it was decided that Mesopotamia, along with Palestine, would be allotted to Britain as Mandates. In the meantime many interested parties were arguing for different outcomes. The British government seemed quite unable to make up its mind about the long-term future. In May 1919, for example, London seemed to be thinking in terms of a system of indigenous states on the model of the Indian princely states. T. E. Lawrence and his allies were pressing the continuing claims of the Sharif and his son, and had strong support within the Foreign Office. Wilson himself wanted a quasi-protectorate for five years, with Sir Percy Cox as High Commissioner and no Arab ruler, but with Arabs in ministerial and advisory positions.[7] Following the principle of the Anglo-French Declaration of November 1918, Wilson ordered a plebiscite in 1919 in which local notables would be asked three questions: should a unitary state be set up, probably including Mosul; should this state have an Arab titular head; and if so, who might be the best candidate? Predictably, since the local officials were ordered to press for an affirmative answer, there was support for a unitary state and an Arab ruler, but no agreement over who that might be. Though well-meant, the plebiscite was probably a mistake since it gave the impression that Britain had no clear strategy and also aroused latent anti-British feeling in favour of some form of independence. London's decision, taken in June 1920, for elections to a constitutional convention to be followed by the creation of an Arab state, came too late to dampen disaffection.

The major rising of July 1920 fundamentally altered the situation. While the Syrian threat to Mosul had been relatively small, that in the Middle and Lower Euphrates region seriously challenged British rule. The revolt had many aspects. The Shiite priesthood, many of them Persian subjects, preached a jihad against the infidel British rulers, aiming at priestly rule over an Islamic state. Tribal rulers were alienated by more efficient tax-collection by the British since 1917 and regretted the relative autonomy they had enjoyed under inefficient Ottoman rule. Many other landowners and tenants were equally affected by taxation and administrative pressures. Finally, reports of British military defeats in the Mosul wilayat encouraged the view that the conquerors could be defeated. The rising began at Rumaitha on the Lower Euphrates, spread rapidly to the Middle and Upper Euphrates but did not have serious consequences in the Mosul region or in the Tigris valley and Basra. It had been repressed by October, but at huge cost: 426 British (and British Indian) troops killed, 1,228 wounded, 615 missing or taken prisoner. There were over 8,000 casualties among the insurgents. A number of British Political Officers had also been killed, among them Colonel G. E. Leachman.[8] The cost to Britain of the British (including Indian) military occupation was about £35 million in 1919-20 and still £32 million in 1920-21; and this had considerable influence on the major policy decisions taken in 1920-21.

The rising had occurred at a crucial point in British-consideration of the future of Mesopotamia. It is clear that one major reason for the crisis was that London had been unable or unwilling to make any firm commitments or even to give Wilson any clear directives. The excuse was that until the San Remo decisions and the allocation of the Mandate it was impossible to take any decisions. Moreover, Mesopotamia was still under the India Office, which in turn had to negotiate with the Foreign and War Offices. In his own account Wilson complains bitterly that from November 1918 to July 1920 his repeated requests for a statement on the future of the territory and guidance on political and constitutional matters were ignored or evaded.[9] He had, therefore, largely to act on his own initiative and follow his own inclinations. The result was to bring to a head the fundamental issue of the future status of Mesopotamia and the disagreement over this between Wilson, supported by many of the British officials, on the one hand and Sir Percy Cox, Gertrude Bell (his Oriental Secretary), and the majority of later historians and commentators on the other. Since this conflict encapsulates the major issues of later Iraqi history it is necessary to examine the two positions.

Wilson, as an old Indian hand,[10] was never prepared to accept that an entirely independent Arab state in Mesopotamia, ruled along traditional Arab lines, would be viable in the modern world. Contemporary evidence supported this view. Mesopotamia had not been a state, or even a single political entity, in modern times. None of the other Arab societies of the Middle East or Mediterranean was then fully independent: all were under some form of European protection or formal rule, and three of the four most recently taken over by Europeans (Egypt, Tunisia, Morocco) had previously come to grief mainly over their inability to cope with international finance. Moreover, Mesopotamia had no natural unity or a potential ruling family. The Kurds were not Arabs, though mostly devout Muslims. There were substantial Christian and Jewish minorities. There was a fundamental division between Sunni and Shia. Hence, to set up an independent state would be to create an artefact, and to appoint an Arab ruler from outside the region would mean finding someone with no natural call on loyalties.

Wilson concluded that if Mesopotamia was to become a state it would have to be built up gradually. In December 1918, following serious nationalist demonstrations in Baghdad in reaction to the Anglo-French Declaration of 8 November (which Gertrude Bell described as 'at best a regrettable necessity in Iraq')[11] Wilson made a positive suggestion along such lines, based on his understanding of 'educated opinion' in Baghdad. In the longer term an 'Arab state under an Arab Amir' was thought desirable, but with a British High Commissioner and British Advisers in all ministries, as in Egypt. There was no agreement over a possible Amir, but Wilson thought that a son of King Husain 'would meet with widespread acceptance'. Wilson thought, however, that the immediate appointment of a member of the Sharifian family would be impractical due to conflict between Husain and Ibn Saud of Riyadh and the fact that Faisal had been 'nominated' for Syria. He concluded that the best interim solution was that 'Sir P. Cox should be appointed High Commissioner for the first five years without any Arab Amir or other head of the State, but with Arab Ministers backed by British Advisers ... Under such auspices self-determination would be a continuous process; and not a precipitate choice between uncertain courses half understood.'[12] In April 1919, when visiting London, Wilson spelt out his ideas in more detail to the Eastern Committee of the Cabinet. Government would be in the hands of a British High Commissioner without an Amir. There would be no central legislature but councils in each of four proposed provinces, whose members would be elected by the nominated members of divisional councils. The main towns would have nominated Arab governors with British advisers.[13]

Wilson never changed his mind on the need for a period of effective British control during which Arabs could be trained in the business of modern government; and at the start many specialists and supporters of Arab nationalism agreed with him. Gertrude Bell, later a deeply committed supporter of Hashemite rule, adopted the same position until late in 1919.

Thus in December 1915 she had written, 'the Arabs can't govern themselves', and in February 1918, 'they can't conceive an independent Arab government. Nor, I confess, can I. There is no one here who could run it.' In December 1918, 'I wish they would drop the idea of an Arab Emir; it tires me to think of setting up a brand new court here'. It seems that in November 1919 Bell was converted by the Sharifian Yasin al-Hashimi to the idea of a Hashemite Amir and much wider Arab responsibilities, though with effective British support for ten years; and thereafter she gradually moved away from Wilson's approach, culminating in a major disagreement in June 1920.[14]

By March 1920 Wilson had decided that his scheme of April 1919 was no longer adequate. He now proposed to set up 'a Central Legislative Council, with the High Commissioner (when he should arrive) as President, and Arab members in charge of Departments, with British Secretaries'. He got no reply from London, so he set up a committee under his Judicial Adviser, Sir Edgar Bonham-Carter, who had been recruited from Egypt and who, in February 1919, had argued for an Arab cabinet and senior civil servants under British supervision along Egyptian lines.[15] The committee's report suggested postponing the nomination of a ruler since no Sharifian candidate would be acceptable to the majority in Mesopotamia. Meantime there would be a nominated Council of State under an Arab president but with a British official majority. The Arab members should be consulted by the British Secretary on matters of importance but the High Commissioner should have a veto on all decisions. There should also be a Legislative Assembly whose members would be elected or appointed by local bodies, which in turn would be elected by constituencies of about 50,000, but with special seats for Jews and Christians. Arab members of the Council of State would be ex-officio members of the Assembly. The Assembly could approve laws issued by the Council and budgets drawn up by the High Commissioner. Its members could initiate legislation (except on tax and constitutional matters) and put written questions. This constitution was to last for seven years, after which the British government would set up a commission to inquire into the operation of the system.[16]

These proposals were in line with Wilson's thinking. Seen in the wider context of British imperial history they clearly represent an amalgam of contemporary Indian and Egyptian practice in that they provided an active, prestigious and educational role for indigenous notables while preserving overriding British control.[17] They were wired to the India Office on 27 April 1920. It appears that the India Office was willing to accept them, but the Foreign Office blocked them until the peace treaty was signed with Turkey and the Mandate awarded. Meantime Wilson was forbidden to publicize the proposals. News of the acceptance of the Mandate (issued 28 April

1920) reached Baghdad on 1 May. Wilson could still not make any public announcement of his intentions; and on 5 May the British government issued a formal statement of the need for immediate measures in consultation with the Councils and with approval of local opinion in all parts of the country to frame definite proposals for 'creating a form of civil administration based upon representative indigenous institutions which would prepare the way for the creation of an independent Arab State of Iraq'.[18] Both news of the Mandate and this bland statement inevitably aroused nationalist opinion in Baghdad and elsewhere. Wilson wired for urgent permission to publish the Bonham-Carter proposals to show that action was proposed, since the Iraqi Sharifians in Syria (still under Faisal) demanded immediate Mesopotamian independence, and by then news of the British retreat from Deir ez-Zor and the subsequent march towards Mosul seemed to many to imply British defeat and withdrawal. London in fact wired Wilson on 7 June that he could now announce his constitutional proposals, but by then it was too late. The nationalist tide was running too fast for a quasi-colonial regime to be acceptable. On 2 June Wilson summoned a group of Baghdad notables, including the fifteen delegates to the previous Ottoman parliament. He outlined his constitutional proposals; but the delegates demanded instead a national convention based on Turkish electoral law to prepare a national government in line with the Anglo-French Declaration of 8 November 1918. Wilson immediately wired London: it was now too late for his proposed constitution. A Constituent Assembly would have to be summoned as soon as the Mandate was finalized. Sir Percy Cox should visit Baghdad on his way from Persia to London to meet the notables. By the end of June the main Euphrates revolt was in progress, and Wilson's scheme was sunk without trace.

Wilson later claimed that, had the India Office been free to approve his constitution in March, the rising might never have taken place.[19] By the end of July 1920 he recognized that the opportunity for the sort of controlled devolution of power which he had wanted had passed. Hearing on 30 July of the deposition of Faisal as King of Syria by the French, he immediately wired the India Office 'suggesting that H.M.'s Government should offer him the headship of the Mesopotamian State'.[20] Justifying his late conversion to this idea he claimed: 'Objections entertained on this side to creation of Amirate have hitherto been primarily that no suitable person could be found. We have always regarded Faisal as booked for Syria ... Faisal alone of all Arabian potentates has any idea of running a civilized government on Arab lines.'[21] Montagu at the India Office welcomed the proposal, which, if announced in Baghdad, might well have taken much of the steam out of the rising. But it was blocked by Curzon at the Foreign Office, who preferred Faisal's brother, Abdullah, while others in London and Baghdad favoured the Basra notable, Saiyid Talib, Naqib of Basra. Nor is it clear what role Wilson would have cast for Faisal. The evidence suggests that he would have expected the Amir to be a largely titular head of state, at least initially, with a predominantly British administration, but with an increasing injection of Iraqi officials and representatives. He was at least clear that Iraq should not be made a sovereign state so long as British responsibilities continued under the Mandate. In his view sovereignty now lay with the League of Nations.[22]

In the event Wilson never had the opportunity to influence later developments. He was forced to soldier on, suppress the rising, and maintain the elements of a bureaucratic military occupation until he handed over to Sir Percy Cox as Civil Commissioner on 4 October 1920, leaving Basra on 5 October. As a result he was heavily criticized, then and later, for having blocked the creation of a 'democratic' Arab state of the type set up by Cox and Faisal from 1921. This was expressed most strongly by those who had been involved in the Arab rising in the Hejaz and who believed that Britain had reneged on promises made to the Sharif. In retirement a decade later, when he wrote his *Mesopotamia*, Wilson still felt deeply aggrieved that he was, as he put it, 'pilloried, week by week, during the summer of 1920, in leading articles in *The Times*, *The Observer*, *The Daily Herald*, and elsewhere as a sun-dried bureaucrat intent on "Indianizing" Mesopotamia'.[23]

This image stuck and had the effect of dramatizing and exaggerating the contrast between the aims and methods of Wilson and those of Cox.[24] In much of the literature it is made to appear that Cox, along with Gertrude Bell, inaugurated a radically new approach to the government of Iraq, dropping a conservative and imperialist strategy and creating a free and democratic country ruled by an Arab prince. This antithesis is clearly false. At most there was a change of emphasis. Wilson wanted overt British rule for perhaps five or so years, coupled with an Arab head of state and a gradually increasing political and administrative role for local people. Cox, on the other hand, had been in London in 1920 before he took control. He was able to persuade the British government that the only way to end rebellion and to reduce the vast British expenditure on its forces in Iraq was to carry out 'a complete and necessarily rapid transformation of the façade of the existing administration from British to Arab'.[25] The ultimate form of the new constitution would be determined by an Arab assembly, thus conforming to the 1918 Anglo-French Declaration, once the country was stable again.

The key word here was 'façade'. In practice, behind an indigenous front, the system created by Cox was as effectively British as that proposed by Wilson. Late in October 1920, Cox set up a Council under the Naqib of Baghdad as president, whose members consisted of other Arabs as nominal heads of the main departments and others without portfolios. The membership was carefully arranged by Cox to include the leading Sharifians, many of whom had been involved in the rising, such as Jafar al-Askari, and to exclude anyone known to retain Turkish sympathies. Significantly there was no portfolio for Shia affairs, though the majority of the population was Shia, a premonition of one of the main problems of the eventual state of Iraq. In November 1920 Cox proclaimed that this Council of nine ministers, and other members summoned ad hoc, was the provisional national government. Elections to a proposed National Assembly were planned in an Electoral Law made by the Council. Cox, however, insisted, against the views of the Council, that there should be a special electoral system for the tribes, as contrasted with urban communities, and that there should be reserved seats for Christians and Jews. Elections to the Assembly were to be managed by elective municipal bodies. In addition, mainly to provide employment for the increasing number of Iraqis who were returning from service in Ottoman forces and civil service, many of them via Syria, it was decided to establish a national army. There would also be a gendarmerie of some 2,000, called Levies, which would come under the Minister of Interior, then Saiyid Talib.

It thus appeared that Cox had almost instantaneously transformed the whole political landscape and laid the foundations for a modern democratic indigenous state. In fact this was, and for another decade remained, essentially an illusion. It was the façade, not the reality, of Wilson's system that had been changed. Ultimate power in Iraq, as Mesopotamia was now to be called, still lay with the British authorities, backed by the remaining, though rapidly reducing, British and Indian troops. In Cox's system the High Commissioner, as the Civil Commissioner was now called, had ultimate control, since, as in British India and other British dependencies, he had a veto on all Council proposals. In addition, each Arab minister had a British Adviser, who was appointed by and ultimately responsible to the High Commissioner. The Advisers could insist on their recommendations being accepted only if their rejection would have serious domestic or international consequences. But in practice, given the inexperience of virtually all their ministers and the overriding authority of the High Commissioner, this was unimportant. For most of the next decade, until the independence of Iraq in 1932, the British were able to govern behind the façade of ministerial responsibility. In addition, as will be seen below, even the appointment of a King and the realization of an elective parliamentary system, did little to reduce the power of the British. In short, the contrast between the gradualist proposals of Wilson and the instant transformation made by Cox is largely an illusion.

The reality of British power becomes clear if one examines the process by which Faisal was made King of an Iraqi state. The key decisions were taken late in 1920, and were closely related to the demands of Winston Churchill.[26] As War Minister in 1920 he had demanded reduction of British expenditure in Iraq, even at the price of withdrawing to Basra. Accepting continued occupation of the three wilayats, as pressed by Edwin Montagu at the India Office and Lord Curzon as Foreign Secretary, he insisted that direct British involvement and military costs must be cut. At the end of December 1920, Cabinet decided that Iraq should be transferred from combined India Office and War Office control to the Colonial Office, which had a good reputation for economic management of protectorates in Africa and elsewhere; that a new Middle Eastern department should be set up in that ministry which would control both Iraq and Palestine; and that Churchill himself would move to the Colonial Office at the beginning of January 1921. This set the scene for the conference held in Cairo in March 1921 which was to decide the pattern of Iraqi government until 1932.

The conference was chaired by Churchill and included Cox, Sir Herbert Samuel as High Commissioner in Palestine, Gertrude Bell and leading military officers. For Iraq the conference had four main aims. It had to choose an Arab ruler; to decide how to treat the Kurdish north of Mesopotamia; to make arrangements radically to reduce British defence expenditure; and to decide how defence should be arranged after the virtual British military withdrawal. In addition, the conference had to consider how to deal with Ibn Saud and the Sharif Husain, who were in fact given subsidies to keep them quiet.

The decision as to who should be chosen to be head of state in Iraq had, in effect, been taken before the conference met. The key fact was that there was no obvious Iraqi candidate, though Talib regarded himself as one, and the Naqib of Baghdad would have been a possible choice had he not been very old and unwilling to stand. Talib was regarded as unacceptable due to his pre-1914 reputation as a murderer and Basra city boss. He was also an uncompromising Sunni, which would be difficult in a country with a Shia majority. That enabled those, such as Lawrence, who believed that the Sharifian family had been unforgivably let down, to press for one of their members. Faisal had initially, in December 1920, refused the offer, on the grounds that his brother Abdullah had a prior claim. According to Graves, Abdullah was persuaded to step down by Lawrence, though the reasons are obscure.[27] He was subsequently given Transjordan, newly carved out of Mesopotamia, as compensation. That left Faisal as the prime candidate. He was thought suitable because he had fought with British backing in the Hejaz, was regarded as able and probably compliant, and his family was not aggressively Sunni. By March 1921 the British government was ready to accept Faisal, even though he and his family had no connection whatever with Iraq, and the conference accepted Cox's proposal that he be pressed on the Iraqis.

The second main issue, of the Kurds, which is very important for the present study, was effectively side-stepped at the conference. The Anglo-French Treaty of Sèvres in 1920 had provided for the creation of a Kurdish state to include areas within Anatolia, Persia and Mesopotamia. It had not been accepted by the Turks under Mustafa Kemal and Cox did not believe they would ever do so. Nor did he think that the Kurds within the British-occupied area of Iraq, whose northern boundaries were still to be fixed, could form an independent state. It was therefore left that the Kurdish region of the north-east of Iraq should, for the time being, be left as a semi-autonomous region not directly ruled from Baghdad.

Much clearer decisions were taken over defence costs. It was decided that British (including Indian) forces should be reduced to twelve battalions by the end of 1921 and that from 1922 the Royal Air Force should take over responsibility for enforcing British control and subduing rebellions. Although this meant withdrawing all British garrisons to the three main cities and was strongly opposed by Cox, it had the advantage of financial economy. Churchill claimed that British defence costs would be radically reduced. To solve the fourth problem, of defence after this cut-back, it was decided that additional land defence would be provided by expanding the existing Arab Levies to include Kurds and the Christian Assyrians who had been forced to leave southern Anatolia during the war and were being supported in refugee camps in Iraq. These non-Arab Levies would be paid from British funds and would be under the direct control of the British GOC and the High Commissioner, thus to some extent compensating for the loss of British troops far more cheaply than if British soldiers were used. Nevertheless, it was clear that so drastic a reduction in effective British military power would leave the High Commissioner heavily dependent on the collaboration of the King and his ministers.

It is important that the Cairo Conference treated Iraq as a British dependency. The only Iraqi representative was Jafar al-Askari and the measures chosen were intended to enable Britain to maintain full effective control, though at much reduced cost. This is where the ambiguity of the future kingdom becomes evident. It would appear to be an autonomous state under its own King and parliament, so that in due course it could be presented to the League of Nations as a state ready for full sovereign independence. Yet the British intention was to treat it as a quasi-colony in which key British interests (then mainly strategic: control of Basra and the route to the east, and access to the Gulf and Persian oil at Abadan, rather than Mesopotamian oil) were fully protected. It was the function of Cox to make these two apparently inconsistent patterns compatible.

On the face of it at least he had achieved this by the time of his final retirement in 1923. The first step was to impose Faisal on Iraq while making it appear that he was invited. Before that it was necessary to eliminate potential rivals and to soften animosities. The Naqib of Baghdad had earlier said that he would not accept the post, but equally that, 'I would rather a thousand times have the Turks back in Iraq than see the Sharif or his sons installed here'.[28] Cox made sure that he would not stand and also that he would now accept Faisal. Talib was a greater problem. He was Minister of Interior and his candidature, probably as a republican president rather than as King, was supported by his Adviser, H. St J. B. Philby. Talib ostensibly supported the cause of the Naqib of Baghdad, probably expecting to succeed him. On 16 April 1921 he made a speech in which he threatened a rising if the British authorities opposed the Naqib. On the following day he was arrested on Cox's order after having tea with Gertrude Bell; he was deported to Ceylon. Nothing demonstrates more clearly the arbitrary nature of British methods: this was their standard tactic when dealing with recalcitrant people in their colonies. Winstone described it as 'an act of social and political insensibility'[29] and Philby was rightly outraged, as were other British officials, such as Lyon.[30]

That left the way clear to promote Faisal; but it was necessary at least to appear that he was invited by the people. On 23 June Faisal arrived in Basra and proceeded by train to Baghdad amid general public apathy. On 11 July the Council unanimously declared him King. Between then and August a determined campaign was carried out to create a favourable atmosphere. All British Political Officers were instructed to hold consultations with notables in their areas and, very confidentially, to put a convincing case for Faisal. Most did so, and were able to report that they had been successful.[31] Gertrude Bell used her considerable influence with tribal shaikhs and the authorities pressed hard on the notables in Baghdad, Mosul and Basra. Since Faisal was unknown in Iraq, the government's strongest argument was that he was supported by Cox and the British government which, at that period after the suppression of the rising, when British forces were still powerful and ambitious people wanted to stand in the government's good books, was a convincing argument. The government was thus able, very improbably, to claim that 96 per cent of those consulted were in favour of Faisal, and he was publicly enthroned on 23 August. Thus Faisal became King virtually by default; as Bell herself put it to the American Chargé d'Affaires, 'We have carried him on our shoulders'.[32] In an imperial context he was as much a British artefact as the so-called 'warrant chiefs' of many acephalous dependencies in Africa.

From a British standpoint, the main purpose of installing Faisal was to create an overtly Arab state but one that preserved British interests, that would be largely self-financing (to satisfy the radical cuts in British defence expenditure recommended by the Geddes Committee of 1921) and in which, because there was now a national government, nationalist feeling would no longer be directed against Britain. As in all such imperial situations this was a very difficult balance to achieve. If Faisal and his government appeared too subservient to the British High Commissioner they would forfeit local allegiance. Alternatively, if they were allowed too much freedom of action, they would erode British influence and eventually make the British position impossible. This balancing act depended on two things. First, British rights and obligations had to be defined and the definition accepted by the Iraqi government. Second, it was essential to obtain the collaboration of Faisal, particularly once he was firmly established and could command the allegiance of the majority of Iraqis. This was very similar to the contemporary situation in Egypt where, after long negotiation with local politicians, Britain unilaterally, and without obtaining a treaty, declared the protectorate imposed in 1914 ended in February 1922, made Egypt a sovereign state, but reserved extensive powers for the British Ambassador. Since no Egyptian government could be persuaded to sign a treaty accepting these limitations on its sovereignty, the British preserved their position by a combination of military power and political juggling between the King and the political parties.

In Iraq, Britain seemed to be in a stronger position in 1921–22 to obtain acceptance of a treaty. Under the Mandate their authority in Iraq was undefined and potentially unlimited. They could therefore offer a treaty with limited British rights as an alternative to direct rule, even with Faisal as King. From their standpoint, moreover, and that of the League of Nations, a treaty would not end the Mandate until the League was satisfied that Iraq was fit to stand alone. The Iraqi politicians, however, took the view that a treaty could only be between two free sovereign states and that, if they signed, the Mandate should end. This became a major source of disagreement until 1932.

Negotiations over the possible treaty began early in 1922, leading to its acceptance by Faisal on 3 October and ratification by the Council on 10 October, subject to its later ratification by a projected national assembly.[33] In form the treaty was between two states, but in reality it was a device to induce the Iraqis to accept effective British control. In particular the King agreed to be guided by the High Commissioner on important international and financial matters and British interests and would consult with him on sound financial policies so long as Iraq had financial obligations to Britain; that is, received subsidies. The treaty was to last for twenty years, though a separate protocol of March 1923 stated that it would expire when and if Iraq became a member of the League of Nations, or not later than four years after the conclusion of a British peace treaty with Turkey. There were provisions for the framing of an organic law which would protect the rights of religious and ethnic minorities. Britain would assist in the defence of Iraq, training the officers of a new army, providing all imported defence equipment of 'the latest pattern' (later an important issue). The Capitulations, arrangements made with the Ottomans from the sixteenth century under which foreigners were exempt from local jurisdiction, were abrogated (under League direction), but courts holding cases affecting foreigners were to have at least one British judge.

Perhaps more important for British control than the treaty itself, a separate agreement defined the conditions and functions of British officials in Iraq. Under the treaty only British subjects could be employed in gazetted posts. The agreement then defined their positions and functions in detail. Though technically employed by the Iraqi government and paid by it, they were 'the servants of His Britannic Majesty' and were to report all their actions to the High Commissioner. There were several levels of such British officials, now to be called 'Advisers' or 'Inspectors' rather than, as previously, 'Officers'. At the centre each ministry was to have an Adviser who must see and approve all ministerial orders and actions and report doubts to the High Commissioner, who had the power to disallow them. In the provinces there would be Administrative Inspectors to advise each Iraqi liwa governor (mutasarrif) on virtually all administrative and legal matters. In addition to these administrative officials there were many more in technical posts to run the infrastructural services. In 1923 there were 569 in all, of whom 361 were not gazetted (that is, without tenured appointments). The total was gradually reduced to 160 in 1931, of whom only 28 were not gazetted.[34] The parallel with the Indian Civil and Provincial Services is obvious. Wallace Lyon was one of the provincial Administrative Inspectors whose position was covered by this agreement.

For a newly appointed King and his more nationalistic supporters, notably the mostly ex-Ottoman officers who had come from Syria, the treaty was unsatisfactory because it severely limited Iraqi independence and did not replace the League Mandate. Its troubled history, until its final ratification in June 1924 by the Chamber of Deputies in the new Constituent Assembly summoned under the Organic Law, provides a microcosm of the problems facing successive High Commissioners in manipulating the King and the political class. It shows the problems facing Faisal as he attempted to establish some sort of independence from the High Commissioner and at the same time gain the confidence of his more nationalistically inclined subjects.[35] It is critical that at the end the treaty was accepted only in secretive sessions to avoid strong opposition and that the Assembly was induced to ratify the draft constitution and Electoral Law only after Sir Henry Dobbs, succeeding Cox as High Commissioner in 1923, threatened that if it was not passed the Assembly would be prorogued and that a new system of controlling Iraq would be put to the League of Nations.

By 1924, then, Iraq was taking the shape it was to retain until 1932 and, in many respects, until 1958. The operation of the system will be described in section 2. The critical turning point, however, came in 1932 when Iraq became fully independent as a member of the League and the Mandate was ended. This demanded a change in the treaty. A first attempt had been made in 1927 as result of the League Commission on the future of Mosul in 1925, which insisted that, if Mosul was incorporated into Iraq, a new treaty should be signed and that both it and the Mandate should run for twenty-five years.[36] The proposed treaty, which offered that Britain would recommend full independence to the League for 1932, was blocked by Faisal and the Iraq government, who objected among other things to the proposed military arrangements after independence. Ultimately a new treaty was agreed in 1929. There would be a common foreign policy with Britain and mutual help in time of war, including the right of Britain to transport troops across Iraq and the use of airfields. Britain would retain two airfields for the RAF, one at Habbaniyah, near Baghdad, one near Basra, which would be leased to Britain rent-free. Subsidiary agreements stated that Iraq would normally employ Britons rather than foreigners in posts not held by Iraqis and that British legal experts should hold specified posts in the judicial system. For the rest, Iraq would become totally independent and would take over all external and internal responsibilities then held by Britain. The treaty was to run for twenty years after it came into force in 1930, though either party could ask for a revised treaty, provided that it still provided for British communications. It was accepted by the League in January 1932 only after strong British pressure and with much hesitation.

In principle, that ended the period of quasi-colonial British rule in Iraq. But, at least until the political revolution of 1941, the reality was somewhat different. Both Faisal and, after the brief reign of his son Ghazi from 1933 to 1939, the Regent Abd al-Ilah, recognized that the new state needed continued British support. Although the High Commissioner was now an Ambassador without the formal power to veto measures or to dictate to government, he still had considerable potential influence, provided he kept in close touch with ministers. In particular the Ministry of Foreign Affairs kept in close touch with the Residency (as the British Embassy was still called) since the treaty provided for co-ordination of British and Iraqi foreign policy. It seems clear, however, that after Sir Francis Humphrys, the last High Commissioner from 1929, and the first Ambassador in 1932, left Baghdad in 1935, his three short-lived successors had little local knowledge or influence, a point strongly emphasized by Lyon (p. 204). On the other hand Iraqi ministers, few of whom had any deep grasp of their departmental briefs, knew that they depended heavily on their British Advisers. The 1922 treaty had defined eighteen posts and their holders continued to act as permanent secretaries in the main ministries. Probably the most important of these was that of Adviser to the Minister of Interior, which was held by Sir Kinahan Cornwallis until 1935 (when he was dismissed because he was disliked by Ghazi) and then by his assistant, C. J. Edmonds. It is clear from Edmonds's papers that he saw himself as serving British interests as much as those of Iraq and that he kept the Ambassador closely informed about all ministerial moves.

Thus, at the highest level, the central government, and also the judicial and technical services such as agriculture and railways, continued to be run, or at least strongly influenced, by British officials. The major change was in provincial administration. An immediate effect of independence was that most of the Administrative Inspectors, the right hand of the mutasarrifs in the liwas and the quaimmaqams in the districts (qadhas) lost their jobs to Iraqis. A few, including Lyon, were kept on in other posts, four of them as Land Settlement Officers, a job in which the assumed neutrality of a foreigner was regarded as essential. Parallel with this the defence system was indigenized. Virtually no British ground troops remained, apart from the 2,000 or so Levies who remained under British pay to guard the RAF airfields. To replace them an Iraqi Army was gradually built up, strongly supported by most politicians as the symbol of national identity and autonomy. By the mid-1930s it had grown to some 12,000. Even so it was strongly influenced by British officers as instructors, and by the fact that many of its Iraqi officers were trained in Britain or India. But the most significant residual element of British power was the RAF. As with most aspects of the new Iraqi state, its position was ambiguous. Before 1932 it had been the main agent of enforcing governmental authority, particularly in the lawless north. As the British Colonial Secretary, L. S. Amery, put it in 1925, 'If the writ of King Faisal runs effectively throughout his kingdom it is entirely due to British aeroplanes. If the aeroplanes were removed tomorrow, the whole structure would inevitably fall to pieces.'[37] After 1932 it was officially in Iraq only for external defence and fell under the authority of the British government, not, as before, the High Commissioner or later the Ambassador. In practice, however, the weakness of the Iraqi Army meant that governments frequently asked for RAF back-up for repressive campaigns, and this was frequently provided.

Thus, from 1932 until the Rashid Ali rising of 1941, after which, until

1945, Iraq was effectively controlled by the British much as before 1932, British power in Iraq depended on a sophisticated exploitation of the limited rights provided by the treaty of 1930 and the influence of the remaining British officials. The balance was delicate; and it is clear that a combination of British weakness internationally in the face of rising German and Italian aggression, and the inability of successive Ambassadors from 1935 to 1941 to exploit their potential influence, allowed British influence to decline to the point at which it seemed possible for a new ministry, dominated by sections of the army, to throw in their lot with the Axis powers.

2. The Iraqi State 1918–44

There are basically two interpretations of the character of Iraq after 1918. The first, which Elie Kedourie has called 'The Chatham House Version',[38] suggests that the great British achievement there was to create a single Arab nation-state out of three Ottoman provinces and to endow it with a western-style constitutional monarchy, democratic parliament, law courts, and administration, with equal rights for all ethnic and religious groups. This makes it possible to analyse the course of politics and government policies in the same terms as would be applicable in a western European democracy. It therefore becomes a matter of surprise and regret that after 1958 Iraq should have become a military despotism and that the interests of Kurds and Shias should consistently have been subordinated to those of the minority Arab Sunnis.[39]

The alternative interpretation, in the extreme version put forward by Kedourie, is that, from the start, post-1920 Iraq was a fraud. There was not, as the Arabists such as Lawrence and Bell alleged, an Arab Nation, nor any coherent political unities after the end of Ottoman rule. The basic units were economic (landowners and peasants), and class differentiation was based on function: officials and non-officials, soldiers and civilians. There was no middle class in a European sense, and therefore no basis for western-style politics. Both the state and its politics had therefore to be created by the British to serve their own interests. The Hashemite monarchy was foisted on Mesopotamia by the British as a solution to the crisis of 1920. Few Iraqis wanted Faisal. Basra notables petitioned against his appointment. In the north only Mosul, with its Sunni Arab majority, wanted him. The strongest support came from the ex-Ottoman officials and soldiers, many from humble Baghdad origins, who had supported Faisal in Syria and who flocked to Baghdad in and after 1920. They were the main beneficiaries of the new regime and they dominated Iraqi politics until 1958, enriching themselves in the process. Kedourie had no respect for Faisal. He recognized that he was in an invidious position since he had both to keep in with the British, on whom his position depended, but at the same time to give the impression of being an Iraqi nationalist by opposing the treaty and demanding full independence. But in Kedourie's view Faisal was weak, inconsistent, greedy for property (since the Hashemites had no land or wealth in Iraq), ambitious for power, and unwilling to oppose such obviously wicked actions as the massacre of Assyrian civilians by the army in 1933.

Kedourie argued that Iraqi politics and government policies flowed from this flawed beginning. The constitution ratified in 1924 by the Constituent Assembly was notionally democratic, providing one deputy in the lower house for each 20,000 adult male tax-payers. But it was in no sense democratic in operation. The fact that between 1921 and 1958 there were no fewer than fifty-seven ministries 'argues a wretched political architecture and constitutional jerry-building of the flimsiest and most dangerous kind'.[40] Moreover, this artificial state was extremely unfair in its treatment of minorities and the poor. Kurds and Shias were always grossly underrepresented in cabinets and ministerial and provincial administrative offices. Minorities, such as the Assyrians and Jews, were very severely treated, the Jews in particular suffering after 1948 from regulations which echoed Nazi strategies before the Final Solution. Education policy was designed to promote Arabic at the expense of, for example, Kurdish, and to inculcate pan-Arabism. Land policy favoured the minority of mainly Baghdad politicians and men of wealth who were able to amass large estates at the expense of the peasant cultivators. In short, Iraq was from the start a patrimonial or prebendal state and it should have been no surprise that it ended with the military coup of 1958.

Kedourie, in fact, largely blames the British rather than the Iraqis for all this. It was they who had destroyed the Ottoman empire and had therefore to put something in its place. In their haste to shake off the costs and inconvenience of direct administration they had established the monarchy and in 1929 pretended to the League of Nations that 'Iraq ... would be in every way fit for admission to the League of Nations by 1932'.[41] In Kedourie's view this was inconsistent with the then British record on colonization, which insisted on building a genuinely satisfactory structure before ending imperial rule; he clearly agreed with A. T. Wilson on this.

Kedourie was born a Baghdad Jew and the terrible treatment of his people in Iraq after 1948 may have influenced his views. Yet there is no doubt that virtually all subsequent research and publication supports his approach. On the political system in particular there seems unanimity that democracy was a farce. Longrigg wrote that, while there was no real indigenous alternative in 1920, given the absence of any traditional ruler such as a Shah or an Ibn Saud, Iraq was not capable of acting like a western democracy. Hence,

> in 1932 the Government of Iraq consisted of a façade of democratic forms behind which operated the actual power of a small ruling class: a class which contained on the one hand more than enough figures capable of filling the ministerial posts available, but on the other too little variety of viewpoint to compete for power by the advocacy of genuinely alternative programmes.[42]

Analysing the character of cabinets and parliaments between 1920 and 1936 (the date of the first military coup, after which cabinets depended mainly on the army), Tarbush provides details of their composition which fully support this analysis.[43] Of the fifty-nine men who held cabinet appointments in these years, only eight were tribal shaikhs, 75 per cent came from the three main cities, and twenty had served in the Ottoman or Sharifian armies. Only 24 per cent were Shias, as compared with 56 per cent of the population. Within this elite were an inner group of fourteen who held ninety-seven of the 179 appointments made, including more than a third who were ex-Ottoman or Sharifian soldiers. Of the eleven Prime Ministers, only one came from the countryside, eight came from Baghdad, two from Mosul. The twenty-two cabinets had very short lives, averaging 8.5 months. This reflected intense personal rivalries. Cabinets were normally changed in order to get rid of one or more personal enemies or because the King had fallen out with them. Policies and parties played little or no part in the process. Promises might be made before elections, but no one was expected to honour them once in office. Conversely, no government resigned because it lost the confidence of parliament.

This fact reflected the nature of the electoral system for the Chamber of Deputies: the upper house was nominated. Most of the members were elected on the basis of their personal allegiance to one of the political elites or of their own social status. When an election was called the government sent instructions to the mutasarrifs to ensure the election of the desired candidates in their liwa. Thus in the 1925 parliament all but eight of the eighty-six Deputies were government candidates, the rest independents. Party affiliations were personal rather than ideological and party objectives tactical, not strategic. Opposition was usually intended to induce the government to offer a ministerial place.

Such detailed evidence fully supports Kedourie's argument. Iraqi politics, both before and after independence in 1932, were run by a small elite which shuffled the rewards of office between themselves and made little or no attempt carry out the reform programmes they offered before elections. From 1933, moreover, with the death of Faisal, politicians increasingly looked to the army to support particular factions. In fact the increasing size and power of the army became the central fact in Iraqi politics and history once British control ended.

In 1921 the Cairo Conference had agreed to the creation of an Arab army of up to 15,000 to replace the withdrawing British forces, leaving only some RAF squadrons, a few British battalions, and the Levies. The primary purpose was to provide for the more than 600 ex-Ottoman officers then in Iraq who needed employment. These were led by Jafar al-Askari, initially in 1920 as Minister of Defence, and his brother-in law Nuri as-Said, appointed Commander in Chief of the then non-existent force. Their aim was to build an Iraqi army as the focus and symbol of a new Iraqi nationalism. They also wanted conscription for other ranks, both because low pay and poor conditions discouraged voluntary enlistment (except to the British-controlled and better-paid Levies), but also because they believed that conscription would create a sense of common national identity among the troops. The British were doubtful about the viability of conscription and reluctant to see scarce resources wasted on a potentially useless force. But Sir Henry Dobbs, as High Commissioner from 1923, agreed to a conscription bill being introduced in 1927. It was met by strong hostility from both Shias and Kurds and was therefore dropped. But it was revived and passed in 1934. By 1936 army numbers had risen from 12,000 to 20,000, two-thirds of them stationed in the Euphrates region and within striking distance of Baghdad. Most of its senior officers were from the ex-Ottoman and Sharifian group and closely related to the dominant politicians, thus, as Tarbush comments, 'making the *coup d'état* [of 1936] in effect a horizontal movement within the same arena'.[44]

The political coup of 1936 marked the virtual end of conventional civilian politics in Iraq and the start of army domination. Since 1932 the army had demonstrated its potential, first by the massacre of Assyrian civilians under Bakr Sidqi in 1933, then by suppressing Shia risings in the Euphrates region as well as a Yezidi rising in the Barzan region in 1935–36. Thus, by 1936 the army leaders felt confident of their importance and ready to use the army as a political weapon.

From then until 1941, and again after 1945, the army was to be the most important factor in Iraq. Khadduri lists and describes six more army political coups between 1936 and April 1941.[45] Its interventions were sometimes caused by links between ambitious senior officers and related political groups, but also by army dissatisfaction with what many officers perceived as the self-seeking and inertia of most career politicians. In this sense Iraq can been seen to fit into a pattern that became common in other parts of the Middle East, post-colonial Africa, and South and South-East Asia after 1945, India, Malaysia and Sri Lanka always excluded. In virtually every case such military takeovers resulted from the over-expansion of the armed forces beyond any reasonable defence requirement, coupled with the instability of political and constitutional structures not based on genuine democracy. In such situations the formal requirements of a constitution become irrelevant.

Whether, in the case of Iraq, there was any historically conceivable alternative is, however, another question. A. T. Wilson and Kedourie both argued that Britain was evading its moral obligations by handing over an unfledged state to what amounted to a handful of military adventurers whose only claim to status was that they had served with Faisal or had military or administrative experience under the Ottomans. Either as politicians or soldiers such men were certain to act in their own interests rather than as responsible statesmen. Hence, Britain as the mandatory power should have retained full control for a considerable period until Iraq had some experience of western constitutional forms and conventions. Yet in practice such a strategy was neither feasible in the early 1920s, nor certain to lead to a better long-term outcome. In 1920–21 the key facts were that Britain could have maintained quasi-colonial control only through military force. That would have cost a great deal of money, and it was impossible to provide this from British funds at a time when British public expenditure was being drastically cut back. In other British dependencies military costs had almost always, except in time of international war, been met from local taxation, notably in India and Egypt. But in the early 1920s Iraqi public revenues were far too small to pay for a substantial army of occupation: it was not until after the oil from Kirkuk began to flow through the pipelines to the Mediterranean in 1934, and substantial royalties to be paid, that the Iraq treasury became affluent. Moreover, in 1920 it had become clear that Iraqi nationalism (probably more accurately Arabism or xenophobia) was unpredictably strong. Hence, the decision to create a notionally autonomous state under Faisal and to rely on British influence, the treaty, local collaborators and the RAF to protect vital British interests was probably unavoidable. Wilson was right in his fears for the consequences, but wrong in thinking that there was a real alternative.

In any case, certainly until 1932, and in many respects until 1958, this compromise or fudge largely satisfied British needs. Apart from the revolution of April 1941, when the army imposed a government under Rashid Ali, replaced the Regent, invited Axis help, and imprisoned or isolated all Britons for a month,[46] Iraq fulfilled the terms of the treaty. Moreover, until after 1932, the internal administration of Iraq was more or less as completely under British control as it would have been had a protectorate been declared. Since this was the milieu in which Lyon and his fellow-political officers, later Administrative Inspectors, worked it is important to understand this structure.[47]

In Baghdad, government was controlled by the Council and departmental ministers along conventional European lines. All were nominally appointed by the King, but until 1932 he required the approval of the High Commissioner. By 1926 most major ministerial posts were held by Iraqis, each with a British Adviser and staff; though some technical departments were temporarily under British heads: in 1926 Irrigation, Tapu (Land Records), Customs, State Domains, Veterinary Services, Public Works, the Port of Basra, and Railways. The British element was gradually run down and was virtually eliminated by the early 1930s. A number of departmental Advisers remained, though after 1932 strictly as senior civil servants rather than as effective controllers of their departments under nominal Iraqi ministers.

Provincial adminstration was controlled by the Minister of Interior, a very powerful figure with much patronage, who also had some military power because he controlled the police and the gendarmerie – those Arab Levies not under British control. Since this was what most people wanted, provincial government reverted to near its Ottoman pattern from the temporary British wartime model of sixteen divisions. From late in 1920 the three main wilayats (Mosul, Baghdad, Basra) were divided into ten liwas, which in turn were subdivided into thirty-five qadhas and eighty-five smaller nahiyas. The liwa was the main unit of local government. At its head was the governor (mutasarrif) who was a central government appointment but often a local notable who had served under the Ottomans. Each liwa had an advisory council inherited from the Turks. Below the liwa the qadha was run by a qaimmaqam and also had an advisory council. The nahiyas were controlled by a mudir. The towns had mayors and elective councils, also inherited from the Ottoman system. Thus in principle local provincial government was indigenous with considerable input from local opinion.

Until 1932, though, the most important man in the liwa and in some qadhas was the British Political Officer or Assistant Political Officer, renamed Administrative Inspector (AI) under reform of the system in 1923. In 1923 there were twenty-four of these men; in 1930, fourteen; and still in 1933 ten, after which they were phased out. Although from 1923 technically only advisers to the mutasarrif and his council, the AI had very considerable powers because, in the last resort, he could call on support from the High Commissioner and the military or RAF. He could not be dismissed without the approval of the High Commissioner. Virtually no aspect of local affairs was outside his competence; moreover, particularly in the tribal north of Iraq and in the Euphrates region, the AI had to deal with tribal problems which involved military action. The AIs did not remain in one liwa indefinitely; they were liable to be moved around to fill vacancies caused by death (frequent in the turbulent early years), absence through leave, or promotion. But on the whole most AIs were likely to remain within the same wilayat: Lyon, for example, remained in the Mosul wilayat continuously from 1918 to 1932, though frequently moved from one liwa to another. In this way most AIs, if they survived, accumulated a fund of local knowledge and built up valuable relationships with local notables.

These relationships were the key to success. With very little physical force at their disposal, except in time of rebellion or riot, the AIs depended on establishing good relationships with their mutasarrifs or qaimmaqams and, outside the urban areas, the tribal chiefs. Since the AIs were representatives of a conquering foreign power and were also for the most part Christian, they were under a double disadvantage, particularly in parts of the north where there remained much pro-Turkish sentiment. In fact, their position during the 1920s had much in common with that of Europeans in newly occupied dependencies elsewhere: perhaps northern India in the late eighteenth and very early nineteenth centuries, and tropical Africa in the early twentieth century. That is, they had to be very close to the people they were controlling; not for them the luxury of the remote dignity of the British raj in its mature form. They were a very mixed lot. Some came from the Indian Army or Political Service, some from posts in Egypt or the Sudan, Edmonds at least from the Levant Consular Service, a few from archaeological work in Mesopotamia before the war. The most successful were those who adapted quickly to the special conditions of the new state. The qualities they needed were adaptability, courage, ability to mix with the local people while retaining their authority, and linguistic skills. In the Kurdish area in particular it was helpful to have military experience since POs/AIs had to take an active part in the many little wars against dissident tribesmen, in the early days encouraged by Turks. Those who lacked any of these skills were unlikely to succeed or, indeed, survive; many of the considerable number of administrators who were killed in the early days, and who were listed by Wilson, suffered because they did not understand local customs or religious principles, did not get to know the politics of the area, or lacked military skills. Conversely, it is clear from the memoirs of C. J. Edmonds, who spent the three years 1922–25 as an officer in the Mosul wilayat, and still more from Lyon's memoirs over a longer period, that these and others were successful because they were very close to those for whom they had responsibility. Although seldom copying Lawrence's adoption of photogenic Arab costume,[48] they had no hesitation in eating, living, shooting, fishing, and generally consorting with local dignitaries, both urban and tribal. Indeed, they and some others were so successful in earning the confidence of Iraqis that they were kept on after independence: Edmonds first as Assistant Adviser, from 1935 Adviser, to the Ministry of Interior, Lyon and three other equally adaptable and trusted AIs as Land Settlement Officers, whose primary qualification had to be honest neutrality and ability to earn the trust of those whose properties they defined.[49] It was such men, along with the many specialists in the technical departments, who ensured the viability of the nascent Iraqi state in the period before independence. Much of the value of Lyon's memoir reproduced in this book is to show how this was done.

The role of the Administrative Inspectors typified the ambivalence of the British element in Iraqi administration in that they were primarily servants of the Iraqi state which paid their not inconsiderable salaries, yet were also, at least before 1932, expected to protect British interests.[50] Much the same ambivalence was true of other government agencies that provided the essential back-up for the administrators.

For the most part the AIs were expected to rely on what, in the nineteenth century, had often been called 'moral suasion' rather than force. In fact, given the paucity of enforcement agencies, this was their main tool. But in so lawless a society, after the rising of 1920 and given the presence of Turkish forces in the Mosul wilayat until the final decision by the League of Nations to award Mosul to Iraq late in 1925, force had often to be used. From the withdrawal of most British and Indian regular ground troops in 1922 the AIs had three possible sources of support: the police, the Levies and the RAF.

The police were built up gradually after 1920 until they numbered about 8,000 in 1932. They were under the control of the Ministry of Interior, but had a British senior officer and initially a total of twenty-two British officers, declining to twelve by 1932, plus fifty-nine Iraqi officers. The force was highly disciplined and generally respected for its honesty. But it was an armed gendarmerie rather than a civil police force of the British type. Under officers with military experience, such as Charles Littledale in Arbil, they were probably the most effective force for dealing with minor breaches of the peace and, mounted, usually on mules, with dissident shaikhs in the mountains.

The Levies were an alternative form of back-up for the authorities. They appear to have grown from the organization of informal groups of *shabana*, or night watchmen, in the Tigris region to provide some security after the collapse of Ottoman authority from 1915. The idea was picked up by the British military authorities who proceeded to recruit them to serve in their own districts under British officers.[51] By the mid-1920s there were over 7,000 Levies, recruited from the Arabs, Kurds and Assyrians. They can best be regarded as irregulars, perhaps resembling the many irregular regiments of early British India. Until 1932 they were paid by the British who regarded them as a substitute for regular British and Indian troops as these were gradually withdrawn from 1922. Their quality was variable; but some of the best were drawn from the Assyrians.[52] These were Nestorian Christians from the Hakari mountains of south-east Anatolia. At the start of the war they had been encouraged to believe that the Russians, as fellow-Christians, would occupy that region and improve their conditions. They rebelled; and when Russian support did not arrive, there was a mass trek over the mountains via Persia, which for the survivors ended in the Mosul wilayat. Their hope was that their region would be included in Iraq so that they could return; but when the Frontier Commission of 1925 refused to recommend this, the Assyrians found themselves homeless and generally unwelcome in Kurdistan. The British made various attempts to find them a suitable home, but never did so successfully. Meantime they recruited some 2,000 Assyrians into the Levies. These were regarded by most of their British officers and by those AIs who used them as the best of all Levy battalions: they were very tough fighters and entirely loyal to their officers and Britain. They were, however, intensely disliked by the Iraqi Army and most politicians precisely because they provided Britain with an independent military force. In 1932 their future seemed so uncertain that their officers resigned en bloc and there was the danger that the Levies would form an independent military force, probably capable of defeating the then untried Iraqi Army. British troops were brought in from Egypt to reassert discipline, but some Levy officers continued to make threats in the north as the Iraq government refused demands by the Marshimun, the Assyrian spiritual leader, for considerable autonomy. The government then decided to act. A pogrom was encouraged in three of the towns in which Assyrians were living, and in August 1933 the Iraqi Army, in its first successful role, massacred 315 Assyrian civilians in Sisayl. In the longer term some Assyrians settled in French-controlled Syria, others were gradually assimilated into Iraqi society. Their fate is widely regarded as one of the more disgraceful events in British imperial history, since the British failed to include guarantees for their future in the treaty. But Britain maintained the Assyrian Levy battalions on British pay, primarily for the defence of the RAF's station at Habbaniyah, where they were to be a critical factor in 1941.

The third possible source of support for British officials before 1932 was the RAF.[53] As a virtually new military weapon it was used in Iraq from the early days of the invasion but showed its limitations in its failure to provide sufficient supplies to relieve the siege of Kut in 1916. It proved much more valuable in helping the ground forces to suppress the rising of 1920, particularly because it was able to bypass the physical obstacles to troop movements in both the riverine regions and the northern mountains. To

Churchill in 1921 it seemed the solution to the problem of how to remove most British ground troops yet retain a significant military presence. At the Cairo Conference it was decided that the RAF should in future constitute the main British military arm in Iraq and that command of all defence forces there should therefore be transferred to the Air Officer Commanding (AOC). He would be directly responsible for internal security to the High Commissioner, not the Air Ministry in London.

For the next decade the RAF was extremely active, in particular ferrying officials around, transporting supplies and bombing dissidents. Like most other aspects of the British regime in Iraq, however, its effects were ambivalent. Given the primitive character of contemporary military planes, bomb loads were small and bombing extremely inaccurate. It could act only as a deterrent or back-up for the men on the ground. Moreover, it was often used to punish for non-payment of taxes, as in the Bani Huchaim Confederation in 1923–24 in the Samowa qadha, when 144 were killed or wounded in retribution for non-payment of taxes, caused by the peasants being deprived of water by the local shaikhs.[54] Such actions, since they were seldom followed up by administrative action on the ground, were merely supporting an unjust social and political system.

After 1932 the RAF took on a different role as almost the only remaining British military force in Iraq, with two bases, a new base at Habbaniyah, 50 miles west of Baghdad, to replace those at Hinaidi and Mosul, and the existing base at Shaiba, near Basra. In principle, the role of the RAF was now external defence rather than internal security, since there was an Iraqi Army and a fledgling Iraq air force. In practice, however, the British government was usually willing, on the advice of the Ambassador, to approve use of the RAF to suppress internal risings. In this way, it has been suggested, the RAF was acting in the interests of those collaborative Iraqi politicians on whom British influence now depended.

In 1941, however, the RAF base at Habbaniyah proved crucial in preventing the success of the anti-British coup by Rashid Ali and his army allies. The base provided the only link with the outside world once the government had declared a state of emergency on 1 April and had turned to Germany to provide support.[55] Habbaniyah was virtually defenceless against an Iraqi Army of some 40,000, of whom some 9,000 troops and artillery were sent against Habbaniyah, and an Iraqi air force recently reinforced by modern Italian planes. It was defended only by 1,300 RAF troops, 100 British soldiers, and 800 Assyrian Levies, with very little artillery. Had it fallen, the way would have been open for German reinforcements to come in at leisure. Why Habbaniyah survived remains a mystery. The Iraqi forces began to withdraw as early as 6 May after vigorous resistance by the defenders. On 18 May some 2,000 British and Arab troops from

Palestine and Transjordan arrived at Habbaniyah after a trek of 500 miles across the desert, along with 500 Indian troops flown up from Basra; and on 30 May a small British force of 1,500 with very little artillery or armour arrived on the outskirts of Baghdad. There were still some 20,000 Iraqi troops near Baghdad and a further 15,000 in Mosul; yet Rashid Ali and most of his political allies fled to Iran. The crisis was over and the British then proceeded to build up their forces in Iraq to the point at which it was again, as in 1918, under a military occupation that lasted until after the end of the war in 1945.

Why precisely the Iraqi attempt to replace British by German dominance failed remains unclear. It is likely that the failure stemmed in part from ministerial indecision at the start of May, which enabled the British to break out of Habbaniyah before the Germans (who had warned Rashid Ali that they could not act so quickly before they had wound up their occupation of Crete) had built up their air force and its supplies in Iraq. Silverfarb argues that this indecision was caused by a split in the Iraqi ruling clique and also within the Iraqi Army. The government received no support from the Shia majority, who had been alienated by the brutal suppression of the rising in the Euphrates region in 1935–36; nor from the Kurds, who were bitter at their failure to achieve autonomy or even a fair allocation of official posts in their region. Shaikh Mahmud, who had suffered considerably at British hands in the past, nevertheless even offered to support the British cause. It seems likely that the Iraqi Army also was split internally. The troops who were besieging Habbaniyah could certainly have taken it, or rendered it unusable with artillery (by destroying its water towers), had they been determined. Freya Stark supports this view anecdotally. She wrote that 'Johnny Hawtrey [Air Vice-Marshal and Inspector of the Iraqi Air Force in 1940] remarked to his ex-pupils how poor their artillery had been against Habbaniyah ... They always retorted that, on the contrary, their aim had been *extremely good*, not many of them had wished to destroy us; and this double current through the country ... was a factor of great though unassessed importance throughout the revolt.'[56]

Whatever the reasons, after 1941 British influence was reasserted in Iraq and remained strong until the revolution of 1958 destroyed both the monarchy and the power of the old Iraqi political elite. British officials such as Lyon reverted in 1941 from being servants of the Iraqi state under contract to being British army officers. But for him, and probably many others of the small remaining band of expatriates, the 1941 revolution, and their very rough treatment as prisoners while it lasted, proved a turning point. Although the treaty remained in operation in revised form until 1958, there could be no return to the certainties of the pre-1941 era.

Lyon was glad to be shot of the place in 1944 and spend the rest of his working life in the Consular Service in Ethiopia.

3. The Kurds and British Over-rule

Wallace Lyon spent most of his career in Iraq in the north-east region of Iraq – the majority of the inhabitants were Kurds – itself part of what is loosely called Kurdistan.[57] It is, however, unclear what either of these terms means. Historically there was never a state called Kurdistan; the term is used to indicate that area within modern Turkey, Iraq, Iran and Syria, the majority of whose inhabitants call themselves Kurds. Yet it is equally uncertain what constitutes 'the Kurds' or what their origins are. In the early period of the British occupation of Iraq it was commonly believed that Kurds, by contrast with Arabs and Turks, were Aryans. Thus W. R. Hay, who served briefly in Kurdish Iraq from 1918 to 1920 and published his experiences, with remarkable speed, in 1921, wrote:

> As a race they are not a genetic entity. They are a collection of tribes without any cohesion. They prefer to live in their mountain fastnesses and pay homage to whatever Government may be in power, as long as it exercises little more than a nominal authority ... The Kurds are an Aryan race, and are supposed to be identical with the ancient Medes.[58]

Lyon also believed the Kurds were Aryans.[59] Edmonds discussed their possible origins at some length and decided that the most likely was that they were descended from the Medes. By the seventh century AD, at the time of the Arab conquests, 'the name Kurd was being applied as a racial term to the Western Iranians established astride the Zagros and to the neighbouring iranicized populations'.[60] Izady is more catholic in his definition: 'As to who *is* a Kurd and who is not, this work respects the claims of anyone who calls himself Kurd ... As to who *was* a Kurd, I treat as Kurdish every community that has ever inhabited the territory of Kurdistan and has not acquired a separate identity.' He also suggests that, as a result of waves of conquerors and migrants, particularly the Medes, '[a]t the close of this period, by 900 BC, the Kurds had become aryanized'. But this has no genetic significance: 'By their physical characteristics alone Kurds cannot be distinguished from their neighbours, as all traits and variations among the Kurds can also be found among any one of their major ethnic neighbors [sic]. Neither is there any uniformity among the Kurds themselves.'[61] McDowall agrees that the Kurds are not and never have been ethnically coherent. As early as the Islamic conquests 'the term "Kurd" had a socio-economic rather than ethnic meaning. It was used of nomads on the western edge of the Iranian plateau and probably also of the tribes that acknowledged the Sassanians in Mesopotamia, many of which must have been Semitic in origin.'[62]

In the face of such uncertainty it seems that Kurds can be regarded only as those people who regarded themselves as Kurds and lived in a region which came to be called Kurdistan. Nor were they united by language or religion. Linguistically the various Kurdish dialects belong to the south-western group of Iranian languages, but are divided geographically. To the north of a line running along the Greater Zab to Lake Urumiya most Kurds spoke Kurmanji, to the south of that line Surani, a version of Kurmanji. Other Kurds speak Zaza or Gurani. Nor is religion a uniting factor. The majority of Kurds follow Sunni Islam, while the remainder are divided between Shia, Alevi (strong in central Anatolia), the Ahl-i Haqq and Yezidi. But most of the Kurds with whom the British and Baghdad regimes had to deal in post-1920 Iraq were Sunnis or Yezidis, with smaller intermingling of other Islamic groups.

There were other major divisions within Kurdish society. A basic distinction was between what can loosely be called 'tribal' and non-tribal Kurds. In principle most Kurds belonged to one or another of the many tribes, defined by Chaliand as 'a territorially fixed social and economic unit, founded on real or imagined blood ties which give the group its structure'.[63] Many, though by no means all, tribes were linked in confederacies, which are listed, with their component members, by Izady.[64] Tribes were divided into clans, which Chaliand calls 'the cornerstone of the social system', and the family as the basic unit. He argues that the main cementing factors within tribes were grazing rights, marriage and revenge, of which the last was probably the most important. Thus in the case of a murder, payment was due to the father or brother of the person killed and had to be paid by the whole of a clan. Inter-tribal conflicts over such matters aimed to weaken rather than to destroy rivals. Leadership within the tribe was in the hands of aghas, traditionally leaders of a group of rural warriors. Their main function, apart from fighting, was to use their wealth to entertain guests; and their status depended largely on their generosity. Each agha had to maintain a diwan (court) in which visitors could be entertained, where tribal meetings could be held, and major events celebrated. To finance such conspicuous consumption aghas had the right to 10 per cent of cereal crops and one-fortieth of flocks. Such men feature largely in all accounts of British administration in this period. But not all Kurds were still 'tribal' by the twentieth century. Many lived in towns or had become tenants or labourers on land in the plains. There the landlord had the title beg, and his tenants did not necessarily belong to a tribe. Finally, by 1918 very many Kurds had ceased to live in Kurdistan, having taken service with the Ottoman government in the army or civil service.[65]

The structure of authority in the Kurdish region was complicated by the existence of very powerful Islamic figures, the shaikhs and saiyids. Shaikhs were leaders of Sufi brotherhoods or branches of them which grew from the early centuries of Islam as mystic variants on basic Islamic teaching. Shaikhs were saintly men who, once they had taken 'the Path', became murshids or spiritual directors. Their disciples were murids. The sons of shaikhs had the same title but had to qualify to become murshids. By contrast, saiyids were a very large group claiming direct descent from the Prophet through his daughter Fatima and her husband Ali. Many saiyids took the Path and became shaikhs. Over the centuries many shaikhs acquired great wealth from gifts of land and valuables and founded dynasties. In modern Iraq the two most important Sufi orders were the Qadiri order, founded by the Shaikh Abdul Qadir al-Gilani in the early twelfth century, and the Naqshbandi order, founded in the thirteenth century but reformed in the fourteenth century by Muhammad Beha-ud-Din (or Baha al-Din). The Qadiri order was the only one in Kurdistan until the Naqshbandi arrived in the early nineteenth century. It was regarded as perfectly orthodox. A descendant of the founder was always primate of the order and keeper of the tomb in Baghdad: in 1920 the current primate, with the Ottoman title of Naqib al-Ashraf, was Saiyid Abdur Rahman, who was chosen by Cox to head the first Iraqi government.

For centuries shaikhs of the Qadiri order built up their power and influence, and this increased greatly after the destruction by the Ottomans of the great Kurdish emirates during the first forty years of the nineteenth century. This led to much conflict between rival tribes, and the shaikhs were able to increase their influence by acting as mediators. They sometimes also acted as leaders of tribal rebellions against the Ottoman authorities. In the period after 1918 several shaikhs played a major role in Iraqi politics and feature extensively in Lyon's narrative. Among these were Shaikh Mahmud Barzinja of Sulaimani, Shaikh Ahmad-i Khanaqah of Kirkuk, Saiyid Taha of Shandinan, and the brothers Shaikh Ahmad Barzani and Mulla Mustafa Barzani. These and many others possessed substantial land and, more important, influence. They were capable of raising tribal support either for or against the Iraqi government. Many shaikhs lived in the more remote mountain regions of north-eastern Iraq, where they could hope to escape into Iran if pressed or, until 1926, get Turkish support.[66]

The most important and difficult question concerning the Kurds in the period before and after 1918 is whether they constituted a 'nation', or thought of themselves in this sense. A critical fact is that before 1914 the vast majority of Kurds lived in a single Ottoman empire, which itself was composed of a very large number of distinct ethnic and religious groups.

Most such non-Islamic religious minorities were treated by the Turks as millets and given special rights. These included Jews and Christians. But the Kurds were Muslims, the majority sharing the Sunni faith of the Sultan and Caliph in Istanbul. They were therefore seen, and most probably saw themselves, as integral with the Ottoman world. Very many Kurds served in the Ottoman military and civil services, adopted Turkish culture and spoke Turkish. Why, then, should they come to regard themselves as distinctively Kurdish? There had, after all, never been a single Kurdish state under a Kurdish ruler, by contrast with other parts of the Ottoman empire such as Egypt, Tunis or Algeria. There was no real or mythical past to which they could appeal.

There has been much debate over how significant nationalism had become in Iraq or the rest of Kurdistan by 1918 and what its origins were. Probably it reflected the current claims to nationhood of other Ottoman groups such as the Armenian and Nestorian Christians, whose claims were supported by European states at the Congress of Berlin in 1878. The first Kurdish adoption of such language is conventionally ascribed to Shaikh Ubayd Allah of Nihri (in eastern Anatolia) who, in raising a rebellion and invading Iran in 1880, wrote to the British Consul-General in Tabriz claiming that 'the Kurdish nation ... is a people apart ... We want our affairs in our own hands.'[67] Whether this was merely a claim for an autonomous principality in Anatolia and Iran, for which he wanted European protection, is arguable. Certainly there seems to have been little sense of common nationhood among the majority of Kurds, and Sultan Abdulhamid II had no difficulty in recruiting an irregular mounted force, the Hamidiya Cavalry, mainly from Kurds, as a defensive force against the Russians and as a means of subduing the Armenians. Yet among the minority of mostly non-resident Kurds there were growing before 1914 the same sort of ethnic societies as were then developing among the urban intelligentsia in other parts of the Ottoman empire, notably Arab societies in Syria and Egypt. Before 1909 there were several such Kurdish societies in Istanbul, Baghdad and Mosul and several journals, though most of these were closed or suppressed by the Committee of Union and Progress (CUP) government in Istanbul after 1909. Indeed, the new centralization policy adopted by the CUP thereafter, with its clear aim of imposing Turkish culture and language throughout the empire, alienated many outside these urban circles, notably provincial aghas, who feared loss of power and perquisites or disliked what they regarded as the irreligious features of the new Ottoman constitution. Thus, in 1909 Shaikh Said Barzinja, leader of the Qadiri order in Sulaimani, started a local revolt there. He was killed while in Mosul to negotiate with the government, and his son, Shaikh Mahmud, took on the cause, raising a revolt among the Hamawand tribe which was still not suppressed by 1914. He thus began a long career of opposition to authority, coupled with claims to be the leader of a Kurdish nation.

It would be difficult, in fact, to argue that in 1914 there was in any sense a Kurdish nation or a strong uniting sense of ethnic unity. The Kurds as a whole fought with and for the Ottomans during the next four years and many on the eastern frontiers suffered very badly from the war against Russia. In the immediate aftermath the concept of a new independent Kurdish state came from the victorious Allies rather than from the Kurds. Much allied diplomacy since 1915 had assumed that the Ottoman empire would be broken up and that client states might be created on the borders of a small Turkish state in Anatolia. In October 1918 Arnold Toynbee at the Foreign Office proposed 'an autonomous Kurdistan ... performing the same functions towards Mesopotamia as the NW [sic] Frontier province provides towards India'.[68] There were other different schemes; and once the Sykes–Picot Agreement had been ditched in 1920, and since the concept of a Russian zone east of the Tigris had disappeared, many proposals were put forward. Foremost among the proponents of an autonomous Kurdish region within Mesopotamia was E. W. Noel, who in 1919 had proposed the creation of three autonomous Kurdish states based respectively on Sulaimani (where he was posted), Mosul and Diyarbakir in Anatolia, all to be under British protection. The British Foreign Office, however, had no interest in these ideas; it wanted to withdraw altogether from Kurdistan. For his part, A. T. Wilson in Baghdad was prepared for a ring of small client Kurdish states, but within the limits of Mesopotamia. The climax of this general strategy came with the Treaty of Sèvres, prepared by the British and French at the San Remo Conference and forced on to the residual Ottoman government in Istanbul in August 1920. Articles 62 and 64 provided for a possible autonomous Kurdish state in eastern Anatolia with the option for the Kurdish areas of Mesopotamia to join it later. After this area had been in existence for a year, it might be made entirely independent if the League of Nations was convinced of its capacity for sovereignty.

Many Kurds disliked this project on the grounds that the proposed autonomous region would exclude large Kurdish areas. In any event, it was made meaningless by the victory of Mustafa Kemal in Anatolia. His new government would never agree to an autonomous Kurdish state within Anatolia and continued to claim the Kurdish territory in northern Mesopotamia until 1926. For all practical purposes, that left Britain to decide how to deal with that part of the Kurdish region that lay within the region it controlled, the old Mosul wilayat. The central question was whether this region, particularly that lying east of the Tigris which was predominantly Kurdish, should be incorporated into a future Iraqi state or should constitute one or more autonomous Kurdish regions under British protection. The matter was thrashed out at the Cairo Conference of March 1921, by which time Iraq had been made a state under the Naqib of Baghdad and his Council. The Colonial Office, by then under Winston Churchill, stuck to the principles of Sèvres. The memorandum submitted by the Middle East Department proposed 'that purely Kurdish areas should not be included in the Arab state of Mesopotamia, but that the principles of Kurdish unity and nationality should be promoted as far as possible by H. M. G.'. This was supported by Noel and accepted by Churchill on the grounds that a future ruler of Iraq with the power of an Arab army 'would ignore Kurdish sentiment and oppress the Kurdish minority'. Assuming that such an autonomous region would be under the control of the British High Commissioner in Baghdad, this was the dominant view at the Conference; but it was opposed by Cox, as the man on the spot, on the stated ground that this would cut off areas in which Kurds were predominant but which were integral to the Iraq of his plans. In the course of the next two years, with Faisal set up as King of Iraq in Baghdad, Cox gradually wore down both Churchill and the Colonial Office. By October 1921 Churchill accepted the argument for the unity of Iraq, provided that 'Kurds are not to be under Arabs if they do not wish'. The Kurdish areas, excluding Sulaimani, were included in elections to the Constitutional Assembly in 1923 and the concept of an autonomous Kurdistan was buried when the Treaty of Lausanne of September 1923 made no mention of it.[69]

Seen in perspective this British failure to maintain the apparently generous policy of 1920 towards Kurdish aspirations was due to two main factors. First, once the fiscal cut-backs of 1921 were in place, it was impossible to maintain sufficient British or Indian forces in Iraq to control and defend it. This made it essential to establish a viable Iraqi state under Faisal; and this in turn depended on incorporating the economically critical Mosul region. From Faisal's standpoint it was also essential to include the Kurds as fellow-Sunnis to offset the numerical preponderance of Shias in the south. The Kurds were therefore sacrificed to the requirements of Iraq, though it was then reasonable to assume that an extended British Mandate would enable the High Commissioner and British officials to ensure that Churchill's prediction of Arab exploitation did not come true. Second, once Mustafa Kemal had won control of Anatolia in 1922, there was no point in Britain attempting to determine the future of Kurds in his territories. Britain urgently needed a peace treaty with the new Turkey, and the Kurds had therefore to be left out of it. After Lausanne all that remained was to determine the frontier between Iraq and Turkey, and that was to be the source of most problems in the Iraqi section of Kurdistan until 1926.

The British decision not to create one or more autonomous Kurdistans can be explained and to some extent justified. In the larger context, of one inclusive Kurdistan as envisaged in 1920, it would have become immediately clear, had such a state been established, that it had no internal cohesion. The Kurds were far too fragmented and their leaders too distrustful and competitive. Every attempt to act cohesively, as in the Shaikh Said rising in Turkey in 1925, fell apart due to inability to combine and organize. Such ideas were therefore entirely unrealistic. It was therefore reasonable to incorporate the Mesopotamian Kurds within Iraq, provided that they received most of the practical benefits autonomy might have given them.

On the other hand, it is much more difficult to justify the British failure to ensure that the Arab government in Baghdad treated the Kurds within Iraq fairly. Until 1932 the British remained in full control. Most Kurds regarded them as their main security against exploitation. What they received was promises but no security for their fulfilment. In face of a serious threat of Turkish power in Sulaimani in 1922, a joint Anglo-Iraqi statement was issued in December of that year. It stated that the two governments

> recognise the right of the Kurds living within the boundaries of Iraq to set up a Kurdish Government within those boundaries and hope that the different Kurdish elements will, as soon as possible, arrive at an agreement between themselves as to the form which they wish that that government should take and the boundaries within which they wish it to extend.[70]

In 1923, during the run-up to the Constituent Assembly elections, the Council of Ministers passed three resolutions to encourage Kurds to take part. First, the government would not appoint Arab officials in Kurdish districts, except to technical posts for which no Kurd was qualified. Second, Kurds would not be forced to use Arabic in official correspondence. Third, the unspecified rights of the inhabitants and religious and civil communities in the Kurdish districts would be safeguarded. On this basis, and trusting British good faith, most Kurdish notables took part in the elections and five Kurdish Deputies attended the Assembly. It was, in fact, the strongly pro-British Kurdish Deputies who in 1924 got the Anglo-Iraqi treaty through the Assembly. Yet before then, in April 1923, Britain and Iraq had agreed a protocol to the 1922 treaty that provided for the integration of Sulaimani liwa into the rest of Iraq. In the revised treaty of 1926, there was no mention of guarantees for the Kurds, except for an annex referring to the League's requirements. In that year the High Commissioner, Sir Henry Dobbs, could smugly inform London that the British and Iraqi governments 'are fully absolved from any obligation to allow the setting up of a Kurdish

Government by a complete failure of the Kurdish elements even to attempt at the time this proclamation [of December 1922] was made to arrive at any agreement among themselves or to put forward any definite proposals'.[71] Nor were there any statements concerning Kurdish rights in the new treaty of 1930, which was to be the basis of Iraqi independence.

These failures did not go unnoticed by those British officials in Iraq who felt a responsibility for Kurdish welfare. In particular C. J. Edmonds, who had served in Kurdistan from 1922 to 1925 and had then become Assistant to the British Adviser to the Minister of Interior (Kinahan Cornwallis), wrote a long memorandum for his superior in 1929 about British failure to fulfil its promises.[72] He recapitulated the Anglo-Iraqi statement of December 1922, statements by the Iraqi Prime Minister, Muhsin Beg, in 1923 promising the appointment of local men to all official posts and use of local languages, the recommendation of the 1925 League Commission on Mosul, and a speech by the Iraqi Prime Minister in 1926 renewing these promises. Edmonds then documented multiple failures to act on these promises, leading to serious alienation among many Kurdish leaders. Edmonds did not at that stage favour Kurdish political autonomy. He wanted full integration of the Kurds; but local government officials, many of them Arab, should observe the rules about the use of the Kurdish language and prepare translations of public documents into Kurdish. He also thought that it was important that symbols should be used to encourage Kurds to feel integrated: a Kurdish symbol on the Iraqi flag, Kurdish stamps, a Kurdish royal bodyguard. Moreover, the liwa boundaries should be adjusted to produce more coherent linguistic and cultural entities. In an undated paper headed 'Further Remarks', possibly sent to the High Commissioner, Edmonds made some less guarded comments. The Baghdad bureaucracy wanted simply to suppress or ignore the Kurdish problem. King Faisal was not interested: he apparently thought that Kurds in the mountains would eventually join either Turkey or Iran, making it possible to integrate the plains of Mosul into an Arabized Iraq. Edmonds thought this quite unrealistic. Kurds would certainly not want to join either neighbouring state since neither recognized Kurds as a separate people. Kurds could not be divided into those who were Arabized and those who were not. Finally, it would be quite impossible to defend the Iraqi plains if the northern mountain barriers were given up. Meantime, the Kurds were kept relatively contented only by the presence of British officials and the hope that the High Commissioner would protect them against the Arabs. Conversely, there was a danger that British withdrawal would result in breach of the pledges, leading to possible Bolshevik influence. Edmonds concluded with a list of examples of British and Iraqi double-thinking.[73]

The following March, 1930, a small conference of British officials, consisting of Cornwallis, Edmonds, Lyon (then at Kirkuk), C. H. Gowan (Sulaimani), G. C. Kitching (Arbil) and A. F. Chapman, met in Baghdad to consider 'the Kurdish question' in the light of statistics of Kurdish and Arab official employment in these liwas and in Mosul.[74] It was clear that, except in Sulaimani, little attempt had been made to respect the pledges made as regards Kurdish officials and the use of Kurdish. Things were worst in Arbil and Kirkuk. In the former, according to Kitching, 'the spirit of the promises had been gravely violated. The Mutasarrif, a Turcoman, was bitterly anti-Kurdish and the whole administration was permeated with anti-Kurdish bias.' Arabic was normally used in the courts, and the education officer for Mosul and Arbil was an Arab and violently anti-Kurdish. Lyon confirmed that most of this was true also of Kirkuk. The conference concluded by drawing up a list of the remedial measures it was desirable to promote.

These papers make it clear that even someone as supportive of Kurdish interests as Edmonds had long given up any idea of promoting Kurdish political autonomy. The most that could be hoped for was a fair allocation of official posts and public expenditure, coupled with use of the Kurdish language in government, law and education. That year, 1930, was propitious, for it was then that the Anglo-Iraqi treaty was renewed in preparation for submission of Iraq's request to the League to end the Mandate and become a sovereign state. Moreover, Nuri as-Said had become Prime Minister in March 1930 and was thought to be more amenable to British pressure than his predecessor, Naji as-Suwaydi. In that year he promised fulfilment of the various pledges; and, with elections to the Assembly pending, the acting Prime Minister and acting High Commissioner toured the Kurdish liwas to persuade the notables not to revive separatist ambitions. They were successful in Arbil and Kirkuk, but not in Sulaimani, where there were riots and where Mahmud, returning from Iran, raised tribal support for separation. He was not defeated until May 1931, and there was the danger of a general Kurdish rising. Hence, in 1931, Baghdad went through the motions of making concessions. A Local Languages Law was finally passed in May, though making knowledge of Kurdish, rather than Kurdish ethnicity, the qualification for administrative and teaching posts. A Kurd was appointed Assistant Director-General of the Ministry of Interior, with special responsibility for Kurdish affairs, and a Kurd was appointed Inspector General of Kurdish schools. But this was mere window-dressing. Arabs continued to be appointed as mutasarrifs and quaimmaqams (such as the Tahsin Ali who features in Lyon's narrative), and this was intended to justify Britain's support for Iraqi independence. By fudging the issue of whether the Kurds had even been offered the option of independence, the application went through the Mandates

Commission and finally the League Council. Iraq became independent in 1932 and the British no longer had any power to protect Kurdish interests. Indeed, in 1932–33 the RAF was used to support the largely ineffective Iraqi Army in suppressing a revolt by the religious eccentric Shaikh Ahmad Barzani and his brother, Mulla Mustafa.

It is easy to criticize Britain for failing to fulfil its pledges to the Kurds. In fact, as was suggested above, this failure stemmed inevitably from the decisions of 1920–21 to set up an Arab state in Iraq as a device for minimizing British costs and obligations. Thereafter British leverage on successive governments was always limited, despite the dependence of the regime on the RAF. The frustration of British officials as Administrative Inspectors in the north at their nominal subordination to senior Arab officials, most of them political appointments made within the patrimonial structure of the Baghdad governing class, is clear in all contemporary documents, and particularly in that of Lyon. But it is important to distinguish between two aspects of this British failure. On the one hand it seems clear that there was never any serious possibility of creating a more or less autonomous Kurdish state, even within the wider ambit of Iraq. McDowall, perhaps rather brutally, sums up the point; 'As for the Kurds, their failure was in unity of leadership and of purpose. Had Zakho, Dohuk, Arbil, Kirkuk, Sulaymaniya [sic], Kifri and Khanaqin produced a common front before 1923, both Britain and Iraq would have had great difficulty in denying them the formation of an autonomous province.'[75] In short, the Iraqi Kurds had no tradition of general collaboration and seemed incapable of learning how to do so under the new political order. On the other hand, there is no doubt that more resolute pressure by the High Commissioner before 1932 might have compelled Iraqi governments at least to put laws on the statute book which satisfied the pledges made by the British and which the Iraqi state was committed to fulfil. They did not. Given the record of most post-colonial states after the decolonization period, it seems unlikely that such earlier legislation would have retained any force. Yet at least the British official conscience might have felt absolved of responsibility.

Between 1932 and the Rashid Ali revolution of 1941, Kurdish nationalism was quiescent. There were small groups of mainly urban intellectuals who campaigned for linguistic and administrative equality, but Edmonds could write in 1940: 'In recent years there has been virtually no manifestation of political Kurdish nationalism in Iraq.'[76] The following year the Rashid Ali revolution demonstrated lingering Kurdish faith in the possibility of British support. Reviewing the Kurdish response to the crisis Edmonds divided Kurds into two categories: those who clung to the belief that Britain might still do something for them and 'the realists' who accepted that Britain would not do anything 'to upset the Arabs for the sake of the Kurds'. Early in May 1941, a number of tribes in the Sulaimani region began to prepare for action in support of the British, and Shaikh Mahmud was prepared to put himself at their head. The notables of Sulaimani refused to organize accommodation for the planned evacuation of the Baghdad Military College there. In Edmonds's second category of neutrals, Kurdish officers in the Iraqi Army planned to prevent the Rashid Ali regime from a reported plan to move to the north as a last retreat. Since Rashid Ali and his entourage took refuge in Iran, neither of these plans came to anything.[77]

During the next four years, when the British in effect took back control of Iraq, they had another opportunity to act in support of Kurdish aspirations. They did little, still concerned to keep governmental support. Wartime shortages had a terrible effect on much of the Kurdish area, and famine was partly the cause of the 1944 Barzani revolt which followed the rejection of demands for fulfilment of the pledges and immediate economic aid. Kurdish misery and discontent raised fears that Kurds might appeal to the Russians, or even still the Germans, for help and resulted in much official investigation. In January 1944 Lyon, then a Political Adviser in northern Iraq, sent reports of local desperation: 'there are vast and insalubrious areas [of Kurdistan] completely devoid of all medical services'; and, after leave in Britain, he returned to Kurdistan and wrote what Edmonds described in his diary as a strongly worded report with warnings of probable trouble if urgent steps were not taken to feed and clothe the people before winter. This aroused deep resentment in official Baghdad. Edmonds noted: 'After the receipt of Lyon's report ARSHAD [sic] sent FADHIL JAMALI [sic] (now D[irector] G[eneral] in the M[inistry] of E[xternal] A[ffairs]) to ask that Lyon should be withdrawn from the North and indeed Iraq.'[78] In fact, Lyon left at the end of that year, fed up with what he saw as the inexcusable refusal of the Baghdad politicians to give due attention to the needs of the Kurds.

Given the refusal of the British to create an autonomous or independent Kurdistan, either covering the whole Kurdish zone or within the prospective limits of Iraq, British administrators in the north found, in and after 1918, that they had to deal with an extremely complicated network of tribal leaders who themselves were in considerable uncertainty about the future. There were two underlying factors. First, the British had never actually conquered or occupied most of the region to the east of the Tigris, between the Greater and Lesser Zab rivers and the Persian frontier to the east, and further north of the Huwaindiz Chai, tributary of the Greater Zab. Since this area was mostly occupied by tribes whose main activity, apart from agriculture and pastoral pursuits, was war, and since they measured authority in terms of the number of rifles available, this meant that they had never been impressed by the potential military power of the British. It took them some years of experiencing first British (largely Indian) ground forces, and then from 1922 mainly RAF air power, to accept the new alien authority. Even so, their traditions and the whole pattern of their existence militated against a placid law-abiding existence. As Edmonds once commented, their 'nationalism is hardly distinguishable from impatience of any kind of administrative restraint'.[79] It would, therefore, be very difficult to fit many of the tribes into any framework designed for the rest of Iraq. Moreover, it was very hard for the British to distinguish between acts of violence directed against the public peace and those systemic to tribal relations, particularly blood feuds. Only some years of patient negotiation, backed by symbolic use of force, and the creation of adequate communications and defensive positions at key points could bring anything like peace to this region.

That was a long-term problem. More immediately after 1918, and greatly exacerbating it, was the uncertainty over the political future of the whole one-time Mosul wilayat. As was seen above, in 1918 the Turks claimed that Mosul was occupied by British forces only after the armistice of Mudros and that the Ottoman empire had a valid claim to that wilayat. This claim was sustained by the Kemalist regime which, moreover, was prepared actively to pursue it. This increased the uncertainty of many Kurds and others in the Mosul area, especially those that spoke Turkish or had been Ottoman officials, about their future position. Since the British themselves remained uncommitted on the issue for some time after 1918, deciding definitely to retain Mosul within Iraq only in April 1920, it was entirely reasonable that leading Kurdish chiefs should hedge their bets. Clearly, they could play the British off against the Turks in an auction to obtain the best conditions, including maximum autonomy. This uncertainty was increased by the rapid withdrawal of most British troops after March 1919, and still more by the military disasters of 1920. Meantime, Baghdad attempted to control the north with a few political officers, of whom Lyon and W. R. Hay were typical, who had to rely on skill in persuasion rather than military backing to keep control. In June 1921 a small force of Turkish troops arrived in Ruwandiz, their numbers rising to 300 by August. By the end of 1921 the Turks were well entrenched there. In June 1922 they were joined by the Turk, Colonel Ali Shefiq (always known as Oz Demir, or the iron fist), who aroused support among several sections of the Surchi, Khoshnaw, Hamawand and Pizhdar tribes and proceeded to occupy Ranya and Koi Sanjaq. They thus controlled much of the eastern part of the region between the Greater and Lesser Zab rivers, with access to the virtually open Persian frontier, and were poised to move on Arbil and potentially even Mosul.

Given the endemic lawlessness of the mountain Kurds and Turkish support, it was not surprising that the first seven years of the British occupation were the heroic age of the British in Kurdistan. During this period there were many forays by small British forces to deal with Kurds and their Turkish backers, which are graphically recounted in W. R. Hay's *Two Years in Kurdistan ... 1918–1920*, in C. J. Edmonds's *Kurds, Turks, and Arabs* covering mainly the period 1922–25, and by Lyon's memoir, dealing with the whole period from 1918 to well beyond the end of the critical period in 1926. Between them these accounts provide detailed and mutually supporting descriptions of events, which therefore need not be recapitulated in detail here.

Broadly, the attempts to impose British/Iraqi control over the region fell into three chronological periods. The first was from the end of 1918 to the Arab attack on Tal Afar in June 1920. In these years British officers, many of them previously officers of the Indian Army or civil service, made visits to the various chiefs in an attempt to obtain their allegiance, usually symbolized by demands for payments of tax. Many of these visits were successful, but there were a number of failures and disasters, particularly where the British officers were ignorant of local conditions or customs.[80]

These and many similar local problems were inevitable, given the unstable nature of Kurdish society and the novelty of British occupation. The second phase began in the summer of 1920, lasted for some two years, and was more serious. In this period the Arab incursion from Syria, coupled with the risings on the Lower Euphrates and the further withdrawal of British troops, again threw Kurdistan into disorder. In April members of the Surchi tribe, north of the Greater Zab, ambushed a military convoy and attacked Aqra. Hay, then PO at Arbil, attempted to prevent the disturbances spreading to Ruwandiz, Ranya and Koi Sanjaq, but found that there were very few Kurds on whom he could rely. Ruwandiz had to be evacuated later in August, and Koi Sanjaq was in the hands of a junta of local notables. Arbil itself was now in serious danger since elements of the Khoshnaw, usually supporting the British, were poised to attack it early in September. A small relief column was sent from Mosul and the attack withered. By the end of September 1920 most of the Koi and Khoshnaw districts were again nominally owing allegiance to the government, but Ruwandiz was left in Kurdish hands.[81] During the next eighteen months, after the suppression of the Euphrates risings and the end of the Faisal regime in Syria, the situation remained much the same, though it was basically unstable, with local tribal risings at Batas, in the Halabja region, and in April 1922 by the Jabbari chief Saiyid Muhammad, joined by elements of the Hamawand under Kerim-i Fattah Beg. In June 1920 two

British officials, Captains Bond, an APO, and Makant, commanding some Levies, were shot after a meeting with Kerim near the Bazyan Pass.

British control thus remained insecure when the third period, that of active Turkish intervention in Iraq, began in 1922. In fact, informal Turkish forces had been active within the Iraqi frontier since July 1921. In March 1922 the Ankara government gave an agent, Ramzi Bey, the title of quaim-maqam of Ruwandiz, and he was followed in June by Oz Demir, who, according to Edmonds, put it about that 'his mission was the reconquest of the whole of the Mosul wilayat'.[82] This, which may be called the Turkish period, lasted until the end of 1925 with the League of Nations' decision to award the wilayat to Iraq.

This posed the most serious threat to British/Iraqi control of the Kurdish area. The Turks, including ex-Ottoman army officers who knew the area, could supply arms and organization and received much support from Kurds with a strong sympathy for Turkish rule. Later in 1922, in addition to their main base in Ruwandiz, the Turks and local allies controlled Ranya and Qala Diza. Early in September British officials were evacuated by air from Sulaimani. An entirely inadequate force of Levies and a few Sikhs was sent from Darband under the code-name Ranicol to retake Ranya late in August. It was denied adequate air cover by the British GOC Baghdad, General Haldane, and proved a total disaster, with heavy casualties.[83] The Turks and their allies then occupied Koi, though it was reoccupied by a column led by Lyon and Littledale.[84] The situation was so grave that Shaikh Mahmud was summoned from exile in Kuwait and, after giving many assurances of good conduct to the High Commissioner, put back in Sulaimani as President of the Council, to operate under the aegis of Noel, who had replaced Soane there, in the hope that he could rally tribes to the support of the Baghdad regime. In December the British authorities issued the famous statement of intent which acknowledged the right of the Kurds living within the boundaries of Iraq to set up a Kurdish government, which would be arranged by negotiation with 'responsible delegates'. Mahmud, predictably, again set himself up as 'King of Kurdistan' and proceeded to milk all available public funds and put his friends and relations into public offices. He was also alleged to have negotiated with the Turks for an independent Kurdistan under his leadership. He was officially suspended from office in February 1923, refused to visit Baghdad, was bombed by the RAF, fled to the mountains, re-entered Sulaimani in July 1923 after a British occupation force was withdrawn, was again harried by the RAF there, and finally withdrew to the mountains.

By that time, however, the tide had turned decisively against the Turks and their allies. Both Edmonds and Lyon date the turn from the transfer of military responsibility to the RAF on 1 October 1922 and the energies of Sir John Salmond as Air Officer Commanding. He immediately discussed possible offensive schemes with the men on the spot and began using the RAF to bomb recalcitrant Kurds and Turks. After an initial military fiasco late in 1922 failed to capture Ruwandiz,[85] better planned and executed campaigns under Salmond's personal direction in 1923 led to the reoccupation of both Ruwandiz and Sulaimani,[86] though Dobbs refused to allow troops to remain to consolidate control of Sulaimani. This led to a vituperative correspondence between Edmonds and Dobbs.[87] Meantime, Edmonds set up what was called a *cordon sanitaire* of chiefs, appointed as quaimmaqams or subordinate officials and paid generous salaries, to administer the region around Sulaimani and, it was hoped, helped by a mobile police force controlled by Edmonds, block further intrusions by Turkish troops or by Mahmud and his allies.

Perhaps surprisingly this strategy worked remarkably well. The tribal areas gradually settled down. This was greatly helped by the final solution to the Mosul question. The League of Nations Commission of early 1925 eventually recommended that the whole of the Mosul wilayat should be incorporated into Iraq, though it was only in 1926, after much legal activity, that Turkey eventually signed a treaty recognizing this.[88] Thereafter, although Mahmud and Shaikh Ahmad Barzani, and his brother, Mulla Mustafa, continued sporadically to raid, and Ahmad twice repulsed the Iraqi Army in 1931 and 1932, a combined strategy of building roads and block-houses in the tribal area, plus RAF bombing, had finally defeated him by June 1932.[89] Mulla Mustafa, however, raised another revolt in 1943–45, and finally retreated into Persia, where he set up the Kurdish Republic of Mahabad.[90]

These, however, were residual problems in Kurdish Iraq, reflecting the fundamentally unstable character of a tribal society. By the time they handed over authority to the new Iraqi government in 1932, the British had succeeded in imposing a general control over the Kurdish areas of the country. They had done so with minimal use of military force, mainly because they had little land force available. As this and other contemporary accounts make clear, pacification was done mostly by the skill of the very few British Political and Police Officers, using techniques for obtaining support from selected tribal rulers that had been developed on the northwest frontier of India. By playing one chief off against his known rivals, by giving their allies official positions, tax-collecting powers and salaries, they had created networks of clients that contained the trouble-makers. This strategy looked very vulnerable in 1920–23, but gradually gathered strength thereafter, helped by the abolition of the Caliphate in 1924 and the long-delayed decision in 1925 that Mosul wilayat should form part of Iraq.

In all this the British officials, judging by the memoirs of Edmonds and Lyon, were reluctantly aware that they were in effect tricking the Kurds into subservience to what would be an Arab regime which would pay little or no attention to Kurdish interests. They had no option. Their positions depended on the British High Commissioner, who in turn was obeying the orders of London. Iraq was to be made safe for a final transfer to King Faisal as soon as possible, and if this involved subduing Kurds and not making sure of the preservation of even minimal Kurdish rights thereafter, then that was their duty. They were also aware that the British High Commissioners and their staff in Baghdad, including Cox, Dobbs and Kinahan Cornwallis, were 'Arabists' whose main experience had been in the Arab world and who regarded the Kurds as a nuisance. It is therefore not surprising that when, in 1932, Lyon had to give up his position as Administrative Inspector on the creation of the sovereign Iraqi state and was made a Land Settlement Officer, he was delighted that he would no longer have any responsibility for carrying out political policies of which he profoundly disapproved. Again, in 1944, after three years of again having political authority during the British occupation, he was glad to resign and take a consular appointment in Ethiopia because he realized that, with the forthcoming end of the war, he would once again be unable to do anything to help his Kurdish friends.[91] It was thus the great irony of the British occupation of Iraq that they used their authority there not only without fulfilling the promises made in November 1918 and December 1922 but by making it virtually impossible thereafter for the Kurds to fight effectively for what they had been denied.

4. Wallace Lyon's Career

Wallace Lyon's career in Iraq can best be understood in relation to his background. Unlike many of his contemporaries in the administration of the British empire in the early twentieth century, he lacked the conventional upbringing of English independent school and university. He had had to make his own way, and to the end of his career was very conscious that his position remained insecure. On the other hand, his early life and experiences during the First World War before he reached Iraq had made him tough, self-reliant and adaptable. These qualities equipped him exceptionally well for the hazards of life in Kurdistan in the period after 1918.

Lyon's family on the paternal side descended from Scots who left the Highlands after the '45 and became shipowners and traders in Bristol. Their wealth declined after the abolition of the slave trade and both his grandfather and father were Anglican priests. His father, the Revd Paul

Lyon, had started as an engineering apprentice, at sixteen had emigrated in search of wealth in Australia, had little success, and decided to return to Britain to enter the Church. Lacking money he sailed before the mast and enrolled to study divinity in Cambridge. There he was recruited by a Canadian bishop to serve in the remote district of Abernethy in Saskatchewan, north-east of Regina, was rapidly consecrated, and sent there to build his own church and establish a missionary enterprise among the first generation of prairie farmers. Four years later he was joined by his fiancée, Wallace's mother, Louise Crawford, descended from a line of British naval officers, the most famous of whom was Edward Pellew, later Lord Exmouth. She also was a very practical and tough person. On both sides, therefore, Lyon's inheritance was service in Church or the armed forces. This gave him valuable contacts in the British middle and upper-middle class, but no inherited wealth.

The Lyon family left Canada about 1890 since Louise Lyon refused to live any longer in the wilderness, and family influence provided a living in the Church of Ireland. Wallace Lyon was born in Ireland in 1892. The parish was near Kanagh, not far from Lough Ree. Wallace, his older brother Roy, and younger brother Gordon, were brought up there. Money was very short, the stipend only £180 a year, but there was a substantial glebe. It is important that the boys grew up accustomed to a tough rural life, expert at shooting, riding, fishing and trapping. Later they were sent to a very rough Church of Ireland school in Dublin, from which Wallace was expelled at the age of sixteen (for breaking bounds to go to the theatre), after which he attended a Jesuit day-school there. He even enrolled in the National University and passed his first-year exams. But there was no money for him to attend Trinity College, and at this point he had to confront the problem faced by very many boys from the professional but un-moneyed Edwardian middle class: how to enter one of the public services without a degree. The standard practice was to use family influence, if that was available, or to attend a crammer and try for entry to one of the home or overseas services.[92] Wallace Lyon opted to try for the Indian Police Service, which did not demand a degree but had a stiff competitive entrance examination. Living with a relative near London he worked for the examination and, for reasons he never understood, failed. It was therefore decided that he should take the place of Roy, who had been found a post in Sierra Leone, and stay with the family's connection, Bob King, who was an administrator working for the Maharajah of Durbanga in Bihar while looking for a job there. He sailed for India in October 1912. Once there, he was recruited by British American Tobacco (BAT), which was then developing tobacco production in India, to work as a manager in their factory in Bihar. After a foolish juvenile prank he was transferred by BAT to Guntur in Madras Presidency, inspecting bales of tobacco. He then applied to become a 'covenanted' (tenured) employee, and was sent to Bristol to be trained. He was there when war broke out in August 1914. In retrospect this short period in India proved very important. Not only did it provide Lyon with a possible long-term job (and he was paid the balance between his military wages and that of a BAT manager throughout the war) but it gave him knowledge of Hindustani and Urdu, which was to determine his career after 1917.

Lyon immediately volunteered for a cavalry regiment, the 19th Hussars, and, rejecting the offer of a commission, probably arranged by a relation, trained as a private. Early in 1915, however, with the war in France reduced to trenches and with heavy casualties among junior officers, Lyon was ordered to Sandhurst to be trained as an infantry officer. As his regiment he chose the Leinsters and eventually arrived with them in France late in 1915. He was there throughout 1916, was wounded at the battle of the Somme and mentioned in despatches, returning to the trenches after recovery. The critical moment for his future career came in 1917. He was then summoned to London and told that, due to high casualties among British officers in the Indian Army, and since he knew Hindustani, he was to transfer to the Indian Army, where he joined the 52nd Sikhs Frontier Force, an elite regiment. He was sent to Mesopotamia late in 1917 with his regiment, which was put to work on the railway from Basra to Baghdad. Early in 1918 he was back in India for a specialized musketry course, and back in Mesopotamia by August to take part in the final push to Mosul. He ended up at Zakho to eject the final Turkish forces.

In retrospect it is clear that Lyon, as he was fully aware later, had been fortunate. He had been withdrawn from France before the bloody carnage of 1917–18, during which his younger brother, Gordon, was killed; he had arrived in Mesopotamia too late to be involved in the Kut disaster; and he was on the spot when Britain had taken full control over the territory and there was urgent need for British administrators. In his own words:

> Meanwhile Colonel Leachman had been appointed by Sir Percy Cox as Governor of the Mosul Province, and he in turn was obliged to recruit Assistant Political Officers to administer the nine or ten districts into which it was divided. In order to get the necessary staff to administer the country Sir Percy Cox under the authority of the Viceroy of India ... had issued an undertaking that no army officer would suffer professionally as a result of accepting secondment to the Political Service, and among others who had joined were Major Bromilow of the 14th Jat Lancers and our Adjutant Capt. Minchin. It was then that Colonel Leachman asked for me.[93]

It is at this point, late in 1918, that the extract printed here from Lyon's memoir begins, and it is not necessary to recapitulate his career to 1944. It is clear, however, that his earlier life had fitted him exceptionally well for the Iraq of the period after 1918. He was a countryman by upbringing who could cope very well with the physical hazards of spending much of his time under canvas or on safari. He was expert at country pursuits such as shooting and fishing, which added zest to his life. He was physically and mentally very tough, able to survive climatic and medical problems that destroyed many of his contemporaries. After four years in the army, with much active service, he was equally at home as a civil administrator or member of a military expedition. He was a good linguist, already competent in Hindustani, Urdu and French, and became expert in the Kurdish dialects and Arabic, though he never learned Persian. He clearly felt a close affinity with the Kurds, particularly those in the mountains, and their way of life, and was most happy when visiting and staying with them. Conversely he despised the formal lifestyle of the Indian sahib, which was one reason why he preferred to stay in Iraq rather than go back with the Indian Army. But he retained his Indian Army commission until he retired from that army in 1935 as a Major, having hung on to it as security against losing his job in Iraq.

His attitude to other ethnic groups was functional rather than racist. He greatly admired the Indian troops with whom he started and was on close terms with them. He had many very good friends among not only Kurds but also Turks, Turcomans and some Arabs; but he despised those riverine Arabs he regarded as effete and depraved, and disliked most of the Arab politicians who took over power after 1920 as self-serving and corrupt. His main fault, as he admitted in his memoir, was an inherited hot temper, that had got him into scrapes earlier and might have had serious consequences at various times in Iraq. Nor was he a desk administrator. Whereas Edmonds, who had had a much better education including a Cambridge degree, was taken from Kurdistan at the end of 1925 to understudy Cornwallis as Adviser to the Minister of Interior in Baghdad, and later succeeded him, Lyon remained, as in fact he much preferred, in his provincial role. On the other hand, the fact that he was one of the four Administrative Inspectors chosen by the Iraqi government as a Land Settlement Officer in 1932, when the majority of British officials were dismissed, demonstrated how much he was valued for his exceptional knowledge of local land ownership patterns and his total honesty and dependability.[94]

In 1941, after the Rashid Ali revolution and the effective reoccupation of Iraq by British forces, he rejoined the Indian Army and served as a Political Adviser in Kurdistan, as is described in Chapter 12 below. He left Iraq at the end of 1944, finally retiring from the Indian Army with the rank of Lieutenant-Colonel early in 1945, and became British Consul at Harar in

Ethiopia. This seems to have been arranged when he was on leave in Britain that summer, his first visit home since 1938, by his friend Sir Chapman Andrews, who had been Vice-Consul in Kirkuk and, in the 1930s, British Consul in Harar. He must have arranged for Lyon to be considered and interviewed; and on 19 August a Foreign Office official wrote to Sir Kinahan Cornwallis, since 1941 British Ambassador in Baghdad, asking if Lyon could be released as a Political Adviser to take up the post.

> We have been looking around for a good man to reopen the Consulate at Harar in Ethiopia and would like to offer the post to Lieutenant-Colonel W. A. Lyon ... The work would be mainly political, i.e. furnishing reports to the Legation at Addis Ababa on what is going on in the consular district and maintaining good relations with the local Ethiopian authorities and the British military administration in Somaliland ... A knowledge of Arabic is almost essential for not only is it the language most commonly spoken in Harar itself ... but the majority of the inhabitants of the province, both settled and nomad, are Moslem.

The pay would not be as much as Lyon was receiving in Iraq, but there were allowances and he had his Indian Army pension. It was temporary, 'but, if Lyon did well at Harar and liked the work we should, of course, be prepared to try and find another suitable post for him if after a few years he wanted a change'. Moreover, his wife would be very welcome there.[95]

Cornwallis made no objection; and at the end of 1944 Lyon proceeded home for demobilization before going to Harar. He eventually arrived there in August 1945 and stayed until 1949; his experiences there are described in the last chapter of his memoir, which is not reproduced here. He found both Ethiopia and the Foreign Service objectionable in different ways, and, eventually, when the British government proposed new and less favourable tax arrangements for people in his position, decided not to ask for another posting. He retired in 1949. As he said of his time in Ethiopia, 'It had been a novel experience, it had kept me off the bread line for 4½ years and proved an excellent preparation for retirement. I had no regrets.'[96] In retirement he lived in Cheltenham and died of cancer in California in January 1977.

Notes

1. See S. A. Cohen, *British Policy in Mesopotamia, 1903–1914* (London, 1976).

2. The following are among the secondary works I found most useful for the diplomatic background: B. C. Busch, *Britain, India and the Arabs, 1914–1921* (Berkeley and London, 1971); J. Darwin, *Britain and the Middle East. Imperial Policy in the Aftermath*

of War 1918–22 (London, 1981); E. Kedourie, *England and the Middle East: The Destruction of the Ottoman Empire 1914–1921* (London, 1956); M. Kent, (ed.), *The Great Powers and the End of the Ottoman Empire* (London, 1982); M. Kent, *Oil and the Empire: British Policy and Mesopotamian Oil 1900–1921* (New York, 1976); E. Monroe, *Britain's Moment in the Middle East 1914–1956* (London, 1965); J. Nevakivi, *Britain, France and the Arab Middle East 1914–1928* (London, 1969); V. H. Rothwell, *British War Aims and Peace Diplomacy* (Oxford, 1971); E. and I. Karsh, *Empires in the Sand: The Struggle for Mastery in the Middle East, 1789–1923* (Cambridge, Mass., 1999).

3. He became High Commissioner only after the declaration of the protectorate.

4. Kedourie, *England and the Middle East*, pp. 65–6.

5. A good account of this campaign is in E. Tauber, *The Formation of Modern Syria and Iraq* (Ilford, Essex and Portland, Oregon, 1995).

6. S. H. Longrigg, *Iraq, 1900–1950. A Political, Social and Economic History* (London, 1953) pp. 111–14.

7. Kedourie, *England and the Middle East*, pp. 178–9.

8. Casualty figures are from P. W. Ireland, *Iraq. A Study in Political Development* (London, 1937), p. 273. The civil officers killed are listed in Sir A. T. Wilson, *Loyalties: Mesopotamia 1914–1917* (London, 1930), p. ix.

9. A. T. Wilson, *Mesopotamia 1917–1920: A Clash of Loyalties* (London, 1931), pp. 260–1.

10. See J. Marlowe, *Late Victorian. The Life of Sir Arnold Talbot Wilson* (London, 1967). Wilson had gone from Sandhurst into the Indian Army in 1905, transferring to the Indian Political Service in 1909. He served in Persia and on the Turko-Persian Boundary Commission of 1913–14 before joining the IEF as Deputy Chief Political Officer in 1915. He became Deputy Civil Commissioner in 1916–18 and Acting Civil Commissioner in 1918 during Cox's absence in Persia.

11. Wilson, *Mesopotamia*, p. 330.

12. Ibid., p. 108.

13. Ibid., pp. 117–18.

14. E. Burgoyne, *Gertrude Bell: from her Personal Papers 1914–1926* (London, 1962), pp. 31–2, 78, 101–2, 116–18, 141; H. V. F. Winstone, *Gertrude Bell* (London, 1978), ch. 19.

15. P. Sluglett, *Britain in Iraq 1914–1932* (London, 1976), p. 33.

16. Wilson, *Mesopotamia*, pp. 242–7.

17. There were similarities with the 1919 Government of India Act (commonly called the Montagu-Chelmsford Reforms). But much of the proposed system copied that in Egypt under Cromer and his successors, though without an equivalent of the Khedive.

18. Wilson, *Mesopotamia*, p. 249.

19. Ibid., pp. 260–1.

20. The text of the telegram is printed in ibid., pp. 305–6.

21. Ibid., p. 306.

22. Ibid., p. 307.

23. Ibid., p. 320. Although it is not clear, it seems likely that the phrase was from T. E. Lawrence and was printed in *The Daily Herald* on 9 August 1920. Lawrence was then entirely unknown in Iraq. Wilson went on leave and then became General Manager of the Anglo-Persian Oil Company at Abadan. After retiring from that he

was elected to the House of Commons in 1933 and remained an MP until the war, improbably volunteering for the RAF, though then fifty-one, and being killed in action as a tail-gunner on a bombing mission in 1940. There is an ironic echo of Lawrence here, though Lawrence was killed on a motor cycle, not in action.

24. The supposed contrast was exaggerated by Gertrude Bell, who fell out with Wilson in mid-1920, demanding a much more rapid Arabization policy, and wrote very critical letters to highly-placed friends in London and Cairo. For a good account of her activities see Winstone, *Gertrude Bell*, esp. ch. 19. Wilson would have dismissed her as Oriental Secretary for improper behaviour had he continued in office after October 1920. Lyon, and probably many other political officers, were highly critical of Bell, particularly on account of her alleged snobbery in relations with Iraqis and eventual hostility to their revered Wilson.

25. P. Graves, *The Life of Sir Percy Cox* (London, 1941), p. 266. Graves had been a *Times* correspondent in Constantinople before 1914 and served in the Arab Bureau and the armed forces in the Middle East during the war, after which he returned to journalism. He probably knew Cox well and agreed with his strategy in Iraq.

26. There is a good account of this process in Darwin, *Britain, Egypt and the Middle East*, chs 7 and 8.

27. Graves, *Cox*, p. 280. P. Sluglett, *Britain in Iraq*, p. 43 states that he was unelectable after the battle of Maysalun on 20 July 1920, when the French forces defeated those of the Sharifian regime in Syria, but gives no explanation. There is nothing in Tauber's *The Formation of Modern Syria and Iraq* to link Abdullah with Maysulun.

28. See his statement to Gertrude Bell in February 1919, reported by her in a memorandum printed in Wilson, *Mesopotamia*, pp. 336–41. But Sluglett, *Britain in Iraq*, p. 93, n. 3, suggests that he later became less sure, possibly because of his dislike of Faisal's candidature.

29. Winstone, *Gertrude Bell*, p. 240.

30. Philby was dismissed by Cox for protesting over this. For his later career in Transjordan and Saudi Arabia see E. Monroe, *Philby of Arabia* (New York and London, 1973).

31. Part II: 'Buyurun Bakinez', a memoir by Wallace Lyon (hereafter: Lyon Memoir), p. 95, gives a clear indication of how artificial this consultation process was in his liwa of Arbil. Major Marshall in Kirkuk refused to press Faisal's claims and reported a negative response. The Sulaimani liwa was not even consulted since it was excluded from the ambit of the Baghdad Council.

32. Quoted E. Kedourie, *The Chatham House Version and Other Middle-Eastern Studies* (London, 1970) p. 242.

33. In A. F. Madden and J. Darwin, *The Dependent Empire, 1900–1948* (Westport, Conn., 1994) pp. 636–8, which reproduces some clauses of the treaty and summarizes others, it is stated (p. 636, n. 2) that the original draft came from Churchill in February 1922 and that he persuaded the cabinet to prefer his draft to that of the Foreign Office, drafted by Major H. W. Young.

34. Ireland, *Iraq*, pp. 366–7.

35. For descriptions of Faisal's inconsistency and manipulation see the many letters during this period by Gertrude Bell, reproduced in Burgoyne, *Gertrude Bell*. The process of negotiation and conflict is described in some detail by Ireland, *Iraq*, chs 19 and 20.

36. This was possibly due to the insistence by one of the Mosul Commissioners,

the Belgian Colonel Paulis, who formed a very low opinion of the 'extremist' Arab government in Baghdad, that a condition of awarding Mosul to Iraq must be that the Mandate was renewed for a substantial period, possibly twenty years. He expressed this view many times to C. J. Edmonds, the Liaison Officer with the Commission, and other British officials. See Edmonds Papers, Middle East Archive, St Antony's College, Oxford, Box 1, file 2B.

37. Quoted Sluglett, *Britain in Iraq*, p. 270.

38. For this and what follows see Kedourie's *The Chatham House Version*, chs 9, 10 and 12.

39. Kedourie attributes this approach, among others, to M. Khadduri's *Independent Iraq 1932–1958. A Study in Iraqi Politics* (London, 1951; 2nd rev. edn, London, 1960) and Longrigg's *Iraq 1900–1950*. In both cases I think he exaggerates their lack of criticism. Khadduri, for example, wrote of the political structure of the 1930s: 'But when analysed in the light of rigid control of the elections, it is clear that dissolutions [of parliament] hardly meant anything save the replacement of opposing members of Parliament by others from among the Government's friends and supporters' (p. 47).

40. Kedourie, *The Chatham House Version*, p. 239.

41. Ibid., p. 262, quoting the British Command Paper *Policy in Iraq* (Cmd 3440) of 1929.

42. Longrigg, *Iraq 1900–1950*, p. 224.

43. M. A. Tarbush, *The Role of the Military in Politics: A Case Study of Iraq to 1941* (London, 1982), ch. 3.

44. Ibid., p. 79.

45. Khadduri, *Independent Iraq 1932–1958*, provides detailed information on all Iraqi Cabinets and political developments.

46. The Residency was isolated for virtually the whole of May 1941. For a detailed account see Freya Stark, *Dust in the Lion's Paw. Autobiography 1939–1946* (London, 1961), chs 6 and 7. Stark was then Oriental Secretary to the Ambassador and was in the Residency for the whole period. There are pictures she took in the Residency during the siege in the Middle East Archive, St Antony's College, Oxford. See also the diary of C. J. Edmonds, then Adviser to the Ministry of Interior, in Edmonds Papers, Box 27/3. For an account of the experience of Lyon, then in Kirkuk, and other Britons there see Lyon Memoir, pp. 213–14. A fuller account is given by his fellow-prisoner, John Brady, an education officer, in his *Eastern Encounters. Memoirs of a Decade 1937–46* (Braunton, Devon, 1992), ch. 18, part of which is reproduced, with his permission, as an appendix to Chapter 11 below.

47. This account is based mainly on Longrigg, *Iraq 1900–1950*; and Ireland, *Iraq*.

48. But C. J. Edmonds, *Kurds, Turks and Arabs* (London, 1957), pp. 228–9, says that J. G. Cook, APO at Ranya, 'had ordinarily worn Kurdish clothing'. He was clearly an eccentric, and Lyon Memoir, p. 100, described him in 1922 as being at the end of his tether.

49. The land settlement scheme was defined by the Land Settlement Law of 1932 and the Law Governing the Rights and Duties of Cultivators of 1933. These were the outcome of British attempts since the occupation to clarify the very confused Ottoman system of land ownership and tax liabilities. Their approach resembled that which led to the ryotwari system set up in much of British India from the early nineteenth century in that it attempted to investigate claims, rights and obligations and award

possession, along with tax obligations, to active cultivators. British Political Officers and AIs were initially given discretion to investigate rights on state land (miri) and to allocate land if no valid claim could be made. The later legislation was based on the report made by Sir Ernest Dowson, an expert in Egyptian land ownership, which, among other things, recommended that small tax-paying tenants should be given secure tenure against the aggression of shaikhs and larger urban landowners. The Land Settlement Department, in which Lyon, A. H. Ditchburn, C. C. Aston and R. F. Jardine were appointed Land Settlement Officers and made Presidents of Land Settlement Committees, was set up in 1932. But the 1933 Act, which would probably not have been accepted by the High Commissioner during the Mandate period, also imposed obligations and penalties on the peasant tenants and leaseholders, gave the larger landowners the power to evict them for deficiencies, and prevented the peasants from leaving the land until their inevitable debts were paid off. The activities of the Settlement Officers are described in some detail by Lyon. For accounts of these developments and assessment of their effects on the peasantry, see in particular Longrigg, *Iraq 1900–1950*, pp. 212–14; Tarbush, *The Role of the Military*, pp. 19–30; Sluglett, *Britain in Iraq*, pp. 249–52; S. Haj, *The Making of Iraq 1900-1963* (Albany, NY, 1997), ch. 2.

50. In the 1920s Administrative Inspectors were paid £108 per month (£1,296 a year) plus allowances, which was very considerable by contemporary British domestic standards. The ministerial Advisers received £172 per month plus 12 per cent in allowances. Ireland, *Iraq*, p. 306.

51. Wilson, *Loyalties*, pp 66–7. Wilson does not use the term Levies in the text but refers to these forces as Levies in his index.

52. There is a good summary of the experiences of the Assyrians and of the substantial literature on their problems in D. Silverfarb, *Britain's Informal Empire in the Middle East: A Case Study of Iraq 1929–1941* (New York and London, 1986), ch. 4.

53. The best source on the role of the RAF as a police force is D. Omissi, *Air Power and Colonial Control* (Manchester, 1990). There is a useful summary of the role of the RAF in Iraq in Sluglett, *Britain in Iraq*, pp. 262–70. A. Boyle, *Trenchard* (London, 1962), chs 13–17 gives intermittent information on the decision to transfer responsibility for defence in Iraq to the RAF in October 1922, under Sir John Salmond as AOC, and its later achievements. This was a result of the Cairo Conference of March 1921 and the need for reduction in military expenditure; but also of the success of RAF operations in the NW Frontier of India and against the 'Mad Mullah' in Somalia. Conversely, the RAF's success in Iraq then provided a strong argument for preserving the RAF against naval and army hostility. Boyle's book is out of date in its account of the British commitment to the Sharif (p. 377) and wrong in saying (p. 477) that the Lausanne Treaty ended Turkey's claim to Mosul.

54. Sluglett, *Britain in Iraq*, pp. 265–8.

55. There are detailed accounts of the events of 1941 in Silverfarb, *Britain's Informal Empire*, chs 12 and 13, and in Tarbush, *The Role of the Military*, ch. 8.

56. Stark, *Dust in the Lion's Paw*, p. 128.

57. Among the most helpful secondary sources I used on the Kurdish question were: D. McDowall, *A Modern History of the Kurds* (London and New York, 1997); G. Chaliand, *The Kurdish Tragedy* (London and New Jersey, 1994); R. Olson, *The Emergence of Kurdish Nationalism and the Sheikh Said Rebellion, 1880–1925* (Austin, Texas, 1989); M. R. Izady, *The Kurds. A Concise Handbook* (Washington DC and London, 1992);

K. Kirisci and G. M. Winrow, *The Kurdish Question and Turkey: An Example of Trans-state Ethnic Conflict* (London and Portland, Oregon, 1997).

58. W. R. Hay, *Two Years in Kurdistan. Experiences of a Political Officer 1918–1920* (London, 1921), pp. 35–6.
59. See Lyon Memoir, p. 85.
60. Edmonds, *Kurds, Turks and Arabs*, pp. 5–6.
61. Izady, *The Kurds*, pp. xii, 32, 73, emphasis in original.
62. McDowall, *A Modern History of the Kurds*, p. 9.
63. Chaliand, *The Kurdish Tragedy*, p. 19.
64. Izady, *The Kurds*, pp. 78–85.
65. Chaliand, *The Kurdish Tragedy*, pp. 20–3.
66. The main sources used for the material on religious orders etc. are those listed in n. 57.
67. Quoted in McDowall, *A Modern History of the Kurds*, p. 53.
68. Quoted in ibid., p. 118.
69. Olson, *The Emergence of Kurdish Nationalism*, pp. 52–84.
70. McDowall, *A Modern History of the Kurds*, p. 169.
71. Ibid., p. 171.
72. Edmonds Papers, Box 3/2.
73. Ibid.
74. Ibid.
75. McDowall, *A Modern History of the Kurds*, pp. 177–8.
76. Quoted in ibid., p. 289.
77. 'The Kurds in May 1941', paper dated 27 July 1941, Edmonds Papers, Box 3/2.
78. Edmonds Diary, para. 413, 9 September 1944, ibid., Box 27/3.
79. Edmonds, 'The Kurds in May 1941'.
80. McDowall, *A Modern History of the Kurds*, p. 155; Lyon Memoir, p. 70.
81. The events of August–September 1920 are described in detail in Hay, *Two Years in Kurdistan*, chs 17–20.
82. Edmonds, *Kurds, Turks, and Arabs*, p. 245.
83. Ranicol is described in detail in ibid., ch. 17. Edmonds accompanied the force, having just taken over as APO Ranya. He lost part of his diary and other possessions in the retreat.
84. This is described by Lyon Memoir, pp. 113–17.
85. The story is told in Edmonds, *Kurds, Turks, and Arabs*, ch. 20. Lyon was not involved.
86. The story of these expeditions is told in detail in Edmonds, *Kurds, Turks, and Arabs*, chs 21 and 22; Lyon Memoir, pp. 119–25.
87. Edmonds to Sec. H. Com., 5 May 1923, Edmonds Papers, Box 1, file 1C; Box 1, file 1B and Box 3, file 2.
88. There are detailed accounts of the Commission in Edmonds, *Kurds, Turks, and Arabs*, chs 26 and 27, and in Lyon Memoir, ch. 5. There is much material on how the British handled the Commission in the Edmonds Papers, Box 1, file 2, including detailed reports by Lyon in his role as 'Local Expert', by the other 'Local Experts' who

accompanied the commissioners, and by Edmonds, who acted as Liaison Officer, orchestrating the whole investigation. It seems clear that the British, being on home ground, outmanoeuvred the Turks and swung the commissioners to their point of view. See also McDowall, *A Modern History of the Kurds*, pp. 142–4.

89. See Lyon Memoir, pp. 152 and 165–6 for descriptions of this process of road and block-house building, which to British historians may recall the occupation of the Scottish highlands after 1745.

90. For the activities of Shaikh Ahmad and the character of Mulla Mustafa, see Lyon Memoir, pp. 189–90. See also Chaliand, *The Kurdish Tragedy*, ch. 5; McDowall, *A Modern History of the Kurds*, chs 8 and 11.

91. See Lyon Memoir, pp 000 and 000. Regarding his final departure in December 1944, Lyon wrote: 'Other tribal chiefs [as well as Mulla Mustafa] were likewise getting restless and as my sympathies were entirely on their side I became ever more conscious of the delicacy of my position. If I couldn't help them I should clear out.' Ibid., p. 228.

92. Roy Lyon had been provided with a place as a clerk in the Bank of England by family influence but found the archaic discipline unacceptable. According to Wallace Lyon in this memoir, he was sacked for taking off his morning coat in hot weather and hitting his supervisor with a ledger when confronted. An alternative family version is that he threw an inkpot at him. Either way he lost his job and seemed likely to remain unemployed; but an aunt who had high official connections managed to get him an administrative appointment in Sierra Leone, where he had a successful career. He was fortunate that the Colonial Office had not by 1914 established a unified Colonial Service and was desperately short of possible administrators in tropical Africa. See A. Kirk-Greene, *On Crown Service. A History of HM Colonial and Overseas Civil Services 1837–1997* (London, 1999), ch. 2 for a description of the way appointments to colonial administrative posts were made before 1914. Wallace Lyon benefited in that Roy had been scheduled to go to India to work with a family connection in Bihar. Wallace Lyon eventually took his place there.

93. Lyon MS, pp. 99–100.

94. He was awarded the OBE for his work in Kurdistan. In 1938, when on leave in Britain, he was induced by his wife to look for employment there. He found that little was on offer for someone with his qualifications, turning down the offer of a commission as a photographer in the RAF, and returned to Iraq.

95. Letter from Foreign Office to Sir Kinahan Cornwallis, 19 August 1944, in Lyon Papers.

96. Lyon MS, p. 441.

'BUYURUN BAKINEZ'

A Memoir by Wallace Lyon

CHAPTER I

Mosul, Dohuk and the 1920 Rising, 1918–20

§ [AT the end of 1918] I had the choice of three careers: to return to the British American Tobacco Company, to stay with the regiment or go on secondment to the Political Service. All through the war the BAT had been subsidizing my pay, until at length my army pay was equal to what I had been getting before enlistment. This was very generous and so when they asked me when I could be expected back, I replied that the army life appealed to me and that I would not therefore return. I thanked them for their generosity, and offered to repay by instalments. But they said the money had been written off. They congratulated me on winning a regular commission and wished me luck in my new career.

There then remained the alternatives, Regiment or Political. I could never hope to be a General in the Political Service, but on the other hand the life promised to be most exciting for we were in what for us was a new country where anything could happen. Without the spur of war, station life in India could be very boring, and frankly I felt uncomfortable at the prospect of repeating the same old drill and training, giving orders to subedars who were veterans before I was born ... So in the end I decided to consult my Colonel, who had always taken a fatherly interest in me.

He explained what a famous officer Colonel G. E. Leachman was when stationed in India before the war with his regiment – the Royal Sussex: instead of going home on furlough he spent his leave travelling around Arabia on a camel disguised as an Arab. The map was criss-crossed with the routes he had taken both in Arabia and in the desert between Iraq and the Mediterranean. He had before the war been imprisoned by the Turks as an unlicensed Arab kebab seller in Mosul. He was a blood brother of the Aniza tribe which roamed the high desert and a life long friend of Hamo Shero, chief of the Yezidis in the Jabal Sinjar. He had accompanied the troops since the beginning of the war, had escaped out of Kut during the siege and frequently operated alone behind the Turkish lines. In short one could not serve under a more distinguished officer. He [Colonel Wynter] considered that I showed an aptitude for dealing with orientals and he thought I should try it. If I found it disappointing I could return to the regiment, but he counselled me to accept only the office of administrator and not Police Gendarmerie, Arab Levies, or such jobs of secondary standing. He thought the Indian Army would be very soon completely Indianized, and though I might be senior to most of the new Indian officers with King's Commissions, I would as time went on find myself in a minority in my own mess. It so turned out afterwards that his prognostications, though correct, were greatly delayed, but all in all I thought his advice sound, and I took it.

In due course Colonel Leachman provided a T model Ford to transport my relief to Zakho. He also laid on 100 coolies in two batches of fifty stationed at the foot and halfway up the pass to drag the car to the summit and I reported in that evening. I had joined the Political Service of Iraq.

Apart from [Captain A. C.] Pearson, APO Zakho, and [Major G.] Bromilow, now APO Tal Afar, the only officers I knew in the Political Service were [Captain H. C.] Minchin, our Adjutant, now APO [Mosul] City, and Captain [C. H.] Gowan, Adjutant of the 13th Hussars, now commanding the Gendarmerie, and Dr Macdougal who was now in charge of the city hospital. The other officers were Mr [E. M.] Drower, a lawyer who had practised in Egypt and was now Chief Judge, Major [L. F.] Nalder, one of the Blues who had governed the blacks in the Sudan, and was now APO Mosul District, and Captain [K. R.] Scott of the 31st Punjabi Regiment who was Personal Assistant to Leachman. He it was I was detailed to assist, and understudy.

Colonel Leachman was a tall wiry man with dark brown eyes, thinning hair and a long seamed and weatherbeaten face. He spoke the pure Arabic of the high desert and needless to say was at home and familiar with all the details of Beduin culture. Impatient, restless and tireless, like Napoleon he could do with very little sleep. He would lead a carousal in the mess till all but he had fled to bed, then perhaps he might rest for an hour or two before setting off suddenly to some unannounced and distant post, without telling anyone where or when he could be expected to return. He would give orders for champagne by the case, and when the bill arrived he would storm at the expense and extravagance and demand an investigation about who was responsible. He would sometimes wake his staff at 4 a.m. declaiming on the dangers of sunstroke; and once he ordered Minchin to label and number all the streets and houses in the city, only to rant about the job not being finished the next day. He summoned the city councillors and ordered them to make a record of all the houses in the city with the full value of each house. This they reluctantly did, and thinking that it must be for property tax, they assessed the houses at a very low figure and their own at rock bottom. When at length it was done, he sent for Captain Boucher, the City Engineer, and drawing a straight line on the map across the city from the bridge westwards to the Sinjar Gate, he told the council to give one month's notice to all house owners and tenants on this line, after which the houses would be demolished, compensation to be paid at the rates just fixed, and a wide street to be built with the rubble.

When we entered Mosul the prison was full. Such was the corruption and lethargy of Turkish justice that many of the prisoners had been awaiting trial for years. Some had never even had a chance to see a magistrate. It was just like the Old Testament all over again. If a man had a nice orchard which he refused to sell to some covetous Pasha, it was a simple matter for the Pasha to trump up some charge, have him arrested, and perhaps detained until he agreed to sell. There were many such cases, and to solve the problem Leachman arrested all the local judges and confined them in prison till all cases were completed by them. He then released them all, judges, prisoners, criminals alike.

During the Turkish regime there had been wholesale massacres of the Armenians, and this had naturally been intensified during the war as they were all suspect. There were two forms of massacre, the red which was bloody and comparatively sudden, and the white which took the form of marching the victims about until they died of exhaustion. As a consequence there were a lot of orphaned children who had taken refuge with the Arabs, and the location and return of these to their nearest surviving relatives was another problem which he swiftly solved. But what gave [Leachman the] greatest pleasure was the hunt for hidden grain stores which the rich had hoarded. These were raised, expropriated at Baghdad – and not at the local inflated prices – and then issued to the starving masses free. He loved to humble the mighty and uphold the weak. He would quell the most lawless rabble with sheer personality, supported only by his cut-down polo stick. Like Marshal Ney he was the bravest of the brave, and unlike Lawrence of Arabia he wasted none of the British tax-payers' golden sovereigns.

When hearing a dispute he would make no written notes, but as soon as each side had stated his case the decision would follow like the recoil of a field gun. In nine cases out of ten he was right for he had lived among the Arabs and knew them. Perhaps it was intuition. As a wartime Political Officer he was supreme, but for an administrator and organizer he was too much of a lone hand; as a master for young officers to model he was disastrous, especially with the Kurds, a mountain race with whom both he and we were now in contact for the first time. As will be seen later, many young officers were to meet their death as a result of trying to copy his methods without having his background or experience; and little more than a year was to pass before he was assassinated.

Colonel Leachman invited me to join No. 1 Political Mess, but having heard from my friend Minchin of the excesses and expense, I asked to be excused on the plea that there was no necessity to add another to the crowded quarters when there was ample room in my old quarters with the 52nd Sikhs who were only a few doors away. This was agreed, and later on, when numbers increased and the regiment moved out, I started up No. 2 Political Mess in a similar house on the riverside further upstream, and here I was joined by the judge, a rather elderly man who sought a quieter life, the civil doctor, and engineer, and the agricultural officer.

The office work was new to me and I found it most baffling. My knowledge of Arabic was very rudimentary, but even the English side of the work seemed disjointed and devoid of any signs of normal procedure. Though I saw a lot of what was happening, I could seldom grasp what it was all about or the reasons underlying the actions taken. I struggled along as best I could to help Scott, but all the time I felt stupid and disappointed. Of one thing I felt certain: it was enough to be close to Colonel Leachman in the daytime without having to keep up with him at night. My sympathies were with the judge and I was glad I was not No. 1 Mess.

By now [April 1919] the Armistice with Turkey had been signed some six months and the general impression was that as in Europe there would be no more fighting. How naïve we were, and how wrong! For us Political Officers on the Turkish frontier there was to be unceasing though unreported irregular warfare for a further six years before peace was signed, and even after that numerous campaigns, alarms and excursions with turbulent tribesmen both in the mountains and plains of the Mosul Province. For the Turks had never honestly accepted our conquest of the Mosul Province – the most interesting of the three that formed the modern Iraq, with its Kurdish mountains, its potential oil fields, and its many varieties of climate, religions, races and sport.

With special officers, supported by religious fanatics preaching a jihad, Bashi-Bazooks [Turkish irregular troops] and irregular troops of all kinds, the Turks proceeded to stir up the tribesmen, fomenting rebellion with many promises, some arms and a little cash. Propaganda, murder and insurrection were the means adopted to force us out; and in addition to setting up a civil government to preserve law and order, it was to combat this that we had been enrolled. To be sure it was a most interesting job, but far less peaceful than a soldier's life in India.

[The trouble] started off in April 1919 with [Captain A. C.] Pearson, the

APO Zakho, who, following Leachman's orders, had gone up into the frontier hills inhabited by the Goyan tribe to seek out and collect Armenian refugee children. On his way back he was ambushed, his body mutilated, and his ears cut off and sent to his master Leachman. This was an insult and a challenge which Leachman was not slow to take up, for Pearson was one of his best and most experienced young officers. Though a conscientious objector and puritan, he had been one of the first to offer his services on the outbreak of war and had faced all risks unarmed. Leachman at once went up to reconnoitre the situation personally, and while doing so was shot at and missed at close range by a Kurdish assassin. He immediately closed with his attacker, seized the rifle, broke it across his back, and left him disarmed and disabled on the side of the mountain track as a warning to others. It was typical of Leachman to spare his opponent and he didn't even bother to have him arrested. But the murder could not be overlooked and so a column was sent up to [hit] the Goyan with fire and sword.

Shortly after this, one Sunday morning I was fishing in the Tigris on the east bank, just opposite the government officers, when an orderly came with a message for me to report to Colonel Leachman. I confess I was a bit peeved at the continual harrying which had to be endured by anyone on Leachman's staff, and anyway this was my day off. He was waiting for me in his office and said, 'There is a Kurdish leader called Shaikh Nuri who lives in the village of Brifkhan about 20 miles east of Dohuk. Go and tell him that I have heard rumours of his recent activities, and say that if he makes any trouble I will hang him on his own verandah.'

So I called my syce and told him to saddle the horses, his and mine, and I took one mounted gendarme who knew the way, and set forth. By nightfall I had got as far as the village of Alkosh, the site of the tomb of the prophet Nahum, mentioned in the Old Testament. It lay at the foot of the first range of hills and was about 25 miles from Mosul, and slightly less from my objective though just as far or further in time since the second half was mountainous. I therefore spent the night in the monastery where I was royally entertained. It lay several miles off the main road to Zakho, and I was the first British officer to visit it since 1914.

The next morning, after a good night's sleep and an early breakfast of hard-boiled eggs, cheese, honey and unleavened bread, I set off accompanied by the syce and the gendarme and made for the pass over the first line of hills. The gendarme rode in front, being the guide, myself next and the syce behind me. The gendarme had a Turkish rifle, the syce an old Snider and I had my automatic Colt pistol. We reached the top and then proceeded down the other side into a valley which was covered with stunted oaks and vineyards. Suddenly round a corner we came upon an armed Kurdish tribesman, with rifle, bandolier and dagger complete. Now

Colonel Leachman had issued a proclamation forbidding the carrying of arms on the roads, so I hailed the tribesman and told him to stop. But instead of doing so he loaded his rifle and ran up the hill and off the road, and I spurred after him closely followed by the syce. He turned, sat down, and fired, so I drew my pistol and fired while the syce also fired from the saddle as we dashed up the hill, when suddenly our quarry dropped his rifle and toppled over on his side. We galloped up, seized his rifle, and then had a look at him. He had a deep wound in his thigh and buttock so we tore off the lower part of his shirt and bound him up. To this day I don't know what hit him, for the Snider fired a big bullet which would make a wound similar to a 455 Colt automatic. Hitting him at all was a tremendous fluke when pursuing him on horseback, and if it was I, then a still bigger fluke, for I had only hoped to fluster him until we could close. The syce had fired of his own volition, and the gendarme had galloped on down the track and now that the firing was over and he could see that we had won he came back. I was naturally annoyed with his conduct, which was cowardly when compared with that of the syce. So I made him dismount, put the wounded man across his saddle, and continue on foot. Eventually we came to a village and there I dumped the wounded man, and proceeded on my own way. And now, the more I thought about it, the more I realized how hasty and ill advised I had been. It was the Leachman tradition, without the Leachman experience, for a tribesman returning home without his rifle would be the laughing stock of his womenfolk. However, there was nothing more to be done about it, and after another 6 or 7 miles we rode up the last slope to Brifkhan where I sent the gendarme ahead to announce my arrival.

Shaikh Nuri had a very pleasant *Qasr* or château overlooking the Gelliroman, or pomegranate valley, beyond which several more ranges of hills were visible. He ushered me into his reception room; and as it was now late afternoon he invited me to stay the night. After serving me the usual sweet tea and cigarettes he inquired politely if I was tired after the journey, and how did I like the Kurdish country, so different from the plains. I said I had enjoyed the journey and the scenery but that it had been interrupted by an encounter with a Kurdish rifleman, who contrary to the proclamation was carrying arms on the highway. To my surprise he told me he knew all about it and that the victim was one of his own men. To this I replied that I was sorry to hear that, but if he cared to send him to Mosul I would see that he received the best medical attention and there would be nothing more said about it. It then occurred to me that news travelled fast, and someone in the village must have gone on ahead of me. He thanked me and said the matter was of too little importance to merit my anxiety. So I thought this was the time to tell him the purpose of my visit and I gave him the Colonel's message as well as I could. He took it all very politely and then asked if I was ready for food. Soon there was a choice tray with chicken and rice cooked in boiled butter, fried eggs and spinach and locally produced crystallized fruit. After a good meal and the usual formalities he withdrew and I composed myself for sleep.

The following morning I was up bright and early and ready for the usual Kurdish breakfast, hard-boiled eggs, cheese, honey and tea with wafer-thin crackly bread. After that I said goodbye to Shaikh Nuri and started back, not, however, without certain qualms for there was lots of cover on each side of the road; so just in case somebody might be waiting up, I turned northwards to Dohuk. Till well out of sight I went at a walk, though I never felt more like a gallop; however, there was no ambush and I reached my destination without incident. On arrival at Mosul I reported to Colonel Leachman, including the incident on the way up for which I expected a reprimand; but he was quite satisfied and said it all went to show we meant business.

I continued for another week or so in the office and then confessed to Scott that I was a round peg in a square hole and out of harmony with it all; so he said I'd best go and tell the Colonel. It was a delicate matter for me as I did not want to hurt the feelings of an officer who had invited me to join him. Scott had arranged the interview and so I was surprised to see Major [L. F.] Nalder sitting in the room. However, it was the Colonel's affair to dismiss him, having just sent for me, and so I thought it best to go ahead. I told him I didn't think I was any good for the work in his office and I therefore requested permission to return to my regiment. The Colonel said nothing but to my surprise Nalder spoke up. 'If you agree, sir, and if he is willing, I would like to give him a trial in my office and if after he still wishes to return to the regiment then let him do so.' To this I was agreeable.

Now Nalder had been a personal secretary to Lord Northcliffe, a district officer in the Sudan Service; a professional administrator by training, he was cool, calm and collected. His procedure was standardized and his actions deliberate: he did nothing without proof and reason, and best of all he was always ready to explain anything to a learner. Like master, like man ... and all his staff were like him. His chief revenue officer Umjad al-Umeri was a local aristocrat who commanded universal respect; his translator Hussein Effendi was a young and rather delicate Arab gentleman, and the doorkeeper Riscoe, an Armenian who knew all the local languages, had been dragoman to the German Consul for years, and was by far the best and most knowledgeable in the whole serai. The atmosphere was a complete change, and at once I felt interested and at ease. I sat beside him and learned a lot; not only what to do but just as important what not to do. But for his tuition I feel sure I would have shared the fate of so many brother officers who were denied it.

Gradually I became helpful, and after a couple of months, it was decided that I should go to Dohuk as Assistant Political Officer [APO] of that district. My Police Officer was Charles Littledale whom I had known when we were encamped at Samarra. We rode up together, ran up the Union Jack on the roof of the government office, and then pitched a tent in a vineyard above the river gorge, for it was very malarious and we sought to avoid the mosquitoes by living above them. We then took a stroll through the bazaar, but there was no deputation to welcome us, nor did anyone take the slightest notice. So we returned to our tent, drank some tea, and went into committee. Something must be done, for were we not members of an army that had defeated the Turks who for years had enslaved these Kurds. We would make an example and thereby let them know who had come to town. Thereupon we returned to the bazaar, and the first person squatting on the pavement who failed to get up received Charles's boot in the backside and went sprawling across the road. He was an elderly man wearing a white turban and the effect was electric. All and sundry got up and salaamed, for though we knew it not, he was a most influential holy man. It was all very rash, and I'm sure Nalder would not have approved. I would never think of doing it again in that way; but we were young, and it was a case of then or never, for I'm sure they were pretending not to see us and now they ... did.

Between the Dohuk district and the Turkish frontier was the district of Amadiya, inhabited by Kurds plus a few Tiyari Christians, normally referred to as Assyrians; and the officer appointed to it was a Mr [R. F.] Jardine, who had joined the Political Service during the war. He was now due for leave, and his place was taken by a Captain [D.] Willey, assisted by a police officer Captain [H.] Macdonald MC. The town lay in the valley just south of the Seri Amadiya (top or head of the Amadiya range) and it was dominated by a fort or serai built on a precipitous pinnacle of rock about 50 yards high in which were situated the government offices and the living quarters of the APO. Now how far they were aware of enemy propaganda I know not, but suffice to say that one hot July night [14 July 1919] the assassins penetrated into their sleeping quarters and daggered Willey while he was asleep. The noise, however, awakened Macdonald who drew his automatic and fired; but unfortunately it jammed and so he closed with the intruders and, taking one under each arm, he left through the ancient embrasure, taking them with him to his death and theirs more than 100 feet below. Sapper Troop, their only British companion, was also killed.

This of course provoked a punitive column, which on this occasion was composed largely of my regiment, the 52nd Sikhs Frontier Force, with some mountain guns and a section or two of ambulances. They duly went forth from Mosul and attacked Haji Rashid Beg's tribe and villages who were held responsible; but, as is usual in such mountain affrays, the tribesmen withdrew when confronted with superior force, and it was mostly their homes that suffered. After the column had returned to Amadiya there was occasion, for some reason I have since forgotten, to send back a small force. This was composed of B Company of the 52nd, a section of mountain guns, and a section of RAMC. The infantry company was commanded by Lewis, a charming and most promising young officer who came from Devon. The column commander was an acting Major of Sappers, a mining engineer by profession, with no experience of mountain warfare, who took command in the absence of his own Sapper commander, away on leave. Because he was the senior officer, he had command of the column, and this was a fatal mistake.

The little column, retracing the route on which the larger column had returned the previous day, headed up hill for the Gelli Mizurka, a pass over the Seri Amadiya, and the advance guard was one platoon under my old friend and companion in Pachmarhi, Jemadar Abdulla Khan, a Pathan with eyes like a hawk's and much experience in mountain warfare. On reaching the mouth of the pass, which was a steep-sided cutting in the hill, he noticed some tribesmen ahead who appeared to be armed, and whose movements were suspect. This he reported back to the commander asking at the same time for the column to halt while he investigated ahead. But the column commander brushed aside this advice saying that they were probably cultivators with their implements, and that there was no time to waste, so the column moved on. All were inside this gulch except the rearguard of one platoon of Dogras under a jemadar, when they were fired on at close range from the rocks above, in front and on both sides. The casualties were appalling; all the British and Indian officers were slain. The only ones to escape were the Medical Officer at the tail of the column and the rearguard, the commander of which seized a hillock, and successfully defended his position till the arrival of reinforcements from Amadiya for which he sent back. It was a black day for the 52nd and especially for me because both Lewis and Abdulla, close friends of mine, and first-class officers, were sacrificed by the mistake of an inexperienced commander.

At that time wheel traffic could penetrate no further than Dohuk, and so it became my duty to collect and organize Kurdish stretcher-bearers to bring down the wounded – nearly all men of my own regiment. It was a sorry task.

About this time [early 1919], Turkish propaganda and Kurdish unrest began to spread throughout the whole of Kurdistan in British occupation, and the next outburst was in Sulaimani to the east and along the Persian border where the British government was trying to work out some form of indirect rule through Shaikh Mahmud, a religious and temporal chief, son of a reverend father who had been martyred by the Turks. But he, taking advantage of the absence on leave of Major [E. B.] Soane who kept him very much in his place, suddenly imprisoned Soane's officers, and declared his independence as King of Kurdistan. It did not last long, however, for General Fraser, known as 'Frosty', with Major [C.] Auchinleck (now Field Marshal) as his Brigade Major, defeated him at the Bazyan Pass, halfway between Sulaimani and Kirkuk. He was found by the Political Officer with the column, Major [C. J.] Edmonds, lying shot through the liver, subsequently cured by the RAMC, court-martialled, sentenced to death, reprieved and banished to India, where he lived in exile for about five years. I was not present at this engagement but mention it to show the extent of the unrest at that time, and also as an introduction to Shaikh Mahmud with whom I had numerous engagements, both hostile and friendly, after his return to Kurdistan.

It was a hectic year for us Political Officers putting up a show on a shoe-string at the daily risk of our lives. Sir Percy Cox was at this time in Persia and Sir Arnold Wilson was acting for him as Civil Commissioner in Baghdad; and he has put it on record that Leachman never seemed to understand the Kurds in the way that he understood Arabs, and had little success with them. They were of course quite different races with different languages, though having a common religion. At any rate Leachman was transferred to the Euphrates area and a Mr [J. H.] Bill, who had been Deputy Commissioner of Bannu on the North West Frontier of India, took his place. Now anyone who has lived [in] or even read about the North West Frontier of India will know that it was a very tough and unruly tribal area, and Mr Bill was a senior officer and experienced, so it is difficult to understand what happened and why. I confess it escapes my memory exactly whether it was a murder or a hold up: but anyway Mr Bill went off with Scott, investigated the case, and fined the tribal chief while still enjoying his hospitality; and on the way home the next day both were waylaid and killed [2 November 1919]. It was an obvious abuse of hospitality.[1]

It was some time before we had the news, for wheel traffic could go no further than Aqra and from there it was a long steep climb with mules

---

1. There is a fuller account of this event at Bira Kapra in W. R. Hay, *Two Years in Kurdistan. Experiences of a Political Officer* (London, 1921), p. 181. Hay says that the two local chiefs involved, Faris Agha and Babekr Agha, 'took offence at something that was said in the course of the conversations' and arranged to kill the two officers after they had been politely escorted out of the village next day, in conjunction with a Shaikh Ahmad.

over the Aqra Dagh mountain, and then down to the valley and again up the Piris Dagh, a higher and still more difficult and blood-stained track, and down the other side to the valley of the Greater Zab, for in parts this was like a staircase and the poor donkeys and mules were usually bleeding at the fetlocks by the time they finished up. The Zab was both wide and swift and crossing in country boats was quite precarious. It was beyond the Zab that they were ambushed and it took some days to recover what was left of their bodies. A few bones, and some blood-stained clothing, with an addition of a few stones in the coffins for ballast, and these were buried with the usual military ceremony. Yet another column went forth to seek out the guilty and in default to [hit] the area in which the murder had occurred; and shortly after this [26 November] Captain [F. R.] Walker the APO. of Aqra died of malaria ...[2]

But all this time, unknown to us simple soldiers, there was the Arab Bureau in Egypt staffed with such people as Dr [D. G.] Hogarth, Miss [Gertrude] Bell, and [T. E.] Lawrence, fanatically dedicated to the cause of Arab freedom as a first and sole objective. When General Allenby had driven the Turks out of Palestine and Syria, Lawrence, without sanction of any superior authority, had dumped Amir Faisal in Damascus and proclaimed him King, an act quite out of harmony with the agreement between the British and French Prime Ministers which, rightly or wrongly (and I think wrongly), assigned the mandate of Syria to France. Consequently it was not long before the French found him a nuisance and booted him out.[3] But the lust for power and riches is nowhere greater than among the Arab demagogues; and thwarted in Syria they turned eastwards. If they could not succeed in Syria then why not try Iraq? As a country it was much richer than Syria both in the fertility of its land and the abundance of its water. In addition to oil prospects, the possibilities of vast irrigation schemes had already been proved in practice by Sir William Wilcox, the famous irrigation expert. Moreover, its people, though less expert at intrigue, were tougher fighters and easily led by Syrian demagogues. True, the British had promised to liberate them from the Turkish yoke, and indeed had done so. But there had been undue delay over a final settlement; a year and a half had passed since the Armistice, yet the people had no say in the government of their own country. The British, military and civil, had possession of nearly all the best houses in the capital, and

---

2. A. T. Wilson, *Loyalties. Mesopotamia 1914–1917* (London, 1930), p. ix, says he died of pneumonia.

3. This is, of course, an oversimplified and biased version of a very complicated story, about which much has been written. For an outline account and references to the main sources see the Introduction above.

the attitude of the British towards the inhabitants was in general much the same as what made them so unpopular in India. The tribesmen were probably the most heavily armed in the world, the notables deprived of the fruits of office, and the country ripe for rebellion.

Now when we first occupied Mosul, Major Bromilow went as APO of the Tal Afar district, which lay about 45 miles west of the Tigris, and with the exception of Tal Afar town, which was mostly inhabited by Turcoman stock, the district was entirely Arab. This was a happy choice for among people who prided themselves on their horsemanship George Bromilow was a master. Champion pig-sticker of India and a top-class polo player, he was not long in introducing the local shaikhs to these sports and they very soon found themselves taken up with the new interests; and though quite outclassed, they could not conceal their admiration and respect for their new ruler and his ways, which were often very unorthodox. For instance, there was a negro slave called Bilabel who in the past had usurped the seat of his master and become Shaikh of the Albuhamad tribe. His lawlessness soon came to the notice of George Bromilow who promptly put him in [prison]; but as Bilabel was a good polo player, he was brought out for practices, taken into Mosul in the back of Bromilow's pick-up to play a match, and then returned to [prison] once more. The better he played the better his chances of remission of sentence.

Again, there is nothing the Arabs like more than an endless dispute, and nothing Bromilow liked less; so when he got tired of their wrangling, he would adjourn the case 'sine die' and suggest they all go off pig-sticking, for which he always had a large supply of hog spears. On one occasion a shaikh could not resist shooting the boar, for which he was fined all the expenses of the hunt; in Bromilow's law this was an offence even worse than sticking a sow. But Bromilow was really much too senior an officer to be an APO, and early in 1920 he returned to command his regiment. In his place came Major [J. E.] Barlow DSO, a distinguished young officer, but one without experience of the East who was fated to be the first victim of the Arab insurrection which was to take more troops to quell than had been used to drive the Turks out of Mesopotamia.

It happened without warning in the beginning of June [1920] when communication with Tal Afar was suddenly cut off. Two armoured cars sent to reconnoitre found the town hostile; and, when trying to force a passage to the serai [the government office], they were hopelessly trapped in a narrow street where they were unable to bring their guns to bear. Eventually they were forced to surrender and the crews were murdered as they did so. It appears that previous to this Barlow and his Police Officer, Lieutenant [B.] Stuart DSO, had endeavoured to make their way out by night but had been caught and murdered [on 3 June 1920]. There remained

Sergeant [A.] Walker and Private [W.] Lawlor, who held out on the roof of the serai for a little longer before being overwhelmed, after which the massacre was complete.

By now Nalder had succeeded Mr Bill as Political Officer of the Mosul Province and I had succeeded Nalder as APO Mosul District. Major General Fraser was in command of the troops and Captain Gowan was in command of the Gendarmerie, and a column equivalent to a brigade was immediately formed and marched forth to Hugna on the way to Tal Afar. General Fraser was in command and Gowan acted as his Political Officer. Intelligence was scanty, so the General decided to halt while further details could be gathered and at the same time give an opportunity for the insurgents to collect into a target large enough to oppose the troops. When eventually, after a few days, the advance was continued the opposition was very distant and disappointing, the tribesmen dispersing in very quick time after suffering very light casualties. So did the leader of the opposition with most of his followers. He turned out to be none other than Jamil al-Midfai, or Jamil the Gunner, one of Lawrence's bright boys from Syria, and some of the British rifles picked up were part of a consignment issued to Lawrence and by him to his Arabs only a few months previously. Our feelings about Lawrence and his stunts can well be imagined.

While this was going on the mukhtar or head man of the village of Tall Kayf came to me with the news that every animal belonging to the village had been driven off by the Girgiri Kurds. This was serious, indicating as it did that lawlessness was being deliberately fomented and must be checked before it spread further. For Tall Kayf was a Christian village, about 12 miles north of Mosul City, containing a population of about 10,000. It was the largest Christian village in the whole country and something must be done at once; but the only troops I could scratch up were one section of Indian cavalry, under a naik (corporal), a platoon of Indian Sappers under a British subaltern, and a few mounted gendarmes who were quite unreliable. I supplemented this with about a dozen mounted and armed Christians and about twenty armed and mounted Yezidis under the command [of] Said Beg their Amir. It was not an impressive array and the more I looked at it the more I thought of 'Slattery's Mounted Foot';[4] however, it was the best we could do and off we went. The plan of campaign was to make a sweep through the Girgiri villages which lay between the hills and the east bank of the Tigris. The cavalry and gendarmes would act as

---

4 The reference is to a popular song of that name about a totally incompetent and highly irregular small military force in Ireland of uncertain period, written and performed by the singer, actor and writer Percy French before 1914. The correct title was 'Slathery's Mounted Fut'.

advance and flank guards, picket each village in turn and arrest anyone trying to escape. The Sappers in front looked impressive and the Christians and Yezidis formed the rearguard. After surrounding a village the mukhtar was summoned and given ten minutes to inform the people that they should bring out their firearms: on the expiry of the time limit the Sappers would search the village, and wherever a firearm was found the house would be burned. When the search was over the mukhtar was arrested and the column proceeded to the next village. Of course speed was essential; and we had got along very nicely when, having completed the search of a village and about to march off, a man who seemed to be an effendi or educated townsman approached me saying that the troops had taken a woollen sock containing £1,000 Turkish sovereigns. It sounded rather a tale to me, but in duty bound I told the officer. He lined up his platoon and said: 'Will the sepoy who has a sock full of gold, take one pace forward.' Much to my astonishment a sepoy stepped forward and produced the sock, complete with sovereigns, out of his pack. We then marched off; but as a safeguard against looting, especially of women's trinkets, in all the remaining villages, I told them to bring out their valuables for safety, and they would be returned on completion of the search.

The operation was most successful. We picked up quite a few rifles, for the Indian Sappers are very efficient at ferreting out hidden arms; we burned a number of houses and arrested all the head men. Their sentence was to be kept in prison till all the animals were returned; and just to ensure against any delay one of them would be flogged daily. There were about fifteen of them and we'd only got about halfway through the pack when the mukhtar of Tall Kayf came in and reported that all their animals, mules, donkeys, cattle and sheep had been found outside their village that morning. The Girgiri mukhtars were then released and the file closed.

So far as we were concerned there was no more trouble; but the insurrection travelled right down the Euphrates and up the Tigris and Diyala rivers till it finally ended in September [1920] at Arbil, thus making a complete circuit of the country. It was an expensive affair both in life and money. Many Political Officers, including the gallant Colonel Leachman, were murdered [14 August 1920] and certain post-war units of the British Army failed to maintain their reputations for steadiness under fire.[5]

The decisions for the future of the Arabs were too long delayed at the Versailles Peace Treaty. Sir Percy Cox was in Persia trying to put over a

---

5. A. T. Wilson, *Mesopotamia 1917–1920: A Clash of Loyalties* (London, 1931), p. 298, commented: 'The British units in Mesopotamia were throughout 1919 and 1920 composed of men who, by reason of their youth were of little military value. It was the Indian Army that endured the hardest and worst brunt of the fighting in Mesopotamia.'

very one-sided treaty with the Persians. The Army HQ had gone up to Karind hill station in Persia and was out of touch; nearly all the seasoned troops that had fought in the war had been demobilized; our intelligence was faulty; and the whole affair quite unnecessary. The Arabs would have got their independence in any case, but now they believed they had gained it by force and this was a great pity.

Apart from this insurrection and numerous other affrays that were to follow, the life of a Political Officer was most interesting and the Mosul Province was by far the best in every way. For sporting purposes the plains of Iraq held gazelle, wild boar, frankolin, bustard, snipe, geese, woodcock, chikoor and sisi. On the eastern face of the highest mountains which went up to 12,000 feet the snow never melted, and there was a variation of climate and scenery unobtainable in the other two provinces. The Greater and Lesser Zabs, the Diyala and their tributaries were magnificent fast-running rivers with fish up to 200 pounds in weight, and everywhere there were good horses to be had at moderate prices. For those interested in archaeology it was a Paradise first explored by A. H. Layard over a hundred years ago in Nineveh, and still holding many so far untapped sources of ancient civilization. For the Political Officer, however, the greatest interest lay in the various peoples, languages and religions in the province. Arabs, nomadic and settled Kurds, likewise nomadic and settled Assyrians in the hills, and Chaldeans in the plains, with a sprinkling of Turkomans said to have descended from the camp followers of Timur-i-Lang scattered along what was presumably his line of march. In the towns there were always a few Jews and some Sabaeans or followers of John the Baptist. Each with their own language and with many varieties of religion especially among the Christians, some of whom held services in Aramaic, the language of our Lord. Not the least interesting were the Yezidis, who practised a secret religion and were therefore dubbed Devil Worshippers. These people had suffered heavily under the Turks and had never failed to afford shelter to the Christians of Mardin when, to escape massacre, they fled to the Sinjar mountain which was the chief Yezidi stronghold.

There were nearly a thousand villages in what was then the Mosul District and I made a point of visiting most of them on horseback during the year. In this way one got to know the people and they in turn had an opportunity of speaking freely in their own villages about matters they would never dare to mention in the headquarters office. They were always eager to accompany me and to entertain me for the night. It also provided a grand opportunity for finding out the best places for shooting and the best pools in the river, of which I was very careful to make notes.[6]

---

6. There is a great deal in Lyon's MS about fishing and shooting, which has had to be cut for reasons of length.

There were, I discovered, three stages in the life of a Political Officer. The first was overwhelming flattery as the best approach to an officer of a victorious army. The second stage was disillusionment, which invariably followed; and the third stage was a realization that there are good and bad in every race. No one should be accepted at face value and judgement should best be deferred till sufficient evidence is available to put the matter beyond doubt.

It was a relief to escape from the rigid rules of caste that formed such a barrier to normal intercourse with Indians, and among the country people of the district there were many interesting and amusing characters, some of whom I can still remember. There was Shaikh Ajil al Yawir, the paramount Shaikh of all the Shammar. He stood about 6 feet 5 inches, was well built and very handsome, with a soft modulated and persuasive voice and a most intelligent brain. He was all for fast cars, cheque books and real estate companies. Out in the high desert he would entertain like a prince; in the capital he would more than hold his own with the smartest of concession hunters. One day just outside the town he happened to meet the British Police Commander. After the usual greetings the Police Officer said, 'And where are you off to today, O Shaikh?' 'I'm off to bomb fish,' said Shaikh Ajil. 'But know you not,' said the Police Officer, 'that by recent proclamation this is forbidden and therefore against the law?' 'Perhaps,' said the Shaikh, 'but the fish don't know it. Come along and join me.'

Down at Sharqat there were the two shaikhs of the Jibbur tribe enjoying the proximity of the supply depot from which their men made frequent thefts; they also enjoyed the friendliest relations with the Supply Officer. One of them called Ali al-Hamada was famous as the first and only man in the tribe to wear socks; the other, Shaikh Shillash, when entertained in the officers' mess, invariably asked for a gin with the 'water of thorns' – a very apt description in Arabic for soda water. When thefts became too frequent I used to imprison both of them until the cases of tea and sacks of sugar mysteriously returned. They were very sporting about it all and it in no way affected their friendship with the British officers.

Further away on the left bank of the Lesser Zab river I had occasion to spend the night with a certain Shaikh Noah of the Jibbur. All he had for supper was some boiled barley with dates and quite a lot of goat hair. When finished, instead of calling for the brikh or water pot with which to wash one's hands, he called his eldest son, a long-haired youth of about fifteen, and wiped his hands in his hair which was unplaited and down to his shoulders. For a moment I was at a loss what to do; then it occurred to me to imitate my host. So I asked if he had a second son and if so please to call him. He came and I wiped my fingers on his hair. The Jibbur were a dirty lot; all suffered from a type of syphilis called Bejel.

Then there was Mejid Agha, the chief of the village of Khorsabad, where in the past an American professor had made some very successful excavations. Before saying farewell to his host, Mejid Agha, he made a Assyrian brick and with a style printed in ancient Assyriac an inscription extolling the many virtues and generosity of his host the chief of the village, baked it, [and] gave it to Mejid telling him exactly where to bury it. Needless to say several years later it was again dug up by a second party of archaeologists; and, being a first-class fake, caused quite a commotion among the learned professors, much to the amusement of Mejid who in the end told them the truth.

About 16 miles from Nineveh on the main road to Arbil lay the monastery of Kidher Ilyas, presided over by the Syrian Catholic Bishop Qalian. He had played the good Samaritan to the wounded and sick prisoners on their march to Turkey after the siege of Kut-al-Amara, and there was a register in his guest book. Naturally the monastery was held in high esteem by us and came top on the priority list for pickings; and when disposing of surplus army bullocks I invited the Bishop to come and choose two pairs for the monastery, which cultivated quite a good-sized area around it. He chose three really good animals but the fourth I thought was a poor type. This surprised me, for he was an experienced judge of cattle, and when I remarked on it he said, 'The fourth is indeed smaller but I think he is a bull and I will cross him with some of our cows, and I will give him the name of Enver Pasha after the notorious Turkish general who forced Turkey into the war and was afterwards killed on the Russian front.' I tried to explain that though he might look like a bull in actual fact it was most unlikely, for the Indian practice of castration was to crush the testicles rather than cut them, and sometimes they remained but were useless. However, the Bishop stuck to his choice, which was justified the following year by the birth of a bull calf.

In Mosul there was a great character called Ibrahim Jissar – or Abraham of the Bridge. He was the expert who maintained the precarious bridge of country boats across the Tigris at Mosul. He was also an expert master of *kelleks* – or skin rafts – a great swimmer, and above all a great entertainer. When the river came down in spate it was he who decided whether to cut the bridge before it broke. Whenever a pilot of the RAF in flying too low hit the telegraph wires it was always Ibrahim who was on the spot to retrieve him from the depths of the Tigris. He had even been known to dive in, release the pilot from his trappings, and while still under water take his watch. He gave wonderful parties in the summer when the river was low. The guests were taken by boat to a selected island where there was a troupe of Arabian dancers with musicians complete. The food was all native, including grilled fish, roast sheep with rice, melons both water and sweet, and the whole washed down by endless glasses of araq. This is a type of eastern absinthe or Greek ozo made of fermented and distilled dates, which turned milky white with the addition of water. I know of no drink better calculated to split a head, even if made of teak, than araq, especially Ibrahim's own brew. When the Air Marshal presented him with a watch, Ibrahim produced two more he had 'saved' in the course of his rescues.

On one occasion I was invited by Said Beg, the Amir of the Yezidis, to come to their spring festival. This was a great annual event held in the plain just below Ayn Sifni. All the Yezidis of Shaikhan and many from distant Sinjar would gather in one great camp for the occasion. Their priests and monks would be there in force, never missing a chance to make a collection, and sometimes an emissary with the secret and holy peacock would be there too. This bird, said to be made of gold, was about the size of a pigeon and kissing it was reputed to earn as much merit as did the Moslems by their pilgrimage to Mecca. It was all very secret and the only non-Yezidi who had ever seen it was a Christian called Ibrahim Karagulla who was several years later to be judicially murdered by a fanatical government. There was much dancing to the drums and pipes; displays of horsemanship and in the evening feasting and drinking. I well remember one Kawal or monk in his black garments mounted on one of the Amir's horses with a bottle of whisky in one hand and a bottle of araq in the other, from which he took alternate swigs as he galloped around until he had finished both bottles neat. I expected him to blow up and fall off long before he was halfway through, and this opinion was supported by Dr Nicholson, IMS who was with me at the time; but he carried on amid great applause, and if he suffered any ill effects afterwards they were not reported.

The Amir was an extraordinary specimen. Aged about twenty-five he was tall and slender with a great long hooked nose, his hair in ringlets that fell to his shoulders and the tiniest hands I had ever seen on a grown man, which Nicholson attributed to many generations of inbreeding by ancestors who had never done a stroke of work in their lives. He was very proud of a new thoroughbred Arab stallion of the Seglowy strain which he had acquired from the Shammar Arabs of the Jezira, and challenged me to race him the following morning. I was then riding a very good Waler mare from the Guides Cavalry which had won several military events; and knowing that there was more than one stone penalty on any Waler as against an Arab horse, I was not slow in accepting his challenge. But when the sun rose the following morning there was no sign of the Amir, so we went round to his family quarters to make inquiries. There we found him lying on a vast four-poster bed with his women all around. To Dr Nicholson's inquiries he replied that the unmentionable (for they dare not speak the word *Shaitan*, meaning the Devil) was in his head and it was obvious that he could not carry his liquor so well as his monk. Under the bed was an enormous chamber pot, and Nicholson, giving him a double dose of Army No. 9 pills, plus half a dozen aspirins, assured him that within a few hours the unmentionable would be driven out of his head and into the chamber pot. To further questions I assured the Amir that Nicholson was King George's own physician and that he had often performed this miracle with complete success on the Royal Master. So he eagerly swallowed the lot and we, suspecting that he might have a bellyache before long, asked leave to depart.

A week later a Yezidis shepherd appeared outside our quarters in Mosul with half a dozen choice lambs. From this we gathered that all had gone well with the Amir.

The work of a Political Officer in those days was interesting, varied and often most exciting. Routine included supervision of tax assessment and collections, education, agriculture, control of the police and maintenance of law and order. As a magistrate there were numerous cases to hear, petitions to be dealt with and now and then one was roped in as a member of a Court of Sessions composed of three, the president being a professional lawyer.

Intelligence included the provision of answers to inquiries from all quarters on all sorts of subjects from archaeology to zoology; and every now and then there was a tribal raid or a frontier affray demanding personal and speedy attention. The Arab tribes had never before had so many rifles and were naturally eager to try them out in the settlement of old feuds; while on the northern frontier in the Kurdish hills the Turks were for ever instigating disorder. On one such occasion the pursuit in armoured cars of some raiders from Syria under Nijiris al-Gaud of the Agaidat tribe led to the ancient and deserted Parthian city of Hatra, situated on the wadi Tharthar about 60 miles west of Sharqat. The city walls of dressed stone were octagonal in design and still bore some of the bas reliefs with which they were originally adorned. There was a great pool of salt water and a small spring of fresh water but nothing else and no habitation nearer than the Tigris some 60 miles away.

In the Kurdish hills too one could never be sure when some ancient Assyrian inscription would be pointed out by the local shepherd. One such we discovered when out hare hunting with the Girdi chief. A recent storm had dislodged the earth on the edge of the Bastura Chai, a watercourse draining into the Greater Zab some 15 miles north of Arbil, disclosing a large stone tablet inscribed in ancient Assyriac. The exact spot was noted and at a later date an Italian professor of archaeology was taken to the spot to interpret the writing. It was to the effect that the King of Assyria had found the people of the hills rebellious and so he had sent his troops to [hit] them. This had been done most effectively in the usual way; men killed, women and children enslaved, houses burned and cattle confiscated. Finally the tablet had been erected as a warning to others. All in all one couldn't help thinking that in some way we had not made much progress in 3,000 years.

During the later stages of the war, and just before the Revolution, the Russians staged a three-pronged advance through eastern Turkey and western Persia, with the object of joining up with our forces which had just taken Baghdad. Coming from the north-east the more western prong was held up in the district of Van; the centre prong got as far as Ruwandiz where, its momentum exhausted, it was unable to force its way through the Gali Ali Beg leading to the Arbil plain and so had to beat a retreat. The eastern prong or column, however, managed to reach Khanaqin, where it joined forces with the 13th Hussars who had been sent ahead to meet them. The Commander of the advance guard, a squadron of Cossack Cavalry, was immediately rushed to GHQ in Baghdad and there ushered into the presence of the Chief of Staff. There, when addressed in French, he seemed at first somewhat puzzled, then he replied in perfect English. It turned out that his name was Gowan, and that his ancestor had been brought over from Scotland by Peter the Great. Of course the British officer who brought him down from Khanaqin was well aware of this but kept it dark as it presented a wonderful chance to put one over the top brass. Before passing on with the story, however, it may as well be mentioned now that the behaviour of the Russian troops in Khanaqin was not such as to endear themselves and the Allied cause to the local inhabitants; and as their morale was now beginning to crumble with news of the Revolution, Sir Percy Cox insisted on their withdrawal.

Now the country through which these columns operated included the district of Hakari and all that rugged mountainous area between Lakes Van and Urmia inhabited by Kurdish tribesmen and Assyrians. These were an isolated remnant of the past who had preserved their language but adopted the Christian religion at a very early stage, and were now in communion with the Church of England. They had indeed enjoyed the benefit of the Archbishop of Canterbury's mission under Dr Wigram, whom I had the honour of meeting and whose book *The Cradle of Mankind* is the most informative work on this extraordinary people. It will suffice here, however, to say that this remnant of ancient Assyria, consisting of about 50,000 souls, living in isolated villages among the most rugged of mountains, was ruled by a leader with the title of Marshimun, who was also their High Priest.

In a remote corner of the Turkish empire, surrounded and interspersed with fanatical Moslem tribesmen, they had clung to their religion and traditions and earned the respect of both the local tribesmen and their Turkish officials. Thus when the war came closer to their homes it was natural for them to confer with their neighbours and decide on a policy for their mutual benefit, for the Turks had suppressed many Kurdish rebellions with much the same cruelty as they had used in the case of the Armenians, while the Assyrians were naturally inclined to the side of the Allies by reason of their common religion. The Russians were Christian, and what was more important, both they and the British now looked like winners. So there was common ground on which to hope for agreement when the Marshimun, accompanied by an escort of about fifty of his rifle men mounted on mules, accepted the invitation of Ismail Agha, commonly known as Simko, Chief of the Shikak tribe, to a conference at his village.

On arrival the Marshimun was treated with the deference due to his rank, the usual banquet was laid on, the situation discussed and finally agreement reached to back the Allies. But as the Marshimun rode out on the way home he was ambushed by his hosts and he and all but a handful of his escort were massacred. This vile treachery had immediate repercussions: the Assyrians gathered together, chased Simko out of his village and burned it; but their success or revenge was short-lived for Simko had been carrying out a well prepared plan; and, as a result, the Assyrians found they were up against all the Kurdish tribes surrounding their homes. So they gathered together, men, women and children, all their animals and as much of their household equipment and food as they could carry; and under the leadership of their general, Agha Petros, they began the long march towards safety and the British troops, very much as Moses led the children of Israel out of Egypt towards the promised land. They were, needless to say, beset on all sides by hostile tribesmen and suffered great losses both in cattle and personnel; but the 13th Hussars came to their rescue, convoyed them to Khanaqin and ultimately to Baquba, where a refugee camp was prepared for them on the banks of the Diyala river about 20 miles from Baghdad. Here during the Arab rebellion of 1920 they were attacked by the Arabs, who very soon found that these people were made of very different metal to the emasculated Christians of the Mosul plain and were repulsed with considerable loss.

After the Armistice there followed a period of nearly six years before peace finally settled with the Turks who during this time spared no pains to get us out of the Mosul wilayat or province, which was one-third, and indeed the best third, of the whole of Mesopotamia, later to be called Iraq. Thus, although we had won the war, our efforts to impose conditions safeguarding the Assyrians in their homelands, most of which were over the frontier, were unsuccessful. A hill people, they were unhappy in Baquba and it was thought that they would do better and be nearer to their own country if brought up to the north. It thus fell to my lot to choose a camp-site for them; and this was my first experience of this brave but unfortunate people, for of all the nations engaged on the winning side in the 1914–18 war they were the only ones to lose their country as a result. The site chosen was on the Khazir river on the south-east tip of the Jabal Maklub, about 30 miles east of Mosul on the road to Aqra. Here they were close to their native hills, and out of the main traffic routes.

Their new Patriarch, chosen from the royal family, was a sickly young man already in the throes of consumption who had been sent to the monastery perched on the summit of Jabal Maklub for convalescence under the care of his aunt the Lady Surma; and in the course of my reconnaissance a visit to him and to the Bishop was necessary. The old Bishop in charge of the monastery was very hospitable and finished up by inviting me to the crypt. There he showed me a line of wooden thrones, each with a corpse sitting in state, clothed in mouldering bishop's robes, all in various stages of decomposition producing a stench of death that filled the whole crypt. Each had been placed in position in the order of succession, and the old man showed me with pride the place which he expected and hoped would be allotted to him. I had seen more than enough death during the war, but this was the first (and last) time I had ever been invited to view it as a showpiece. I was glad to say goodbye and get into the fresh mountain air.

The sickly young Marshimun did not last long and after his death a successor was duly elected. It seems that any lady of the family qualified for production of an heir to the holy office must become a vegetarian as soon as she becomes pregnant; thus the Marshimun is under a great physical handicap for not only must he remain a celibate, but he is meatless from conception to the grave.

The return of the Assyrians to their homes in Turkey by diplomatic means was not possible for there was only an armistice with Turkey and peace did not come till six years later. By then Turkey had experienced a drastic revolution, the Sultanate had been abolished, the Greeks had been defeated by [Mustafa Kemal] Ataturk, and the new Turkish Republic was adamant in its refusal to make any arrangements for the return of a people which had taken sides against Turkey in the recent war. Moreover, the support of the Greeks by Lloyd George and the snobbery of Lord Curzon, our Foreign Secretary, in his dealings with the Turks made conditions still worse. It was therefore agreed to allow volunteers from the Assyrians to cross into Turkey and Persia on their own, rather like Joshua and his party spying out the land of Canaan. However, Jehovah was evidently not with them: they came into collision with the Kurdish inhabitants across the frontier and the operation failed. So, except for those whose homes were on our side of the frontier, the Assyrian nation were left homeless in rest camps; and to alleviate their lot, the administration recruited most of the able young men into the Levies, in which they served with distinction. In all they amounted to about three battalions, commanded by British officers, and under the administration of the Royal Air Force which subsequently [October 1922] took over the defence of Iraq from the British Army. The remainder sought employment in the railway, the Iraq Petroleum Company, the local hotels and such-like menial jobs. Such was the beginning of the end of an ancient, brave and warlike race of mountaineers. They lingered on for another twelve to fifteen years and more will be heard of them later; but the fact [that] they had joined the victorious Allies and lost everything as a result was the primary cause of all their subsequent troubles, and historians will no doubt have great difficulty in excusing the Allies – particularly the British – for the way this small and gallant nation was let down ...

So far as I was concerned, however, [by September 1920] twenty-one months had passed since the Armistice ... and it was three and a half years since I had left home; and so when I was told it was now my turn for leave I was glad to go ...

The return to Mesopotamia was by a Strick cargo boat starting from Hull and calling at Genoa. My father had introduced me to a local colonel who had some well-bred field spaniel pups for sale, and so I bought one and put it on the boat in charge of the ship's butcher at Hull. At the same time I put on board my heavy kit, which included new suits for all civilian occasions, new saddlery, a new set of fishing gear, and most prized of all a new shotgun, price £40, which I had had specially fitted at the London Shooting School. This exhausted all the residue of my current pay and war bounty, and about ten days later, just before Xmas 1920, I said goodbye and set off by train for Genoa. The voyage was pleasant and without incident and I reached Baghdad about a month later.

CHAPTER 2

Arbil: The 'Election' of King Faisal, 1921

§ HAVING reported in at the Baghdad military rest camp I went across to the Maude Hotel, which in those days was the most popular resort for army officers, and there I met Nalder, now an acting Lieutenant Colonel, who proceeded to give me all the latest news.

Sir Arnold Wilson the [Acting] Civil Commissioner, having been chosen as the scapegoat for the rebellion, had left the administration [4 October 1920] and gone to Abadan as local managing director of the Anglo Persian Oil Company.[1] Sir Percy Cox, now installed as High Commissioner, was entrusted with the formation of a provisional government under the terms of the recently devised Mandate by which the British became responsible to the League of Nations for the protection, education and eventual independence of the newly-created state of Iraq, previously referred to as 'Mesopotamia in British Occupation'.

All this involved a great and general clearing out of British officers whose places wherever possible would be taken by Iraqis. Thus apart from technical officers responsible for health, railways, telephones, irrigation, public works and police etc., only a very few of the Political Officers governing various divisions or liwas and subdivisions or districts were to be retained, and these would act in an advisory capacity.

There was, however, one exception – Sulaimani, a completely Kurdish province which had already tried independence under Shaikh Mahmud and, after his rebellion, defeat and subsequent exile, had been and still was to be ruled for the present by British Political Officers. The inhabitants

---

1. This is incorrect but reflects Lyon's respect for Wilson and his policies. The decision that Cox should return as Commissioner was taken before the start of the 1920 rebellion. See Wilson, *Mesopotamia 1917–1920*, p. 260. Wilson had offered to resign in favour of Cox earlier.

were hill men, Aryan by race, Kurdish in nationality and language, and belonged to the Sunni or Orthodox branch of the Moslem religion, and thus altogether different from the majority of the other Iraqis: plainsmen, Semitic by race, Arabs in nationality and language, and belonging to the Shia sect of Islam.

Pending any future arrangement that might be found possible, this province, which had refused to go in with the Arabs, was to be governed by half a dozen British officers of which I was to be one. Although the province, which was very mountainous, had much to recommend it, especially in the field of sport, I did not feel like taking up the appointment, because it meant service under the chief Political Officer there, Major [E. B.] Soane. He was a very able officer, a good Persian scholar, an enthusiastic supporter of those who favoured an independent Kurdistan. He had left the Imperial Bank of Persia before the war and, changing his name to Ghulam Hussein, had assumed native costume and taken service as a Persian Secretary to Adila Khan, the widow of Usman Pasha, chief and ruler of the Jaf tribe – one of the largest in Persia or Iraq and inhabiting a large area in both countries. Soane's experiences are given in his book *Through Kurdistan in Disguise*, and at the outbreak of war he left the service of the lady and joined the expeditionary force. He was, however, like Sir Richard Burton, a man with gypsy blood in his veins. He had a very cruel streak in his character, suffered from tuberculosis, and his treatment of his officers was often dictatorial and sometimes even tyrannical. Moreover he was not a regular officer; and if he reported well of me it would carry no weight, but if on the contrary he reported ill it would harm me in my career in the Indian Army. I therefore decided against it; and on Nalder's advice I went off to the Ministry of Interior where [H.] St John [B.] Philby was installed as Adviser. I told him of my decision and the reasons for it; and when I had finished he said he quite understood and asked me if I would accept the post at Arbil. This was a liwa with 80 per cent Kurdish inhabitants, a few Turkomen and Christians, and hardly any Arabs. It was partly mountain, partly plain. It lay between the Tigris, the two Zab rivers, and the Turkish and Persian frontiers and I would be cock on my own dung hill, dealing directly with the Ministry in Baghdad. To this I readily agreed. He drafted a posting order accordingly, and I picked up my Indian bearer, and caught the train from Hinaydi to Kingirban, which was the railhead for Kifri, on the fringe of the Kurdish foothills about 80 miles from Baghdad.

The heavy baggage consisted of two heavy packing cases and a cabin trunk which were loaded into the baggage van with my bearer, who was detailed to sleep with or on them. The pup Rupert and the bedding roll or officer's valise were all I had in my compartment; and after the train had spent most of the night shunting about in and around Baghdad, I woke up in the morning to find that it had only got as far as Baquba, a mere 30 miles: and on visiting the van I found it empty; and all my efforts with the various police, railway, city and district [authorities] failed to trace the kit, nor could the Indian bearer give any helpful explanation. He had either left the wagon and didn't want to admit it, or else the kit had been stolen while he slept. There was of course no insurance as no company would at that time accept a risk in Mesopotamia, a country with such a dreadful reputation in war and, after the recent rebellions, an even worse one in peace. Thus after six and a half years I now had fewer possessions than when I first sailed for India [in 1912] with hopes so high of a future so vague. Gone were the new suits, the saddlery, the fishing rod and the shotgun on which I had set such store. On the other side of the account, however, I had repaid my grandmother for my uncle's financial help. I had three stars on my shoulder and Rupert who was a grand pup. With these thoughts I comforted myself for the rest of the day till the train reached the railhead, where I was met by Judge [Major J.] Pritchard who was holding Court at the nearby town of Kifri.

As this was one of the last places to be mopped up in the recent rebellion, the surrounding country was still very lawless and there were many cases awaiting trial. The local judge had funked sitting on the Court of Sessions and so, as I had magisterial powers, Pritchard roped me in to sit with him and the qadhi and so make up the quorum. The Court was sitting in an upper room from which the prisoners' cell was visible; and I found it hard to forget that only five months previously [28 August 1920] Captain [H.] Salmon had been shot through the bars of the cell door very much as the lions in the Cairo Zoo were shot by King Fuad twenty years later. What with this murder haunting me and the recent pillage of my kit, I have since realized that I was in no condition to act as an unbiased judge, especially as there were one or two cases of murder and several of brigandage. However, after several days it was over, and with Pritchard I went on to Kirkuk, the liwa capital some 70 miles north, where I was introduced among others to Stephen Longrigg, who was handing over to Major [C. C.] Marshall, and to Captain [A. F.] 'Pa' Miller his assistant, who was to stay. Here also was Dr [W.] Corner in charge of the liwa health.

Longrigg was a scholarly and able young Political Officer who would have been much more popular had he been at more pains to conceal his superiority.[2] Marshall was an elderly army officer with a DSO and many

---

2. Longrigg lost his job in 1931 as part of the reduction in the number of British administrators, but later became an important historian of Iraq. See in particular his *Iraq 1900–1950. A Political, Social and Economic History* (London, 1953).

years' service in the Sudan. His Arabic was elementary, his ethics high and his personality loveable, even to those who could not understand his halting, broken and mispronounced Arabic. Miller was much older than Longrigg, under whom he served as assistant. He was fluent in Turkish, was stout and fond of his food and drink; he had a generous nature and [was] a great mixer at parties with the notables. He was a tireless and willing worker for anyone who commanded his respect and was always ready to meet any call on his services provided it did not include equitation. Corner was a serious, thorough and courageous officer devoted to his profession and an outstanding example of the type that have made Scottish doctors famous throughout the world.

The country between Kifri and Kirkuk and onwards to Arbil, Mosul and across the Turkish boundary to the north, consists of rolling steppes, bounded on the right or east by the Kurdish foothills and on the left by the Tigris. It is intersected by many watercourses, including the Greater and Lesser Zab rivers; and along the road to Mosul and onwards to Turkey are numerous villages inhabited by people of Turkish origin speaking the Turkish tongue, who are quite distinct from the people on either side. It is presumably a relic of the old Turkish line of communication with Baghdad but tradition has it that these people are descended from the camp followers of Timur-i-Lang [Timur Leng]. At any rate Kirkuk and Arbil are outstanding examples, and after a day or two I set forth to Arbil with Major Marshall who had taken it over from Major Hay after the recent rebellion had been crushed.[3]

Although the distance was not more than 70 miles, there was no consolidated road, no culverts or bridges over the many wadis or watercourses in wet weather, any of which might take hours to cross or even prove impassable. Halfway was the little town of Altun Kopru – or Golden Bridge – built over the Lesser Zab, which was the boundary between the two liwas. Originally it had been a very high arched stone bridge, the toll of which was leased annually by public auction, and the fabulous fortunes alleged to have been made by the lease holders gave rise to its name. It was also a fortunate bridge for the British for it was the scene of one of the few really smart actions of the war.

It so happened that after the capture of Baghdad [in 1917] the British pushed their right flank northwards to Khanaqin where they made contact with a small Russian column, as previously recorded, and then onwards through Persia to Teheran; but finding their transport unable to sustain such a long line of communications it was decided to withdraw from

---

[3]. See Hay, *Two Years in Kurdistan*, for a detailed account of his experiences and the defence of Arbil.

Kirkuk. But as withdrawals invariably encourage enemy to pursue, it was advisable to arrange for enough obstruction to give our troops a fair start. Accordingly a Brigade of Cavalry was sent off to mount a feint attack on Altun Kopru. This worked wonderfully, for as soon as the Turks saw our troops deploy under cover of a light barrage, they blew up the bridge and so formed an excellent obstruction, which, alas, they saw too late was to our advantage, as our troops then made a leisurely and unhampered withdrawal back to Tuz Khurmatii about 80 miles back.

Arbil town is situated in a fertile plain bounded on the east by the Kurdish hills and on the west by the Kandinawa foothills, to the north by the Greater Zab river and to the south by the Lesser Zab. The older part of the town, known as the Qala, is built on a tumulus about 90 feet above the plain and has the reputation of being the oldest continuously inhabited town in the world. The name is said to derive from 'Arab Al' or four gods, but in Kurdish it is called Howleir. The Goddess Ishtar was said to preside over it in the days of ancient Assyria, and it was probably for this reason that Alexander the Great spared it after the defeat of Darius. It should therefore be a treasure house for some future archaeological research as the presence of inhabited houses has so far precluded a proper survey. However, even a small and shallow excavation about half the size of a tennis court carried out in my time, for the foundations of a pure water tank for the municipality, yielded quite a number of coins of the period of Alexander, which is recent history compared to the many layers of Assyrian ages which lie underneath.

The Political Officer's bungalow which was to be my home for more than three years was about one kilometre north of the town. It was an isolated single-storey building of sundried brick with broad verandahs and two wings. The roof, which was the usual flat mud variety resting on spindar poles, served as sleeping quarters during the hot weather. Around the house was a spacious compound divided into two compartments by a mud brick wall. The nearer to the outer gate contained a line of rooms for servants' quarters, stables, garage and kitchen; the second compound contained the bungalow and the garrison tents. The wall was provided with a firing step and loop-holed strong points. When the bungalow was first occupied it was unfortified and an assassin had made an attempt on Major [W. R.] Hay's life by shooting at him through the window while he slept; and as this was the second attempt on his life it was decided to surround the bungalow with the wall, strong points, [and] barbed wire, and [to] garrison it with one company of the 15th Sikhs. The garrison commander was Major [J. E.] Barstowe, one of the best officers I had ever met, who was a charming companion besides commanding the respect and affection of his native officers and men. In addition to him there was a Dr [H.] Williamson, the civil surgeon, and [Captain] Charles Littledale who commanded the police. There were also three other officers whose districts had just been taken over by qaimmaqams or native district officers and were now on their way out, either to their regiments or to demobilization, and one of them was kind enough to sell me his shotgun, for which I was very grateful. I also took over a good Arab horse.

Having introduced me to the British officers and to the notables of the town, Marshall wished me luck and returned to Kirkuk. I was then able to survey my province, which consisted of four districts: HQ, Mackmur, Koi Sanjaq and Ruwandiz. There was a mud road or track, passable only in good weather, to Kirkuk and to Mosul, each about 70 miles away; and the latter involved crossing the Greater Zab river in a native ferry, a procedure that might take anything from half an hour to three hours according to the height of the river, and was sometimes quite impassable. There were no wheel tracks to any of the districts, two of which were in the mountains, and there was no telegraph to Mosul, and only a very unreliable one to Kirkuk. Except for about half the population of the town, which was Turkoman, the rest of the liwa inhabitants were all Kurdish tribesmen, owing allegiance only to their chiefs, who acted as intermediaries in all matters affecting the administration. There were two completely nomadic tribes, the Herki and the Khalhani, which owned vast flocks of sheep and goats and migrated annually from the plains where they passed the winter, to the snow-covered mountains along the Persian and Turkish frontiers where they remained in their black tents till autumn.

The mutasarrif or governor was Ahmad Effendi Usman, who as mayor of the town had been a loyal supporter of my predecessor Major Hay, and there was the usual complement of staff in three of the districts. The fourth district, however, Ruwandiz, had never been reoccupied since the rebellion, when the British officers of the district had been forced to evacuate it. Indeed the whole countryside had barely recovered from the previous year's upheaval, and no one knew what was to become of the country or who was to rule it. I had been told to show the flag, so I lost no time in touring the province on horseback, visiting the districts and making the acquaintance of the tribal chieftains with whom I often spent the night. In order to save them unnecessary expense I usually took just a roll of bedding, and a mounted escort of half a dozen police. These, under Littledale's able tuition and leadership, had reached a high standard of military efficiency and had already proved their worth in several affrays during the rebellion. Though officially known as police, they were to all intents and purposes mounted infantry — those in the plains on horses, and those stationed in the hills on mules. There were also foot police in the headquarters of the province, the districts and sub-districts. They were likewise armed with rifles and trained in mountain warfare. In addition to the company of Sikhs camped in the compound there was a squadron of Mounted Levies, commanded by a British officer, stationed conveniently near to the landing ground and about one kilometre beyond our house.

In the house there lived Dr Williamson, who was in charge of all the health, civil and military, Charles Littledale, and myself. I had inherited a good memsahib-trained Indian cook and a first-class Indian Cavalry-trained Kurdish syce. The nearest NAAFI store was over 100 miles away, across the Tigris at Sharqat, and we had three camels that made periodic journeys which took about ten days for the round trip. Considering the number of times the camels couched, plus the hazards of crossing the Tigris in a country boat, we were lucky to get 75 per cent of the stores unbroken. We had many calls on our hospitality for there was nowhere else between Kirkuk and Mosul where officials or army officers could stop. Besides our own normal consumption there had to be a bottle of whisky available for the Sikh officers' monthly reception.

This was an established ceremony which usually took place on a Friday. The senior officer, a huge bearded subedar, accompanied by one or two jemadars[4] in parade order would solemnly march over to pay their respects to the Hakim Siassi, as I was called. I would receive them on the verandah, escort them in and sit down with them at a table furnished with one bottle of whisky and enough glasses to go round. Having poured myself a tot they would then join in drinking our mutual healths till they had finished the bottle neat. They would then arise, salute and depart. They were grand chaps and their friendship and co-operation was later to serve me in good stead.

In those days there was no town water supply, no electricity, no radio, no local butter or fresh milk, but we made do with a bhesti who brought spring water in goat skins on a donkey, buffalo cream in lieu of butter, goat and buffalo milk when available, packed snow from the Suffin Dagh to cool our drinks, paraffin lamps for illumination, wood and charcoal for cooking, a gramophone and any books we could get hold of for the long winter nights' amusement. But usually we were so active during the day that we did not stay up long after the evening meal. The home mail took anything from six weeks to two months via Basra and Bombay. Our servants were a happy lot and were always willing to do their best night or day. With them it mattered not whether one was early or late, or three more or two or three less: there was always enough and served with a smile. What they liked most was time off between breakfast and lunch

---

4. A subedar was the senior Indian officer of a unit, a jemadar the Indian equivalent of a lieutenant in the British Indian Army.

when they could do the shopping, visit the tea shops and pick up the local gossip. There were of course times of passing distress, such as when Qaderok the sweeper got bilharzia and had to be half poisoned in the process of cure, or when Hamid's wife died in childbirth and we had to buy him a replacement; but usually they were a happy collection, and by their faithful service more than repaid the interest taken in them.

I had not been long in Arbil before I discovered the numerous facilities for sport. There was excellent shooting of all kinds from ibex down to snipe and quail; we also started a bobery pack and hunted jackals, foxes and wolves: in the summer there was fishing in the two Zab rivers and polo on the airfield ...

The local notables were a mixed lot of Turkish-speaking origin, not nearly so interesting as the tribal chiefs. Politically they favoured the return of the Turks to the Mosul wilayat, the fate of which was not to be finally decided for another three or four years. Culturally they had nothing to recommend them and physically they were weeds. This was largely their own doing. Once a lady was married she was immured in the dungeon-like house of her husband from which she was never allowed out. So they bred unhealthy children and usually died of tuberculosis.

The most influential notable in Arbil province was Abubeker, a rich and holy Moslem cleric who was always referred to as Mulla Effendi. He followed both world and local politics with great interest, and his wide knowledge of most subjects from astronomy to botany was extraordinary in view of the fact that he had never travelled outside the province. After his first few wives had died of tuberculosis he had sense enough to leave the Qala and build himself a villa on a stream about a mile south of the town. Here he set up his own chapel, his library of Persian, Turkish and Arabic books, his garden and guest house, and seldom left it except for the Friday Prayer in the big mosque in the Qala. Whenever I returned from leave, a long absence in the mountains from a frontier affray, or escaped an ambush, he would call on me in the office and invite me to a banquet at his villa. He was a most charming conversationalist and a lavish host. The lunch was usually a fourteen-course affair, composed of nearly all the principal Turkish, Persian and Arab dishes, to which we did full justice.

There were times when he would call on me to warn me that in the near future he would have to lead a deputation pleading for mercy for some notorious criminal. Would I receive the deputation politely and agree to consider the case, but on no account was I to allow this to influence my ultimate decision, because in fact the criminal in question was a notorious blackguard who well merited whatever was coming to him. I was to understand that as leader of the notables he had to do his duty etc., etc. He had great influence with the tribal chiefs who were always going to him for advice, and a line from him would be sure of a favourable reception from an otherwise bigoted and unco-operative public. He could reassure them about drinking water from a clean source pumped by infidel engines to the top of the Qala, and when the first troop of Boy Scouts was looked upon with suspicion as the beginning of conscription, it was Mulla Effendi who told his sons to join. The rest followed like sheep.

At this time [October 1920] Sir Arnold Wilson ... had left the civilian administration and gone to Abadan as general manager to the Anglo Persian Oil Company. The son of the Bishop of Worcester,[5] he was a great scholar, one of the bravest of the brave, and a leader whose personality inspired all his officers; he was sadly missed by all. Subsequently [1933] he became an MP for Hitchin, made an unhappy impression on the House of Commons, and finally, during the Second World War, joined the RAF as a tail-gunner and was lost over the Channel [in 1940].

In his place came Sir Percy Zachariah Cox, who was much more of a cold-blooded diplomat who had spent most of his service in Persia and the Gulf before appointment as Chief Political Officer to the Mesopotamia Expeditionary Force. Since the Armistice he had been in Teheran negotiating an exceedingly one-sided treaty with the rulers of a country which had been over-run and trampled upon by British, Turkish and Russian armies alike and so in very poor shape to face the representative of the victors. However, the Persians have great experience in such matters and at the time it was common gossip that Sir Percy spent half a million gold pounds in winning the assent of the principal deputies who then, with one accord, resigned and arranged not to be re-elected. Thus the new parliament refused to confirm the treaty and Sir Percy was back where he started in Baghdad, but this time it was to set in motion a provisional government under the Naqib of Baghdad as a first step towards Home Rule for Iraq [October 1920].[6]

The country which under the Turks had consisted of three wilayats, Baghdad, Basra and Mosul, was now divided into thirteen provinces or liwas each under a mutasarrif [governor] with a British Political Officer at

---

5. This is inaccurate. Wilson's father, the Revd J. M. Wilson, had been headmaster of Clifton College, where A. T. Wilson was educated. He then took holy orders and was archdeacon of Manchester before being a canon of Worcester in 1905, becoming a distinguished antiquary. There is a biography of A. T. Wilson by J. Marlowe, *Late Victorian. The Life of Sir Arnold Talbot Wilson* (London, 1967).

6. For Cox's career see P. Graves, *The Life of Sir Percy Cox* (London, 1941). Graves had been a journalist in the Middle East before 1914 and *Times* correspondent in Istanbul. He joined the Arab Bureau in Cairo in 1915. The biography is useful but uncritical.

his elbow to advise, support and stimulate as necessary.[7] The Minister of Interior presided over the administration and, as in all Middle Eastern countries where law and order take priority, his was the most important portfolio in the Cabinet, not least because it was he who controlled the elections.

The Mosul wilayat consisted of four liwas or provinces, Mosul, Arbil, Sulaimani and Kirkuk, in each of which it was my fate to spend several years, and the set-up was to say the least of it [uncertain].

There was no peace treaty with Turkey, now rejuvenated under Mustafa Kemal, flushed with success against the Greeks, and unwilling to accept our occupation of the Mosul wilayat. Though two Kurdish uprisings and one Arab rebellion had been suppressed yet no real tribal disarmament had taken place. The [British] troops were disgruntled at the extended post-war service in a country devoid of the normal facilities for their enjoyment and where no families were allowed. The British government was naturally anxious to reduce their commitments and expenses in accordance with post-war economies. The people had no certain knowledge of what was to be the fate of their country or those who helped us to rule it, and this was especially the case for the inhabitants of the four provinces of the old Mosul wilayat still in dispute. If it came to the worst we Britishers could go home but where could they go? The Turks had hanged everyone in Kut-al-Amara who had in any way assisted us, and this was not easily forgotten.

Saiyid Talib Pasha of Basra was appointed Minister of Interior. He had always been friendly to us since the troops first landed in Basra, and the legend that he had murdered no fewer than three Turkish governors was in the present circumstances all to his credit. He was also rich. The thirteen provincial governors were all ex-Turkish officials of local origin, respectable, conservative, and men who had continued to serve on the administration since the exit of the Turkish Army. To advise, support and stimulate them a British Political Officer was attached to each. So, though nominally an adviser or Administrative Inspector [as he was now called] was without authority, yet in practice it was the British officer who had to put the tick into the new clock. There were times when a political personality or a tribal chief had to be restrained; and, as it would be asking too much of a local governor to risk a future family feud by taking the necessary action, the British Adviser stepped in and acted for him. The police were still commanded by British officers and the ultimate sanction of force by the

---

7. From 1920 Political Officers were officially called Divisional Advisers, and from 1922 Administrative Inspectors, to reflect the end of the military occupation and creation of an Iraqi state.

employment of troops or aeroplanes had to be recommended by the British Political Officers and approved by their chief and the British High Commission.

During the war [as was seen above] there had been set up in Cairo a department called the Arab Bureau which was originally intended to provoke rebellion by the Arabs so as to hamper the Turkish operations and lines of communications while facilitating our own ... After the Armistice, however, the 'raison d'être' of the Bureau no longer existed. Hogarth returned to Oxford, leaving Miss Bell and Lawrence to plead the cause of the Arabs. Miss Bell [had] come to Baghdad as Oriental Secretary to the Civil Commissioner [in 1917] and subsequently to the High Commissioner, Sir Percy Cox. Lawrence felt himself under an obligation to the Amir Faisal, who had been ejected from Syria by the French, and in Miss Bell he had a fervent supporter, for in fact she in a platonic but nevertheless intense degree had become a worshipper of Faisal and his cause. Thus it was that the British government was persuaded to put him on the throne of Iraq by the pleadings of Lawrence and Hogarth, while Miss Bell, like St John the Baptist, went ahead to Baghdad to prepare the way and make his path straight.[8] To the inhabitants of Iraq and to the British officers serving there, however, this decision was not revealed. Instead an official notification was issued to the effect that the country would be ruled by a King to be elected by the people. Thus Saiyid Talib Pasha who, though Minister of Interior, was quite unaware of the plan decided that he would enter for the Royal stakes. He gave a dinner party to all the most important people, Iraqi and British alike, including the *Times* correspondent, and at it he told them of his intention and hopes for their support.

As soon as Miss Bell heard of this she rushed round to Sir Percy Cox, with the result that the next afternoon [17 April 1921] Saiyid Talib Pasha was arrested when leaving Miss Bell's house after a cup of tea and a friendly chat. He was bundled into an armoured car and out of the country without further palaver. Philby, to his credit be it said, was furious on hearing that his Minister had been banished, and dashed round to see Sir Percy. What sort of procedure was this? Banishing the Minister of Interior without reference to his Adviser, etc., etc. But all Sir Percy said was, 'I

---

8. The decision to promote Faisal was in fact taken at the Cairo conference in March 1921, chaired by Winston Churchill, newly appointed Secretary of State for the Colonies. The basic objective was not to reward Faisal but to create a viable Iraqi state and so enable Britain to reduce its very large expenditure there. Faisal seemed the best available candidate, despite the fact that he and his family had no connection with Iraq. Lyon's account reflects the reactions of incompletely informed British administrators to this whole devious strategy.

perceive that there isn't enough room in this country for both of us'. So Philby left.[9] The next notification published the fact that the British government's candidate for the election was Amir Faisal, and to all of us Political Officers there came a top secret coded telegram instructing us to use all our influence, personal and official, to persuade the people to elect Faisal.

For me this was a tough assignment, as the great majority of the people were Kurds who cared little for any Arab prince, and like all hill men despised the dwellers of the plains. Had I been older, more experienced, or even known at the time of the dubious methods employed to confront the people with a Hobson's Choice while telling the world it was a free election, I feel I would have stood aside. But at the time I was a young military officer, tempered in war and accustomed to carry out orders without demur, but inexperienced in the wiles of politics.

The tribal chiefs and city elders were gathered together and asked to sign the petition for Faisal. An Arab prince, descended from the Prophet, who had supported us in the war against the Turks from whom they were now liberated, etc., etc. They were reluctant and asked about other candidates; and I was compelled to admit there was none, but that Faisal was Lloyd George's candidate, and who would know better than him? Would the British be annoyed and perhaps send out columns of troops if they didn't sign? I said I didn't know but presumed they would be disappointed. In the end after a very long, hot and tiring day, I returned to the bungalow to find two strange British Colonels had arrived for the night. They were [Colonel Kinahan] Cornwallis and [Colonel P.] Joyce [both one-time members of the Arab Bureau]; like Joshua and his companions they had come to spy out the land.[10] Later one [Cornwallis] was to take the place of my Chief, Philby, the other [Joyce] to found the Iraqi Army. After I had checked their credentials, they asked me how the election was proceeding, and I told them that as most of the inhabitants were Kurds it was no easy matter to get their representatives to sign for Faisal; however, after much persuasion, I had succeeded in carrying out the orders and as far as I was concerned the election was over. Later I heard that Major Marshall had refused to use any persuasion in the Kirkuk liwa, and as a result the people there, who were mostly of Turkish and Kurdish origins, had refused to elect Faisal. He was older, and more experienced, and he was right where I was wrong. The Sulaimani liwa was completely Kurdish, the centre of Kurdish nationalism, governed as a separate province under the British High Commissioner and

---

9. For Philby's career before and after 1921 see E. Monroe, *Philby of Arabia* (New York and London, 1973).

10. Joyce had fought with Faisal in the Hejaz campaign.

consequently left out of the election; though subsequently when, for want of British support, the Kurdish aspirations faded out, it was included in the remainder of Iraq.

The coronation was arranged to follow swiftly on the 'election' and the Naqib of Baghdad, an old and saintly gentleman who commanded universal respect, was only too willing to hand over the leadership of the provisional government; and in due course all the notables of the country were summoned to Baghdad to witness the coronation of Faisal. Perhaps coronation is the wrong word, for among the Arabs there is no such thing as a crown and the ceremony consists of leading the King to his throne. This was done by the Naqib under the supervision of Sir Percy Cox, and in the presence of all the notables assembled to witness the ceremony and to pay homage to him when seated [23 August 1921]. Apart from his relations who accompanied him to Iraq, the new King's supporters were Cornwallis, Joyce, and the ex-Turkish officers of Iraqi origin and Arab blood who had been captured by us during the war and who had elected to support the Sharif's rebellion under Faisal. The most important of these were Jafar al-Askari and Nuri Pasha as-Said, and always, though often behind the scene, the faithful and ubiquitous Miss Bell.

As soon as the ceremony was over a working party arrived to dismantle the platform and throne which, stripped of its regalia, was seen to have been hurriedly put together from sections of Japanese beer crates with the stencil marks 'Asahi' and 'NAAFI' still showing on the seat. For the few junior British officers who remained behind this provided a hilarious anti-climax to the solemnity of the occasion, though as an omen it could hardly be interpreted to predict solidity for the foundation of the Hashemite rule, nor its adherence to the orthodox Moslem attitude towards alcohol. But junior Army officers were not in the councils of the great and consequently did not concern themselves with political prognostications. They did not know that the King was foisted on Iraq by the British government ... They were not to know that the election was rigged, still less could they foresee that every subsequent election would be rigged until the final collapse of counterfeit democracy with the violent deaths of the Hashemite family and all its principal supporters [in 1958] ... Thus as soon as the King had been crowned, the orders came for consolidation of the country by showing the flag.

The Armistice was now several years old, yet there was no peace with Turkey, now rejuvenated by Mustafa Kemal through his successes against the Greeks, whom he had driven out of Anatolia, and was still claiming the Mosul wilayat. There had meanwhile been two campaigns against Kurdish insurgents in the Amadiya district of Mosul and in the Sulaimani liwa – the centre of Kurdish nationalism, and of the Arab insurrection of 1920 ... Thus it will be seen that the political state of the country was far from settled, especially in areas which had not yet been reoccupied. Such an area, by far the most formidable, was the district of Ruwandiz in the Arbil liwa. It was here that the Russian Cossacks had failed to penetrate the mountain ranges separating it from the Arbil plain; and being on the north-east corner of Iraq it had frontiers with both Turkey and Persia.

The nearest sub-district of Ruwandiz was called the Desht-i-Harir, about 50 miles off, inhabited for the most part by the Surchi tribe. So a letter was sent to Ali Beg, their local chief, to say I would be paying him a visit. The escort consisted of one squadron of Kurdish cavalry under the command of Captain O'Connor with Lieutenant Boyce as second in command, plus about a dozen mounted police. We crossed the Arbil plain and spent the night at Dera with Mejid Agha, one of the chiefs of the Girdi tribe about 25 miles from Arbil and beyond the first foothills. Next morning the column proceeded through the hills to the pass of Duwin Qaleh, which is locally believed to be the birthplace of Salah-ad-Din, the famous opponent of Richard Coeur de Lion. Beyond Duwin Qaleh the track lay through a narrow valley covered with stunted oak trees to the next pass called Babachichik, beyond which lay the Desht or plain of Harir. All went well till the advance guard supervised by Boyce was approaching the pass, when suddenly it was subjected to heavy rifle fire from the front and from both sides. This sudden and unexpected attack naturally caused some confusion at first, but after a minute or two Boyce got the advance guard into dismounted action formation. O'Connor, at the head of the main body, on hearing the firing, took up a defensive position, with horses led to the rear, while I went to see what it was all about.

On reaching the vanguard I found that the pass was held in strength and the enemy had luckily opened fire on the point before turning their fire on the advance guard itself. Had they waited in their concealed positions and held their fire till the column was halfway through the pass it would have been another calamity like that at the Gelli Mizurka in 1919. As it was there were three or four casualties out of fewer than a dozen men, including Lieutenant Boyce who was wounded in the arm and had lost his horse. With the enemy – dismounted tribesmen – now advancing in strength under cover of rocks and trees on the ridges each side of the valley, there was small prospect of forcing the pass with mounted troops, but considerable risk of being ultimately surrounded. So I put Boyce on my horse and we withdrew to the head of the column; and coming under fire, O'Connor then sent a dismounted section out on the ridge each side of the valley to halt the enemy while he withdrew the column, and this was accomplished with only a few more casualties. This was a most unpleasant rebuff, but under the circumstances there was no alternative but to withdraw and have another go when we had gathered more information about the opposition.

In due course it was reported that a Turkish officer with some Bashi Bazooks or *franc tireurs* had arrived in Ruwandiz on a mission to foment rebellion among the tribes with the object of facilitating the return of the Mosul wilayat to Turkey. He had got the support of Shaikhs Obeidulla and Raqib of the Surchi tribal section across the Zab river in the Aqra district; and it was these plus the local Surchi under Ali Beg and an assorted lot of recalcitrant tribesmen who were responsible for holding us up.

After due consideration it was decided that mounted troops in such a confined and mountainous area were unsuitable, so instead we decided to use dismounted police under Charles Littledale, supported by the RAF Bombing Squadron in Mosul. We planned a different approach, with air cover from the point where we intended to deploy into the Harir plain at dawn. Littledale knew the country well, having fought over it during the 1920 rebellion; our liaison with the RAF squadron was excellent as we knew all the officers personally and they were all keen to take part; and last but not least the High Commissioner and the AOC in Baghdad had given us their blessing. This time, however, our mission was secret and punitive, unheralded by any message of greeting. Instead we equipped ourselves with various coloured flares and a Popham Pannel[11] for sending simple signals to the covering planes.

On the appointed evening we set forth under cover of darkness and made our approach undisputed to the edge of the plain, into which we deployed in open order with the first two planes overhead as arranged. Our first objective was the village of Batas situated on a low outcrop, beyond which at about one kilometre lay the village of Harir at the foot of the precipitous range known as the Harir Dagh. As we approached we were greeted by desultory rifle fire, so the planes were signalled to go in with bomb and machine-gun, under cover of which we rushed in, the tribesmen withdrawing to Harir under our combined fire. We then sorted ourselves out while waiting for the next planes, consolidated our position, and prepared for the next phase for which Harir was the objective. This proved to be a much tougher proposition as there was a lot of cover for the tribesmen in the gardens and walls; moreover being so close to the foot of the mountain made it more difficult for low-flying planes while providing extra cover for the riflemen. As a result of this one machine was

---

11. A Popham Panel was a set of flat sections that could be set out in different patterns to signal to aircraft, using a code.

hit and made a forced landing in a rice field behind our position. The pilot, F/O Teagle, and his air gunner were unhurt; but knowing the machine could not be salvaged he set up the rear gun at about 20 yards range and opened fire on the tank, which exploded, covering him with burning petrol. This also set off some bombs still in the rack which wounded the air gunner. Though neither appeared to be in a serious condition it was embarrassing for us on a tip and run show to take extra casualties, so we marked out a suitable landing strip and got them off by air. Though Teagle made light of his burns and refused to go to bed at once on returning to the mess, he became worse next day and died on the third day afterwards. The sight of the burning plane put more heart into the tribesmen who now put up a fierce counter-attack; and as a result we had to withdraw after having only partially burned the village. The last phase was the withdrawal from Batas after having first set all the roofs afire. We got back to Arbil the next day, tired but satisfied that we had wiped off the Babachichik insult and shown Ali Beg's tribesmen that treachery had its price. But as time went on reports showed that the trouble was much greater than we had at first supposed; and gradually there emerged a definite picture of a Turkish-organized fifth column campaign conducted by an officer [Colonel Ali Shefiq] known as Euzdemir [Oz Demir] (Iron Shoulder) distributing money, arms and promises of rich rewards to all who would make trouble. This soon spread to the neighbouring Kurdish liwa of Sulaimani.

Here the British had experimented with the idea of Kurdish self-rule under Shaikh Mahmud, with Major Soane as his bear leader, assisted by British Political Officers in the several districts, who were expected to set up some sort of a framework of democratic administration. Soane was an enthusiastic but ruthless type who had no love for Shaikh Mahmud. His officers, whom he had himself selected, were, with few exceptions, what might be described as 'tough guys'.

Shaikh Mahmud was a thoroughbred trouble-maker and the most tyrannous of a tyrannical family of Barzinja Saiyids – i.e. a family claiming descent from the Prophet Mohammed. He was totally inexperienced in administration, hated Soane, and had seized the opportunity of Soane's absence on leave to raise the standard of revolt in 1919. He had been defeated, shot through the liver, restored to health by the RAMC, sentenced to death, reprieved and exiled to India. But Soane had gone home to die of tuberculosis, and now his place had been taken by Major [H. A.] Goldsmith. Though he also suffered and finally died of tuberculosis the analogy there ended; for he was a mild-tempered student-like type, the antithesis to his predecessor, and thus out of harmony with Soane's rough lieutenants who showed him or his orders little or no respect.

There was [Captain J. G.] Cook in the Godforsaken and malaria-stricken district of Ranya, 80 miles east of Arbil, whose sole means of communication were a mule track and a rickety telephone. His feuds with various chieftains were almost unbelievable. His nerves were in such a state that he shot one of them in his office ... Sometimes he would ring me up at Arbil for want of company, and each time his prospects of holding out seemed less. Eventually he was succeeded by Major [C. J.] Edmonds, a scholarly officer of the Levant Consular Service, who had a very short reign [May–September 1922].[12]

In the Halabja district was [Captain] George Lees, an artillery officer who flew in the RFC during the war and had a taste for archaeology. It was his duty to play ball with the Queen of Halabja [Adila Khan]. She was the widow of Usman Pasha, Chief of the Jaf, and she ruled the tribe with a rod of iron. Having employed Soane before the war as a personal secretary when he was in disguise as a Persian, she was now somewhat peeved at being sometimes restrained by one of his junior officers. She was up to every sort of trick, not excluding seduction. She would warn Lees that her nephew Hamid Beg, whom she disliked, intended to assassinate him; then she would follow it up by sending two of her riflemen to shoot up Lees' house by night. He on his part would warn her that if she did not come to heel Soane would probably send the RAF to bomb her. Having delivered this warning Lees would go off, borrow a plane from one of his RAF pals and circle her house at tree height, the while he let off a stream of threats in Kurdish interspersed with a few warning shots from his revolver. Eventually Lees, a highly intelligent officer, saw that the game was not worth the candle, so he went home, qualified himself as a geologist, and ultimately became chief of that department in the Anglo Persian (now BP) Oil Company. Thus the Halabja post was left untenanted; but as the Jaf tribe were anti-Turk, anti-Arab, and anti-Shaikh Mahmud, and anti-everybody but themselves, it didn't much matter.

Then there was [Captain L. O.] Bond in the Chamchemal foothills, halfway between Kirkuk and Sulaimani. He was the son of an Istanbul boat-builder, born and bred in the Middle East and proud of his British blood, as is usual with such [men], and tough as they are made but over-

---

12. On Cook (though his name is not spelt out) see C. J. Edmonds, *Kurds, Turks and Arabs* (London, 1957), pp. 228–30. Cook went home on leave in May 1922 and did not return. Edmonds took his place at Ranya for five months and was later that year appointed to succeed Marshall at Kirkuk. He remained there until he was appointed Assistant Adviser to the Ministry of Interior in 1925, finally replacing Cornwallis as Adviser in 1935. He was a close friend of Lyon throughout and went climbing with him.

The 'Election' of King Faisal · 101

confident in himself. It was his duty to deal with the Hamawand, a tribe of notorious reivers [robbers] who in the past had ranged from Mosul in the north to the gates of Baghdad and eventually so disrupted trade with Persia that the Turks dispatched an expedition to round them up, men, women and children and herd them into exile at Tripoli in Libya some 2,500 miles off. But even there they could not be contained for long, and soon they had stolen enough arms and transport animals to enable them to escape. Thus, leaving their families in the care of the Shammar Arabs in the Syrian desert, they rode back to their homes and renewed their forays until the Turkish authorities were obliged to pardon them.

This was the general administrative set-up in the Sulaimani province, which now came under increasing pressure and was soon to upset the whole structure, leaving me, as it turned out, with all the bits and pieces with which to start afresh. But as that came later I now return to personal experiences in the Arbil liwa.

Here, though we had given the opposition something to think of, there was still a general atmosphere of political unrest. The two Surchi Shaikhs Obeidulla and Raqib, who belonged to the Aqra district of Mosul, had broken the conditions of residence agreed with Colonel Nalder on the conclusion of the 1920 rebellion and had crossed the Zab to take up permanent residence in the Desht-i-Harir. Moreover Oz Demir's continued presence and propaganda in Ruwandiz was attracting refugees from justice from all the neighbouring administered areas. Finally I got news that two of the Dizai Chiefs from the large tribe inhabiting the Arbil plain had been in correspondence with him about joining forces to isolate Arbil by cutting the only bridge over the Lesser Zab, on the line of communication to Kirkuk and Baghdad. As there were no bridges over the Greater Zab on the north, nor the Tigris on the west, this was a threat serious enough to merit further investigation. I soon got confirmation from a most reliable source and Ahmad Effendi, the local governor and ex-mayor of Arbil, approached me about it. He was genuinely anxious to avoid trouble but did not wish to take any action himself which might lead to subsequent bad feelings on the part of tribal chiefs with whom he would have to live, whether the province was ultimately left in Iraq or returned to Turkey. He told me that Ahmad Pasha, a loud-mouthed and brutal type of chief, had openly boasted of what he would do and that his neighbour, Haji Pir Daud, was to give him his support. So I proposed that the governor should summon all the Dizai chiefs, both loyal and suspect, to headquarters and leave the rest to me.

The serai courtyard had a single entrance through a great wooden door, with the various offices built round the four sides and all doors and windows facing inwards. On the appointed morning the station house officer, Charles Shepherd, was to drill the police in the courtyard as was customary, but on this occasion there would also be an inspection of arms, ammunition and equipment. As soon as the Dizai chiefs arrived he would close and bolt the great door and continue to drill until he got the signal from his commander, Charles Littledale, to load with ball ammunition. The chiefs were to be shown into my office where, after the usual exchange of greetings, I would refer to the political situation and provoke Ahmad Pasha. As soon as I got him annoyed and abusive I would accuse him and Hajir Pir Daud of treachery and press the bell in my table, whereupon Charles would give the signal to load: he would then knock on my office door and come in, whereupon I would give the order for the arrest of the suspect chiefs. A section of armoured cars would then be flagged up from where they would be waiting in dead ground, about a quarter of a mile down the Mosul road and out of sight of the town. The two chiefs would then be taken to Mosul and thence to exile. All the details were carefully thought out to carry out the operation in theatrical style and so effect maximum impression on the remaining tribesmen. To make sure there would be no mistake Charles went round and confiscated all the bells in all the offices except mine and we then reckoned that the stage was well set.

In due course the chiefs arrived and after being greeted first by the governor were shown into my office, where I opened the proceedings with a review of recent happenings. All was going according to plan and my provocation of Ahmad Pasha was warming up nicely when suddenly a bell rang. There was an unmistakable sound of ball ammunition going into rifle magazines followed by the clashing home of the bolts, quickly followed by the entrance of Charles Littledale with hand on holster. To say I was surprised is to put it mildly; as for the chiefs, swarthy as they were, they paled visibly beneath their tan. Charles had a very decided cast in his right eye which, although sightless, seemed to cover everybody in the room; and this, coupled with his reputation with the revolver, was enough to cow the stoutest of hearts. He gave me an inquiring glance, thinking naturally that I had rung the bell. I was annoyed and disappointed at the way this premature signal had ruined the theatrical effort of the showdown, but the show must go on and so I quickly finished my peroration with an accusation of the two culprits and ordered their arrest. Except for that damned bell everything went off according to plan. The armoured cars drew up, whisked the two chiefs off to Mosul and thence to Palestine, after which there was an immediate drop in the political temperature.

THE EPILOGUE: About a year or eighteen months later, when Mosul Province had been awarded to Iraq and a Peace Treaty signed with Turkey

[1926], Ahmad Pasha and Haji Pir Daud returned from exile and were kind enough to pay me a courtesy call. They freely admitted their guilt and even said they were now glad of my intervention which saved their tribe a hearty bombing. During their exile they had taken the opportunity to make the pilgrimage to Mecca and had drunk the water from the holy spring of Zemzem which Ahmad Pasha – now Haji Ahmad Pasha – assured me, tasted like camel's piss. From a religious point of view this description would, by most sincere Moslems, be considered blasphemous, though to him it was merely a disappointing incident in an otherwise successful tour, for he confided to me that, with the co-operation of his son Kidher, who was an expert car driver and gold smuggler, he had done quite nicely while abroad. He concluded by presenting me with a very fine string of amber beads.

But who rang the bell? It was on the typewriter of my Indian clerk in the next room!

Having removed the risk to our rear it was now [late 1921] decided by the authorities in Baghdad to make another show of force in the Desht-i-Harir under the command of a new officer, Brigadier Sadleir Jackson, a very distinguished cavalry officer, as brave as Marshal Ney and as cocky as Conan Doyle's military hero Brigadier Etienne Gerard, fresh from service in North Russia and eager to try out the troops of his new command. He arrived in Arbil bringing with him the regiment of Kurdish Mounted Infantry stationed at Kirkuk and proceeded to review the two regiments and to make a plan. This was for one battalion of Assyrian Levies to march from Aqra to Bujil, the home of the two Shaikhs Obeidulla and Raqib, which they would attack and burn. Then crossing the Greater Zab on *kelleks* (rafts supported by inflated goat skins) they would enter the Desht-i-Herir from the north – sweeping along the base of the Spilik and Harir-Dag mountains until they joined up with the mounted Levies, which would approach from the east via Shaqlawa and Sisawa. Thus on the evening of 13 December [1921] we assembled to dinner in the Political bungalow, thirteen officers including Dr Corner who had come up from Kirkuk to supervise the medical arrangements.

As host I noted the number and lest there be any who might notice the number and date and feel ill at ease, I told the head boy to set out two separate tables, one of six and the other of seven. But in spite of this simple precaution bad luck dogged our activities almost from the start. We set out in the dark soon after dinner, O'Connor with the advance guard, Sadleir Jackson and myself at the head of the main body, Charles Littledale and Dr Corner with some police and stretchers forming the rearguard.

No sooner had we gone a few miles across the Arbil plain than O'Connor sent back a message that he was not sure of the road. So I cantered up to confirm the right track, and in doing so my horse put his foot in a hole and came down. Neither of us had any broken bones but I had a nasty and unexpected jar, and in getting up the horse had rolled over me. However, we carried on, crossing the Bastura Chai, the foothills, and then on to the Pirmum Dagh, which could only be climbed up a rocky path in single file. This involved waiting on the top till the column closed up, by which time it was nearly dawn and very cold with the top covered in snow. We went on the next day past Kora and Shaqlawa and over the next range, beyond which lay the Desht-i-Harir with Sisawa the first village in the plain and the last of those belonging to the Khoshnaw tribe. We had now done nearly 60 miles and it was quite dark before we got near the village. Here O'Connor sent back word that the village was hostile. This infuriated Sadleir Jackson. 'I have heard no shooting, how in thunder then can it be hostile?' said he. So I went forth once more and eventually got to the door of the Chief's house. This was the usual type of fortified khan with courtyard, loop holes and only one entrance. It belonged to Abdul Rahman Beg, one of the Khoshnaw Begzada, and so I rapped on the door and called upon him to open, saying who I was. There was a long pause and considerable whispering before the door was opened a few inches only. As this was not a friendly welcome I put my foot in the doorway and drew my pistol – just in case. He was one of the Chief's retainers who said that his master was with his women and not to be disturbed. So I told him to call his master and say we would be his guests for the night. By then the Brigadier had caught up with me and we then went inside. We had been on the march for about twenty-four hours and were very cold and hungry; so as soon as Abdul Rahman Beg appeared I told him to kill a couple of sheep and boil plenty of rice and barley for the troops. The diwan khana or reception hall in which we found ourselves was dark and smoky but warm. As soon as Charles arrived with the rearguard and police I told him that I had ordered food which should be ready in a couple of hours, and then, being very tired, I dozed off, to be awakened two hours later by revolver shots. Charles had demanded the food, and when it appeared that preparations had not yet begun and the Beg's retainers got cheeky, Charles went into action and shot them as they tried to escape into the women's quarters. This we followed up by arresting the Beg, and soon the household were busy preparing the food.

As soon as it was light the next morning I went outside with my Kurdish orderly and a samovar that he had found and started to make tea, when suddenly there came a burst of rifle fire from the mountain and one of the bullets hit the orderly below the knee. However, after we had taken cover on the other side of the house, he continued to make the tea and made light of his wound. Then after a hasty breakfast of Kurdish bread and cheese the Brigadier summoned his officers and explained the plan. Lieutenant Devenish was to take a troop up the Harir Dagh to the crest of the mountain and then move along the top and, if possible, get behind the party that had started shooting. The remainder, less a reserve of one squadron, would move in extended order dismounted towards Batas till they joined forces with Colonel Barke's battalion of Assyrian Levies. They would right turn and attack the village and gardens of Harir. Devenish had by far the most formidable task as the mountain was very steep and covered with large boulders which gave excellent cover to the enemy. Nevertheless his operation was by far the most successful. The remainder were very slow and, when the time came to attack, most reluctant. The Brigadier was furious and dashed after them throwing stones and shouting at those who refused to get up with their officer when he advanced. However, after much delay they got there in the end. Barke's Assyrians were of course much better and quickly subdued any opposition, which in their case was light. Towards the close of the day the order was given to withdraw; and it was after they got back to the Batas ridge which was parallel to the Harir Dagh, and at least one kilometre from its base, that both [Lieutenant R. A.] Surridge and [Captain J. P.] Carvosso, two promising young officers, were shot. Dr Corner, in mufti with a Red Cross armlet, was always at hand careering over the battlefield regardless of danger, and he spent the night in Sisawa comforting them as best he could but both were hopeless cases and died before the dawn [27–29 December 1921]. In view of the fact that the light was failing fast and the nearest enemy was then more than a thousand yards away it seemed extraordinary bad luck that they would have been hit and I never felt certain that they were the victims of enemy bullets. Their own troops were reluctant, tired and untrustworthy, and in such conditions what better way of avoiding further risk and discomfort than by putting a bullet into the British commander.

It was a sad march back to Kora, where we spent the night, and the following day we reached Arbil. Apart from the two British officers the only casualties were one native officer and six or seven men wounded.

The next day we buried both officers in the Christian village of Ankawa which lay about a mile north of my bungalow, and the units collected for the operation returned to their stations. Did the sinister date and the number of the officers sitting down to dine have anything to do with it? I wouldn't know. But the fiery Sadleir Jackson was very disappointed in the quality of his command and soon there were new officers commanding the mounted Levies in Kirkuk and Arbil. The Viscount Gough, a one-armed Major of the Irish Guards, took over the Kirkuk unit and Major Wild of the Oxford and Bucks took command of the Arbil regiment. Lord Gough came of a famous Irish family and was known as the 'Lord'; Wild was the son of an Oxford don and had served with the Brigadier in the North Russian campaign under General Ironside.

The operation could hardly be classed as satisfactory, though from my point of view as the Political Officer on the spot the answer to our problem was a simple one. Just get together an adequate force, push the Bashi Bazooks out of Ruwandiz and reoccupy the district. But there was no peace treaty as yet with Turkey; the fate of the Mosul wilayat – i.e. the northern third of Iraq – was yet undecided; the home government did not want to risk further military commitments; and this attitude penetrated from the War Office down to the C-in-C Baghdad, who would be the authority responsible for collecting the necessary force.

It was just then, and before any change in strategy or tactics became known, that Major Marshall, the Divisional Adviser in Kirkuk, went on leave to the UK, and on his recommendation I was ordered to take over his post in addition to my own. This was a great compliment to me, but not for 'Pa' Miller, who was Marshall's Assistant, considerably older than me, fluent in Turkish, the language of the four main towns in the liwa with which he was very familiar. I felt uncertain of his attitude and indeed who could blame him for feeling jealous at being passed over? He did not speak Kurdish or Arabic, however, and being unable to ride and too stout to walk his activities were strictly limited to the few places to be reached by wheeled transport. So I decided to deal with all tribal matters and leave the municipalities and their affairs to him. In the result it worked out well for no one could have given me more loyal support at a time of increasing unrest.

CHAPTER 3

Arbil and Kirkuk: Tribal Risings and the Campaign against the Turks, 1922

§ IT will be recalled that the inhabitants of the Sulaimani liwa, being Kurdish nationalists still unsatisfied politically after the failure of Shaikh Mahmud, had not been consulted about the election of King Faisal, whereas those of Kirkuk, where the Turkish element predominated, had definitely rejected him. True there were some Arabs in the Kirkuk liwa – the nomadic Obeid who wandered in the plain between the Kurdish foothills and the Tigris, also the syphilitic Jibbur who like river rats clung to its banks – but though the Kurds were the most numerous, it was the Turks whose political influence was strongest. Thus, although these Turkomans, as they were called, were a more law-abiding element than either the Arabs or Kurds, they formed a definite flaw in our claim for the retention of the Mosul Province still in dispute. Though one could not blame them for not wanting to be separated from Anatolia, they amounted to an opponent's strong point behind our political lines and as such required careful handling. Luckily the Kirkuk liwa had no frontier but was bounded on the east by the Chamchemal district of the Sulaimani liwa; and it was there, before I had time to look around, that the trouble started.

Under the stimulus of Euzdemir [Oz Demir] this took the form of increasing acts of lawlessness, till raiding parties from Shaikh Mahmud's supporters in the Avroman tribe [began] making the caravan routes unsafe right up to the precincts of Sulaimani town itself; and as the suppression of these activities was proving beyond the competence of the somewhat unreliable local police and Levies, the Political Officer, Major [H. A.] Goldsmith, applied for and got the assistance of the mounted regiment of Levies commanded by Major the Viscount Gough which formed the Kirkuk garrison. It was while he was away in pursuit of these raiders to their lair in the village of Bani Banok (top of the little roof) situated near the Persian frontier in the precipitous Auroman mountains that Captain [L. O.]

Bond, the Political Officer of the Chamchemal district, suddenly appeared in Kirkuk. He had recently returned from home leave to find the Hamawand chiefs arrogant and out of hand. They had just murdered Bond's local sub-district officer, an action which was not only a serious crime but an insult to the administration and to Bond himself. He implored me to lend him a posse of Arbil Police; reliable and well trained by Charles Littledale, they were easily the best in the country. I said I was sorry I could not oblige, for both Arbil and Kirkuk liwas were now under the jurisdiction of the Minister of Interior in Baghdad, whose permission would be necessary for an operation of this sort. I suggested that he apply officially and I would support him. But he said he'd be damned if he'd ask a favour of any Arab. As an alternative he could ask his superior Major Goldsmith to hold Viscount Gough, now on his way back after [attacking] Bani Banok. He would have to pass through Chamchemal in any case and I could think of no one more willing to hit the Hamawand than this distinguished fire-eating Irish Guardsman. But no, he [Bond] was too proud to ask his superior Goldsmith for any help. As his district was adjacent to the Kirkuk liwa and lay across the only wheel road to Sulaimani, the matter was bound to have repercussions in Kirkuk, so I suggested he talk it over with the governor of Kirkuk. Fattah Pasha was a charming old retired Turkish Brigadier who, incidentally, had been concerned in the rounding up of the Hamawand when he was a junior subaltern in the Turkish Army and was bound to know quite a lot about them. But Bond was too proud; so I dined him, wined him, and [gave him a bed for the night], and in the morning I wished him luck and off he rode. A few days later, accompanied by Captain [R. K.] Makant of the Sulaimani Levies and a couple of orderlies, he made an assignation with Kerim-i Fattah Beg, the guilty Hamawand Chief, at which both officers were murdered [18 June 1922]. This started a vendetta which lasted several years and in many respects, except for its finale, resembled Kipling's famous 'Ballad of Bodathone'. Pursued from pillar to post, but never cornered or brought to action by a superior force, he became a focus for all outlaws for miles around.[1]

It was not long afterwards [July 1922] that the next outbreak occurred. This was in Ranya, Cook's old district, now tenanted by [C. J.] Edmonds. The most northerly district of Sulaimani, spanning the unbridged Lesser Zab river, it lay between the Koi Sanjaq district of Arbil and the Persian frontier. It was approached only by pack transport and second only to Ruwandiz as an ungetatable spot, and so ideal for the Turkish troublemakers.

---

1. See Edmonds, *Kurds, Turks and Arabs*, pp. 247–62 for details of the hunt for Kerim-i Fattah Beg and the Ranicol expedition.

Tribal Risings and the Campaign against the Turks · 109

The district was inhabited by a miscellaneous confederation of small tribes dominated by the Pizhdar, a proud and unbroken family of squirelings whose territory spread right up to and across the Persian border. In all these Kurdish frontier areas it was customary for each tribe to be politically divided. They would of course never dream of fighting each other, but it was a convenient policy in an area where the ultimate winner, whether Persian or British, was still undecided. In this way, whatever power gained the upper hand, there was always a loyal section of the tribe in a position to mediate for those on the losing side. Thus it was that Babakr Agha's section remained friendly, though otherwise neutral, to Edmonds while the other section, headed by Babakr's cousin Abbas-i Mahmud, favoured the opposition. And so the situation degenerated until Major Goldsmith was again obliged to ask Baghdad for help. Accordingly Colonel 'Spookey' Hughes went forth with two companies of the 15th Sikhs, one section of mountain howitzers, and the Sulaimani Levies to support Edmonds.

Leaving a picket of Sikhs on a mound overlooking the river Zab to ensure the water supply the column [code-named Ranicol] crossed over and camped at Ranya about a mile distant from the right bank. During the night [31 August 1922] the picket was rushed by the hostile tribesmen and next day the situation became serious as the troops were now denied access to the river, which provided the only clean water supply. The enemy, now encouraged by their successes, came closer and began sniping the camp, so the commander decided to retire the following night. But the path led through a very boggy rice field and in the confusion some of the transport stampeded and one of the two mountain howitzers was lost and Edmonds had a bullet through his topee. By daylight the situation was serious. The mounted Levies had not waited for the rest of the column, the Sikhs had rallied together and, surrounded by tribesmen, were fighting a rearguard action across the plain towards the pass over the Haibas Sultan mountain on their way to Koi Sanjaq and safety. From Kirkuk No. 8 squadron, commanded by 'Beery' Bowman, were busy as bees, bombing and machine-gunning the enemy and thus producing air cover which enabled the column to get through.

Happening to be at Kirkuk at the time I went up with one of the officers, 'Crasher' Pett, and after chaperoning the column to the foot of the Haibas Sultan, I asked him to put me down at the Arbil landing ground to enable me to arrange accommodation and rations at Koi Sanjaq for the column. Pett's cognomen was not unearned for, after over-shooting the landing ground twice, we hit the ditch on the third attempt and turned upside down. Although the plane was out of action neither of us was hurt. So I arranged for the food and accommodation for the troops, transport to Kirkuk for the wounded, including one British subaltern –

now a retired General – and awaited decision by the headquarters in Baghdad. I felt sure there could be only one decision, i.e. to collect a larger force based on Koi Sanjaq and under cover of the RAF go up to the Pizhdar country and lay it waste. But to my amazement the order came for the troops to withdraw, and I realized that after such a defeat, if the troops left Koi Sanjaq there was nothing I could do to save it from the enemy; so I ordered Charles to send a Police Inspector with a strong party of police to remove the records and treasure chest and withdraw as soon as the tribesmen came on. This they did and as I anticipated Koi Sanjaq was lost. I was very disappointed about all this; but worse was to come, for news came through in cypher that the Army Command was being handed over to the RAF, and there being no troops available to safeguard the British and Indian administrative staff in Sulaimani, they were all to be evacuated with the families by air. Squadron Leader Maxwell, who had recently evacuated the British staff in Kabul with great success, was now in Iraq and he at once repeated the operation. There was much publicity in the press about the air lift, but so far as I was concerned it was a 'Dunkerque' for we had now lost the whole Sulaimani liwa, [and] the opposition were now about 50 miles nearer to the towns of Arbil and Kirkuk, the capitals of the two liwas for which I was responsible.[2]

In Sulaimani Goldsmith had handed over the administration to Shaikh Qadir, a brother of Shaikh Mahmud, a weak personality and over-shadowed by his wife Hafsa Khan, the lady who had been so fond of Major [A. M.] Daniels during Shaikh Mahmud's uprising in 1919. Meanwhile, for want of a better solution, the High Commissioner decided to bring back Shaikh Mahmud, this time accompanied by a British Adviser, ... Major Noel, who it was hoped would be more successful than his predecessors in curbing Shaikh Mahmud. But it was not long before Noel saw how useless it all was and handed over his charge to Captain [A. F.] Chapman, who in a short time became a hostage if not an actual prisoner of the Shaikh, who proved as tyrannical as ever and lawlessness continued unchecked.[3]

About this time [October 1922] who should arrive on the Arbil/Persian frontier but the notorious Ismail Agha – known for short as Simko, Chief of the Shikak – who since the murder of Marshimun had been roaming round the north-west of Persia with a collection of outlaws and deserters from the various armies of Russia, Turkey, Persia and India numbering at one time several thousand and even including a battery of guns. He was undoubtedly the biggest brigand of modern times and had he been politi-

---

2. For a full account of the Ranya disaster, at which he lost part of his own diary, see Edmonds, *Kurds, Turks and Arabs*, ch. 17.

3. For a fuller account see ibid., pp. 305–8.

cally minded he might have headed a Kurdish nationalist movement, especially as he was accompanied by Saiyid Taha, whose father had raised the Kurdish standard of rebellion in the Bhadinan district of Turkey. But Simko was only interested in looting the Persian countryside from Urmia to Saujbulak; and eventually the Persian Army led by a Russian General defeated him, so that now, deserted by his followers and deprived of his loot, he was driven out of Persia with a mere fifty or so of his bodyguard.

Now as Shaikh Mahmud had proven an impossible leader, the High Commissioner, Sir Henry Dobbs, advised by Noel and Edmonds, saw in Simko and Saiyid Taha a possible way out of the Kurdish imbroglio and a cheap way of re-establishing authority in Sulaimani liwa and in the Ruwandiz district of Arbil, now illegally held by a Turkish official by the name of Ramzi Bey who had come in support of Oz Demir. Accordingly Simko and Saiyid Taha were invited to come in and discuss matters. Edmonds, representing the High Commissioner, came along and, together with Charles Littledale and Ahmad Effendi, the Governor of Arbil, I set out to meet them at Dera, a village in the foothills about 20 miles from Arbil. Knowing Simko's reputation for treachery I arranged for Charles to provide a picked party of armed police to provide a bodyguard and, in addition, to picket the hilltops around the meeting place.

I had also arranged with the Mosul squadron to send over a few planes to the Arbil landing ground in the event of Edmonds taking them to Mosul and on to Baghdad for further discussions. Charles and I knew that both Mosul and Baghdad aerodromes were guarded by Assyrian Levies who would most assuredly shoot Simko on sight for his treachery to their Chief, but we thought it best to say nothing. Edmonds would be all right, and there was no blood feud with Saiyid Taha, who had always enjoyed good relations with the Assyrians in the Bhadinan district from which he had been expelled by the Turks. We agreed it would be a most suitable liquidation of a treacherous brute in a way which would give complete satisfaction to 40,000 Assyrians and to all the other Christians in Iraq; and so we thought it prudent not to discuss the matter in case objections be raised, but to let Providence take its course.

So off we went by car [on 6 November 1922] to the Bastura watercourse from which we went on by horse till we came to [the village of Bahirka, near] Dera, to find that Simko and Saiyid Taha had already arrived. After the usual greetings Mejid Agha, the local chief, produced the usual meal and we then started the discussions. Their party consisted of about a score of tribesmen with tall head-dresses, bell-bottomed trousers of native manufacture, thick woollen cummerbunds holding daggers, pistols and bandoliers. All were mounted on scraggy horses which showed signs of long journeys and rough treatment. Simko was a slight figure, clean-shaven with a small moustache, Cossack riding boots and the usual accoutrements. Saiyid Taha was an enormous man of about 6 feet 4 inches, weighing all of 18 stone. His manner was suave and not without charm; by contrast Simko was ill at ease and his deportment fidgety.

The talks followed, mostly in Persian, a language with which I was unfamiliar, and I am bound to confess I was not very interested in it at all, partly because I felt sure Simko would be shot if he came in, partly because I did not consider the situation would be remedied by anything except force; tribal forces (*lashkars*) were all right when one was winning but otherwise most unreliable; partly because I didn't think any good would result from the employment of such a treacherous villain as Simko; and finally it was not my suggestion but [that of] Edmonds and Noel, and if anything came of the scheme it would be their task not mine to see it through. They were both senior to me, and at the moment unemployed,[4] whereas I was over-employed with two liwas to look after. Anyhow, as the talks dragged on Saiyid Taha appeared to be the best bet while Simko only agreed to come in with great reluctance; and on this understanding we broke up the party and rode off to the car, a few miles distant on the Arbil side of the Bastura watercourse, leaving Ahmad Effendi, the governor of Arbil, to escort the visitors. To this day I don't know what happened; whether Simko got wind of the fact that there were Assyrian Levies on the aerodrome, or whether he suddenly realized he had been talked over against his innermost judgement to take part in something constructive for the first time in his life. But anyhow, when within about three miles of Arbil, he saw the planes coming in to land, turned tail and cantered back towards the frontier. Nothing that Ahmad Effendi could say would change his mind, and so Sir Henry Dobbs and myself were both disappointed, though for very different reasons. But while on the subject of Simko I may as well conclude with his epilogue.

After visiting most of the important chiefs on the Persian frontier both in the Arbil and Sulaimani liwas, including Shaikh Mahmud, he eventually returned to Persia. There [in 1930] he received an offer of safe conduct from one of the district governors. Accompanied by Khurshid Agha, Chief of the Herki, he rode into the compound of the Persian governor's headquarters; the gate was slammed and they were both riddled with bullets ... I was sorry for Khurshid Agha: he was a most able and reliable Chief of a large nomadic tribe which, with upwards of 100,000 sheep, made the annual trek to the high Persian grazing grounds after spending the winter

---

4. This was before Edmonds was appointed to Kirkuk and after Noel had left Sulaimani. There is an account of this meeting in Edmonds, *Kurds, Turks and Arabs*, pp. 305–7, though he says nothing about Simko leaving.

in the Arbil foothills.[5] He was the unfortunate stork among the geese. As for Simko, it would have been better if the Assyrians had had the satisfaction of slaying him, but anyway he got what he deserved.

But to return to [the narrative]. Saiyid Taha came along, and eventually after a conference in Baghdad with Sir Henry Dobbs and certain financial refreshers, he agreed to try and use his influence to raise Kurdish feelings against the Turks and so evict them from Ruwandiz. His father had been hanged [by the Turks] after the suppression of his rebellion, and as there was no hope of him ever returning there the prospect of increasing his lands in Ruwandiz was better than nothing. Noel and Edmonds were his advisers and to their enterprise they gave the name of 'Rowlash', signifying a tribal force (*lashkar*) whose objective was Ruwandiz. But contrary to their expectations little or no progress was made in winning over active support from the local Kurdish tribes; and the end came when, on Saiyid Taha's request, Noel got the RAF to bomb the Herki while I was in Kirkuk organizing the salvage of the Chamchemal district, which I had got transferred to Kirkuk. There was no excuse for the bombing which was a flagrant abuse of the RAF for the personal motives and prestige of Saiyid Taha. The governor of Arbil had not been consulted about it, nor had I; so I immediately went to Baghdad and delivered an ultimatum. If the High Commissioner wanted to appoint Noel to my post he was welcome to do so and I would be quite happy to rejoin my regiment in India; but if he wanted me to stay, there would be no more free lances in the liwa. There could be no question of two cocks on the same dung hill. On this Rowlash was dissolved, Edmonds was appointed to Kirkuk as Major Marshall died in Baghdad [6 December 1922] before returning there from leave in the UK. Noel returned to India and Saiyid Taha to his small group of villages on the Iraq side of the frontier.[6]

While in Baghdad I was summoned to an interview with the Commander-in-Chief. The army had by now handed over to the RAF and Iraq was its first independent command. Sir John Salmond, then an Air Vice-Marshal, impressed me as the brightest and most alert general I had ever met. He had already got a detailed knowledge of the Kurdish situation, its tribes and its geography, and he fired questions at me for the best part of an hour. He then told me that he intended to assemble a brigade of Levies and with air support reoccupy the lost areas, starting with Koi Sanjaq, and

---

5. Ihsanullah Agha had protected W. R. Hay in 1920 in Arbil. See Hay, *Two Years in Kurdistan*, ch. 19. There is a fuller account of Simko's murder in A. M. Hamilton, *Road through Kurdistan. The Narrative of an Engineer in Iraq* (London, 1937), pp. 162–4.

6. For a full account of 'Rowlash' (so named because Ruwandiz was then commonly called Rowunduz), see Edmonds, *Kurds, Turks and Arabs*, ch. 20.

asked for my comments. I told him that with the support of one bomber squadron I could reoccupy Koi Sanjaq without any Levies but using the armed police of Arbil. As for Ruwandiz and Sulaimani, I thought it would require a bit more than the Levies as they, except for the Assyrian battalions, were nearly all Kurds and not very reliable. There was of course one battalion of Marsh Arabs, but they were quite unsuitable for mountain warfare. He would be able to judge better after seeing how things turn out at Koi Sanjaq. He then cross-examined me about the plan for Koi Sanjaq and so I suggested the operation should take place in three phases:

First Phase. Drop proclamations on Koi Sanjaq ordering the inhabitants to evict the Turkish *Chittas* within a time limit under pain of bombardment.
Second Phase. Unless they reported it clear, bomb the fort and government offices.
Third Phase. Charles and I with about 100 armed police would go in under RAF cover while the planes bombed Ranya, the headquarters of the next district from which Edmonds and Ranicol had retired. This bombing to take place the day before we arrived at Koi as well as the day we attacked.

At first he seemed doubtful as to whether the ground force was enough, but I persuaded him that the Arbil police had been well trained by Charles. They were well used to hill warfare and much more reliable than Levies. Also I knew the people of Koi Sanjaq well and felt that with a show of force they would co-operate. Jemal Agha, the local governor, was a reliable man and a great personal friend and I did not wish to inflict any casualties that could be avoided. It would also be a much more economical operation than using Levies. In the end he agreed and I returned by air to Arbil where I got Charles to collect the police while preparations of the proclamations and the bombing were set in motion from Baghdad. It wasn't long before D-day arrived and taking upwards of 100 police, mounted and foot, we set forth for Koi. We also took a Popham Panel for simple signals to the planes overhead, two Lewis guns, and a telegraph linesman to repair the telephone wire as we went along. Koi Sanjaq was about 50 miles distant, of which over 40 were through rocky foothills, there being no wheel road at that time. The first night out we camped at the village of Semak Sherin where we invited the head man, Saiyid Kakil Agha, to provide us with a good hot meal, the while I sent a messenger on to Jemal Agha, the governor, to come out and meet me. He duly turned up before midnight and we got into a 'huddle' as the Yanks have it. I asked him about the strength of the *Chittas* and the attitude of the people. He said that there were not more than a score in the town, though there were many more in Ranya and Ruwandiz. He could get the people of Koi Sanjaq to co-operate under one condition, and that was that we would stay when we got in and not make a tip and run affair of it. By that time we had got the telephone working back to Arbil, so I confirmed that we would advance at dawn and asked the RAF to co-operate as arranged. Jemal Agha was then told to go back, gather the notables, give a glorified account of our strength, and tell the *Chittas* to clear out. We then wished him luck and went to sleep.

In the morning we started off with the mounted police on each flank and the infantry and ourselves in the centre. The left flank was to go along the lower slopes of the mountain till it got behind the town, the right flank was directed at the airfield. When we got within range there were a few shots but we went straight on and did not reply as we didn't want to hit any of the townspeople by accident; and soon with our glasses we could see the *Chittas* going up the pass over the Haibas Sultan to the Ranya plain. We immediately occupied the fort and put down a T on the landing strip. Soon one of the planes landed and I sent back a signal that the operation was complete and all was well. The only casualty on our side, I regret to say, was one RAF officer called Horrocks, who was machine-gunning Ranya and was unfortunately shot down and his plane – a 'Snipe' – was burned. Some months afterwards when we reoccupied Ranya I looked for his body or grave but failed to find it, and the inhabitants said it was burned up in the plane when it came down.

As soon as we had reoccupied the police station and the old Turkish fort, Jemal Agha, the qazi, the officials and notables came along to greet us, and Jemal Agha as usual sent up half a dozen servants with a good hot meal. The people were glad it was all over and I assured everyone that the British would never let them down, and a lot more to the same effect and equally untrue. However I meant it as far as I was personally concerned. There were two principal families in the town – the Howaizi and the Gaffuri – and they usually lived in a state of internecine strife rather like the Montagues and Capulets in Shakespeare's *Romeo and Juliet*. However, on this occasion there was no quarrel or bloodshed as they rivalled each other in taking me round to see the bomb holes, which had greatly impressed them.

So the administrative officials and the normal police garrison were duly installed and life returned to normal as every few days we sent back a batch of police to their usual posts in the Arbil town and liwa, and in the meanwhile I suggested that Levies be sent up to take over – one squadron would be ample. But as the days passed and I could get no satisfactory answer, I got [tired of] staying in Koi Sanjaq when I had plenty to do elsewhere, so I asked for a plane and an interview with the C-in-C in Baghdad, which was granted. I then had to submit to a second viva voce examination, after which he inquired about my reasons for wanting relief. I told him that Koi Sanjaq was only one of the four districts of the liwa for which I was responsible. In the present state of instability the worst interpretation would be put on my absence and the administration would suffer as a result. I had carried out my part in the operation but I could not stay on indefinitely, neither could Charles; and I explained how many of the police posts had been weakened to build up our operation, and their absence would soon result in increased lawlessness. 'Did I really think a squadron of mounted Levies would be enough,' he asked. Then seeing he was showing signs of agreement I told him that in fact, apart from the normal complement of police for the town and district, all had already been returned to Arbil headquarters and there were now in the fort half a dozen mounted police and one sergeant with Charles and myself. Surely one squadron in relief would be ample! He had a good laugh at this and gave his consent. Before leaving I made another point with him. I pointed out that up to now he had twice sent for me and examined and cross-examined me about various local points in connection with proposed operations. I had had no previous warning or time to study his questions and so it could easily happen that some detail or alternative action could be overlooked that might make all the difference to the success of the operations. I would feel much more confident if he sent me his questions and I would send him back the answers. Sir John immediately saw the point and as a result many a time in the future an aeroplane would land with a despatch and the pilot would have orders to be my guest until the reply was ready for him to take back.

I then returned by plane to Koi Sanjaq, and after a few days a squadron of mounted Levies with one British officer turned up. Charles and I stayed on a couple of days to introduce them to the local gentry and to their surroundings. There was one bastion in the fort which contained a copy of the Koran and in Turkish times had been used as a mosque. Among the locals it was said to be haunted by the ghost of an Imam or Moslem priest, but though we had camped down there on many previous visits we never saw or heard any ghost. The very first night one of the Levies left his post, crying that he had been visited by the Imam. This was serious and denoted a very low standard of morale which, if not checked, could easily infect the whole squadron. The young officer did not know quite what to do and so he consulted us. This was right up Charles' street. 'Keep him in the guard room tonight,' said he, 'and tomorrow morning put him on a ladder and give him a dozen on the bare backside with a stirrup leather. And make an order that anyone else who leaves his post at

Tribal Risings and the Campaign against the Turks · 117

the sight of a ghost will get two dozen.' The sentence was duly carried out and no more ghosts or Imams were seen.

We stayed an extra night 'just in case' and then returned to Arbil. I was glad to be rid of Kirkuk where Edmonds was now installed and had got the job of keeping the vendetta going on Kerim-i Fattah Beg, the Hamawand Chief who had murdered Bond and Makant. This for the most part amounted to bombing every village which sheltered him, and without close and continuous co-operation from ground troops was not very satisfying, but doubtless better than complete inactivity. Then one afternoon in December [1923] – it was the 23rd – a plane suddenly appeared on the Arbil landing ground and out stepped the pilot with an urgent and heavily sealed despatch for me. It was a personal letter from the AOC saying that on the 24th there would be a dozen RAF officers and about the same number of other ranks staying the night. Would I please arrange to house and feed them. No one was to be told and he himself would be with them.[7]

So I gave the pilot a receipt and he flew off. I told our Indian cook Hamid to kill three or four turkeys, of which we had plenty, and to make enough plum duff for a platoon. He was a good cook, and like all of his kind invariably rose to an occasion without a murmur. Charles supplemented our beds with stretchers from the hospital and blankets from the police store, and next day all was set for action. Neither of us could possibly think of what it was all about, and especially on Xmas Eve. But we were no worse informed than the various officers as they began to arrive. They were from various squadrons stationed in Baghdad, Kirkuk and Mosul, who had been simply told to go to Arbil and await orders. Eventually the AOC arrived in his own plane piloted by his ADC, John [Jones-]Williams. Afterwards [came] some RAF trucks with mechanics, fitters, riggers and armourers, for the trucks were loaded with bombs, the largest yet used, 250- and 500-pounders.

We were then let into the secret. It seems the air staff had a brainwave. It was that December 25 being Christmas Day Shaikh Mahmud would think the RAF would be having a day off for the usual celebrations and unlikely to be active. So it was decided that a flight of De Haviland 9 As, manned by picked officers under the command of Wing Commander Harris – since famous as Bomber Harris – would raid Sulaimani and bomb

---

7. Lyon's chronology is wrong here. The Christmas 1923 bombing of Sulaiman came after the two Koikoi operations which are described below, which took place in April–May 1923. By the end of 1923 Mahmud was back in or around Sulaimani town since the High Commissioner had refused to establish a permanent administration there after the brief military occupation of May 1923. For details see Edmonds, *Kurds, Turks and Arabs*, pp. 318–38.

the Shaikh's headquarters. So the rest of the day was spent preparing the planes' bomb racks for the unusually heavy bombs; some of the aircraft carried two 250-pounders and some a single 500-pounder. They had decided to carry out the operation from Arbil, although further from the target than Kirkuk by some 40 miles, because it was less obvious and because the element of surprise was of first importance. We provided them all with a good meal, bedded them down and waited for the morning, which turned out to be cold and clear. After a very early breakfast we set off for the landing ground. Two of the officers had come without overcoats so we lent them ours and off they went.

In those days it was customary for aircraft to take off one at a time, juniors leading, each waiting on the ground till its predecessor was well up, and circling round to gain height till all were airborne and in formation. Judge of our dismay then, when the second machine was barely off the ground, there came unmistakable sounds of engine failure from the first which was then a couple of miles off. But the pilot jettisoned his 500-pounder in a dry river bed and made a forced landing back on the air strip. There was no mistake about the explosion, it was easily the best we had seen or heard, and we were duly impressed. However, undeterred by this misfortune, the other three, plus the AOC took off and were soon out of sight. It was lucky the AOC was with them as it turned out, so I [will] ... describe the operation.

In order to maintain the element of surprise till the last moment it had been decided to make a wide sweep and come into view suddenly from the east over the Azmir pass, which was about two miles from the town and about 5,000 feet above sea level. So to clear it they had to fly in very cold air and as a result when they flew over the town the release action was frozen and so they had to make a second run, by which time the population were swarming on the rooftops waving and cheering, for believe it or not, they thought the British were coming back and were glad to see them. No such luck, however, though as far as I remember there were no serious casualties, the only bomb anywhere near the target dropped in the garden of the government offices which I was later to occupy.

On the way back only about 10 miles from Sulaimani one of the planes force-landed in a dry rice field, which was the only comparatively flat spot in the area, and pilot and observer would undoubtedly have been taken prisoners had not Sir John landed alongside and taken them off in his own machine. It was afterwards learned that the Shaikh was not even in the town at the time, but he was sporting enough to put a guard on the machine till the eventual reoccupation about six months later. Thus, although the operation failed in its primary objective, it certainly demonstrated the power of the RAF; and as for the RAF personnel nothing could have given a greater boost to their morale than the knowledge that the AOC himself might at any time be accompanying them on their missions, however daring and dangerous. Compare this with the experience of the troops in the First World War, when no officer higher than a brigadier was ever seen in the front line, and it will be readily understood how quickly the confidence of the RAF grew. The aircraft did not return to Arbil but each to its own station, so it was several days before we heard the news, which for us had a special interest because, but for Sir John's gallant action, we would have lost our overcoats.

The AOC, however, was not going to rest on his laurels but was determined to drive the Turkish *Chittas* out of the Mosul Province; and so with the coming of spring [March 1923] there was a gathering of the troops, which this time consisted of two brigades: one of Kurdish and Assyrian Levies under the command of Brigadier [H. T.] Dobbin, who had succeeded Sadleir Jackson, the other was made up of the Cameronians, the Yorkshire Regiment and the 15th Sikhs, and one battery of mountain howitzers – under the command of Brigadier [B.] Vincent, an old Gunner veteran of the South African war. At that time the railhead for Mosul was still at Sharqat, so the two British battalions had to march from Sharqat to Mosul, cross the Tigris by the bridge of country boats – a rickety affair which had to be cut at high flood – and then proceed to Quweir, another 30-odd miles, to the site of the ferry over the Greater Zab. This was normally a single country boat poled and rowed across by an Arab crew, but was now augmented by several more. Nevertheless, when the river was high, as it was now in early spring, a round trip might take anything up to three hours, so there was a delay of about ten days before all were over. This pause was not without its highlights, though I am glad to say no one was drowned, which was a remarkable achievement, considering the propensity of the British Tommy for getting into trouble even in quite shallow water. However, two of them took a small boat by night in order to desert and had reached Sharqat before they were caught by our police.

But that was not the only effort. A party of the Cameronians was loading a boat as an extra punishment fatigue under the provost sergeant when one of them suddenly said, 'Sergeant, can you swim?' and on getting an answer in the negative, gave him a sudden push in the back with the words, 'Then you can now bloody well try.' Within seconds he was out of his depth into fast running water and most assuredly would have drowned had not a Sapper officer dived in and eventually brought him ashore several hundred yards downstream.

As soon as all were assembled at Arbil Sir John came up and made his Advanced Headquarters in my bungalow [8 March 1923] ... The operation was to be in two parts: the Levy Brigade [Frontiercol] was to march up through the Desht-i-Harir and onwards to Ruwandiz. To this column Jardine was posted as Political Officer with Charles Littledale as local guide and expert. The other part [Koicol] was to [be] the British Brigade composed of the Yorks, the Cameronians, the 15th Sikhs and a mountain battery, all under the command of Brigadier Vincent. It was to drive the *Chittas* out of Ranya, then cross the Lesser Zab and [hit] those tribes, including Abbas-i Mahmud's section of the Pizhdar which had joined the *Chittas* in the defeat of Ranicol; and I was appointed as Political Officer to accompany the column.

I took with me a couple of local police as guides and messengers and Hama the syce perched on my roll of bedding on top of the grey mule which he always rode when accompanying me on local tours. And as the usual army contractors were shy of going into the hills, I arranged with the shaikh of the Obeid tribe for several hundred baggage camels to carry the troops' baggage and rations. The drivers were all tribesmen and so had the advantage of being more immune from attack than the normal transport workers in so far as a casualty would entail the subsequent payment of 'Dia' or blood money under tribal custom, failing which a blood feud involving a tribal counter-attack would result. For crossing the Lesser Zab I had hired our old friend Ibrahim Jissar (Abraham the Bridge-maker) with several of his raft-men and their outfit, which consisted of several hundred deflated goat skins, powdered pomegranate rind and leather thongs with which to bind them. The poles with which to make the frame of the rafts could always be obtained locally – if necessary from house roofs.

The assembly of the column was not without its incidents. There was a chaplain attached to the British regiments who was obviously new to the job as he became most indignant when issued with a mule by the transport officer. Had he any idea of the country he was to cover he would have been more than satisfied, but his ignorance was as great as his dignity: he did not realize that in mountainous country a mule was by far the most suitable mount; and when finally he said he would appeal to the Column Commander, the Transport Officer, a well seasoned veteran called Jock Campbell, told him, 'If Jesus Christ could ride to Jerusalem on a donkey surely a mule is good enough for you.' I don't think the padre's prestige ever recovered from this shattering remark, which ended the argument.

When a column has to depend on pack transport, especially when much of it is hired, it is advisable to follow the Persian caravan custom of moving out only a few miles the first day. This brings to light any shortage in transport equipment, misfits in loading and any readjustments that may be desirable in the order of the various contents of the baggage train which can be remedied while still close to the base. The troops have to learn how to pack baggage in half loads, stacked in double lines, with adequate spacing for the camels and mules and their drivers to approach and load with maximum speed and minimum fuss and commotion. Experience has proved that British troops are seldom much good with mules, and the less they have to do with camels the better. So we set out and camped on the watercourse of Benisilawa a few miles outside the town of Arbil and the next day headed for Koi Sanjaq. But no sooner had we started than it began to rain and kept on solidly during the two days' march, so that when we got near the town the Brigadier asked me to go ahead and arrange for shelter for as many as possible of the troops; and so, taking a colour party from each unit, I pushed on and, with the help of Jemal Agha, the governor, found shelter in the old fort, the school and customs khan, at that season empty of tobacco bales. He also invited the officers to a banquet, which was up to his usual high standard, and for many of the young officers quite a novelty to sample good Persian and Turkish dishes. Unfortunately during the night there was a little distant sniping, made worse by the pickets replying to the fire, and I felt that I was among very raw and inexperienced troops, for in my regiment on the North West Frontier of India we had been trained not to reply, for the chances of hitting the sniper were infinitesimal, whereas the noise of additional firing only played into the hands of the enemy by depriving the troops of their sleep.

The morning broke bright and sunny and immediately after breakfast the column moved on over the Haibas Sultan mountain and reached the village of Sarkuma, about 20 miles distant on the south side of the Ranya plain and about 10 miles from our objective, which was the village of Ranya held by the *Chittas*. A cordon was immediately thrown round the village to stop all traffic either in or out; and then the Brigadier with his staff officer, the three battalion commanders and myself, repaired to the top of the tumulus which dominated the surrounding country, and there proceeded to explain his scheme. Our objective, which could be seen through field glasses, lay at the base of a rocky spur which ran from the mountains in the north to the river Zab. The direct approach was by a track crossing a stream below the village and thence in a straight line over the plain; and it so happened that while we were studying the route a man with a donkey crossed the stream and I was able to draw the attention of the officers to the exact location of the ford. The Yorkshires were to start about midnight along this track so as to arrive within effective rifle range of the village of Ranya with the first streaks of dawn, and block the exit to the Zab. The Sikhs would march up the right bank of the stream till they got to the outskirts of the village of Sirkabkan, then crossing the stream they would turn to the right, seize the spur which ran down behind

Ranya, advance down it till they got within range, and await the arrival at dawn of the Yorkshires. This was a sort of left hook to catch the enemy escaping from the frontal attack. It involved a much longer and more difficult approach by night, but the Sikhs were seasoned troops and eager to get their own back for the casualties they had suffered on Ranicol. Moreover, on arrival at Sarkhuma I had found Mamind Agha, the Chief of the Aku tribe, paying a visit to Sowar Agha, so I enlisted his services as guide to accompany me in the Sikhs' column.

In this sort of operation exact timing is of primary importance if the enemy is to be surprised; for given time they naturally bolt before the arrival of a superior force. So, after co-ordinating our watches, I set off with the Sikhs at about 11 p.m. leaving the Yorkshires to leave later as they had the shorter and easier march. All went well with our column and we duly arrived in our positions in good time before dawn and without going near enough to set the dogs barking; but when dawn broke there was no sign of the Yorkshires. This was most disappointing, for if we flushed the village, the *Chittas* would be able to escape before the Yorkshires got into position to close the gap, so we had to wait. Eventually, about an hour and a half later, we saw them coming across the plain and so did the enemy, who immediately started to bolt. It was now obvious that they would escape before the Yorkshires could close the gap, so the Sikhs' commander gave the order to attack and this they did with great élan. I thought I was pretty fit in those days but it was all I could do to keep up with a Sikh sepoy who was carrying a Vickers gun. We gave them a good dusting to be sure, but the operation was not the success for which we had hoped. The Brigadier was furious with the Yorkshires, who had bungled the crossing at the ford in the dark, and so had failed to arrive on time. However, owing to the uncanny ability of a section of Madras Sappers and Miners who searched the village, we found buried under the floor of the mosque the 3.7 mountain howitzer which had been lost by Ranicol. The gunners soon had it cleaned up and in a few days' time had the satisfaction of firing it in action. Meanwhile we reconnoitred the Zab crossing and then returned to camp at Sarkhuma [15 April 1923].

Here we learned that the Levies Brigade had been held up on the Spilik Dagh. This was the northern continuation of the precipitous Harir Dagh, and across it lay the track leading to the entrance of the Gelli Ali Beg or Ruwandiz Gorge, and it was thought that if they could not force the Spilik without heavy casualties then the chances of getting through the Gelli Ali Beg or Ruwandiz Gorge were remote. This gorge was about 8 miles long through the Kurek Dagh; in parts it was very narrow following the course of a river; in some stretches the track was only wide enough for one mule creeping along the face of a cliff, on one side a straight drop of over a thousand feet, on the other a towering massif several thousand feet up. This was the formidable obstacle which, defended by a few Turks, had stopped the advance of the Russian Cossacks. Indeed there was one corner, their furthest point, called Russian Post. So it was decided to alter our plan of campaign in order to assist the Levies Brigade. Instead of crossing the Zab to the Pizhdar country we would go from the Ranya plain up the Balisan valley to its head, and then over the eastern end of the Kurek Dagh by the Bejan pass and so down into Ruwandiz as it were by the back door, thus outflanking the enemy's left wing and turning his front. The movement entailed a march of about 50 miles through increasingly mountainous country over the Bejan Pass some 6,000 feet above sea level and still under snow.

Next morning we started off with the Yorkshires, the Cameronians and the pack battery, leaving the Sikhs in camp at Sarkhuma. As we approached the mouth of the Balisan valley we were subjected to sniping from both sides. The Brigadier immediately called up the guns and a few shots aimed to fall just round the bend at the valley entrance soon silenced the opposition. I afterwards learned that a howitzer shell landed right on top of a party of the leaders having tea, where they made the mistake of thinking that, as they were out of sight, they were safe.

We bivouacked that night about halfway up the valley and the following morning stood by for an air drop of rations. The battery commander had asked for more mule shoes and by an extraordinary coincidence the sack containing them fell right on his bivy. It was just as well he was not inside at the time, though his kit was wrecked. Some of the officers thought this a great joke, though he was far from seeing it. As meat was running short and we wanted to conserve our iron rations, at my suggestion we got the RAF to fly around and spot the nearest flocks of sheep and goats so that we could send out a party to round them up. In this way we collected a number of sheep and goats, some of which were in milk, which was most useful for the field ambulance, for now we were paying for our stay in Koi Sanjaq with an outbreak of amoebic dysentery which was especially prevalent among the Yorkshires. The next day we pushed on to the head of the valley, where we again encountered resistance which delayed us for about an hour, after which we continued to the head of the valley where we settled for the night. The next day we climbed the Bejan Pass, which was lightly held, till the advance guard, preceded by a few howitzer shells, reached the crest. The guns and the camels and the Yorkshires were then left and, with the Cameronians and a minimum of mule transport, we slithered down the steep mountainside track into Ruwandiz village, by then in occupation by the Levies. The outflanking move of our column had scared the enemy off the Spilik Dagh and the Levies column had then advanced through the Ruwandiz Gorge without further opposition [22 April 1923]. The *Chittas* had evacuated the town and the Levies sent a party up the track to Kani Resh on the Turkish frontier just to make sure they had gone. It was just about five years now since I had gone up the road to Zakho on the same errand just after the Armistice, and as it turned out this was the last affray in the unofficial war with the Turks.

Sir Henry Dobbs, our High Commissioner, had decided to appoint Saiyid Taha as quaimmaqam or district governor of Ruwandiz and a battalion of Assyrian Levies was posted to Ruwandiz to see him settled in and give him the necessary backing. There was nothing more for our column; and so, as food was very short, we lost no time in marching back through the Ruwandiz Gorge as it was much easier than climbing back up the steep slopes of the Bejan Pass.

On our way we passed the famous Bekal spring. It was a gigantic fountain of ice-cold crystal clear water of a capacity of about 5 cubic metres per second, bursting out of the precipitous side of the Kurek Dagh at a height of some hundred-odd feet above the track. As we halted to refresh the troops amid the clouds of spray and the thunder of the water as it hurtled down the gulch, leaving a rainbow above, to crown all, I entertained the troops by telling them of the local fable of its origin. It was said that once upon a time a very holy mullah was passing along the track when the sun was at its zenith, and therefore the time for the midday prayer. Having spread his prayer mat he asked Allah, as a prelude to his prayer, to excuse him for not performing the usual ablutions, there being no water available. Hardly had the words left his mouth than there was a crash of thunder and out of the hillside there gushed this vast supply. The troops listened patiently till I had finished when a nearby Corporal remarked in broad Scots, 'It's a pity, sir, he didn't make it Beer while he was about it.'

After about three hours we emerged from the gorge, turned left-handed up the Alana stream till we reached the saddle separating it from the Balisan valley, and rejoined the rest of the column. The following morning on our way back we sent a party to clean up the village of Balisan which had been the scene of opposition on our way up. As the camel men had done so well and been so steady under fire I suggested to the Brigadier that they should be rewarded at the expense of the enemy; and with his agreement I gave them permission to loot the village, which contained a large quantity of last year's tobacco crop, and this they did with gusto. All the camels, which were no longer needed for carrying rations since consumed, were loaded with bales of tobacco, and we all proceeded back to Sarkhuma in good heart.

On our return to camp the programme was once more changed. The Yorkshires were by now riddled with dysentery, and so the sick and wounded had to be evacuated by air to Baghdad. Instead of crossing the Zab as previously intended, the column marched down the right back of the Lesser Zab to Altun Kopru where there was a bridge and wheel transport. Before reaching Altun Kopru I checked over the camel transport for casualties requiring compensation, for some of them had been shot and some had slipped on muddy slopes and broken their breast bones. Those carrying loot were advised to disperse before we arrived at Altun Kopru unless they wished to pay excise on the tobacco, and needless to say they took the hint. On arrival at Altun Kopru I paid off the transport and, taking my leave of the Brigadier, I rode back to my duties in Arbil. I was sorry not to be able to [hit] the section of Pizhdar which had supported the enemy; but now the column was to march to Kirkuk and thence to reoccupy Sulaimani, with Edmonds taking my place, as it was now in his province.[8] As it turned out there was no further action; and though the column subsequently went through the Pizhdar country there were no broken heads, burned villages or looted tobacco, for though the troops were willing, Edmonds was a kindly and forgiving chap, so perhaps it was just as well I was not there. By the time I got back to my bungalow the RAF Advanced Headquarters had left. I received the usual warm greeting from the servants and from my spaniel Rupert ...

By now the spring [of 1923] was well advanced in the plains, and now that we had got shot of the Turkish *Chittas* from Iraqi soil I was able to resume my administrative duties, but these were not without an occasional opportunity for amusement.

The Sikhs had now left and instead we had a regiment of mounted Kurdish Levies commanded by a very pleasant young Australian officer called Captain [S.] White, who messed in the Political bungalow with Charles Littledale, Dr Ridge Jones and myself. And it was about this time that the powers in Baghdad decided to procure data of local conditions on which to base terms of employment under the new Iraqi government for those officers still in the country whom they proposed to employ. For this purpose a certain Major was detailed to make a tour of inspection in the out stations; and, as this was a matter of personal importance to all of us, we went into committee and decided on a plan of action which would highlight our hardships ...

The bungalow was an isolated sort of semi-fort about one kilometre

---

8. On the occupation of Sulaimani and Edmonds's disgust at the failure to establish a permanent Iraqi administration there see Edmonds, *Kurds, Turks and Arabs*, pp. 330–8, and his vituperative correspondence with Sir H. Dobbs in Edmonds Papers, Middle East Archive, St Antony's College, Oxford, Box 1, file 1B.

from the town; there was no water supply other than by sheep skin on a donkey, and of course no water carriage latrines. [There was] no white bread or white flour, no milk or butter, canteen, European goods, [or] cinema nearer than 70 miles, no electricity and no European women north of Baghdad, some 250 miles away, and very few there. Even the home mail took over six weeks and often much longer; and behind all lay the history of battle, murder and sudden death, including an attempt on my predecessor while he slept in the bungalow.

Our visitor on the inspection was a Major; and though a regular officer, [he] had spent most of the war as a local purchase officer and so commanded scant respect from the four of us who had seen plenty of front-line service both during and after the war; and perhaps that accounted for the harshness of the reception planned for one who had lived among the fleshpots.

The doctor arranged for the drinking water to be grossly over-chlorinated and the bath water to be muddy as well. Charles arranged for a police guard to stamp up and down on the concrete verandah outside the guest room, and Captain White laid on a false alarm and 'stand to' with Verey lights in search of invisible attackers at 2 a.m. My job was by far the most difficult for I had to explain with full details to Hamid the cook how to put on the worst possible dinner when he had up to now been frequently urged to do his best. He did not understand going into reverse. However in the end he understood that we had all gone a bit daft and entered into the game somewhat reluctantly. The only drink laid on in the mess was to be araq, and any of us who felt like a proper whisky and water was to have it in his own quarters ... Our guest duly arrived and we put on our hard luck and misery act, and indeed I believe we made quite an impression: certainly he had a most uncomfortable night and made no suggestion about staying to lunch after a rotten breakfast. When he had gone we threw a terrific celebration party over the way everything had worked out according to plan.

Some few days after, it was Easter; and as Judge Pritchard was staying with us on his circuit and was the proud owner of a new T model Ford, we suggested going in it to Kirkuk where we would greet Pa Miller and wish him a happy resurrection. It was a nice sunny day and the car went well. Pa Miller put up a splendid meal with lashings of drink in his usual hospitable style and as usual we discussed local topics. It seems the Major remarked on our very low standard of living in Arbil compared to that in both Mosul and Kirkuk, where Miller had thought it best to entertain him royally, which we felt was giving the game away. My superior in Baghdad however had no difficulty in recognizing it as a leg pull and in the end we failed to get any special hard living allowance or danger money.

Tribal Risings and the Campaign against the Turks · 127

Before leaving Kirkuk after tea we had managed to get a case of Japanese beer from the canteen, which we broached and drank en route, and eventually arrived back about 2 a.m. after many punctures, some of which I am afraid to say were the result of *feu de joie* pistol shots from the back seat. Pritchard was not at all amused but Hamid the cook had an excellent meal ready for us; and after that, and a promise of compensation, his wrath abated ...

About this time the authorities in India discovered that they had too many officers in the Indian Army who had seniority dating from the expansion during the 1914–18 war; and as this was likely to cause a bottleneck in future promotions, it was decided to use the axe. Officers would be graded A, B or C. Those in A grade would be retained, those in C would be paid a lump sum and dismissed, and those in B grade were liable to be dismissed or retained according to the circumstances prevailing after getting rid of all the Cs.

My regiment had long since returned to India and the first I heard of it was a notification informing me that I had been assessed B. This came as an unexpected shock and I was furious, for the future of Iraq was not yet decided and it suited my book to have the Indian Army to fall back on if I could not get good terms in the new service or if the service as such collapsed. I had qualified in all my courses and professional tests. I had commanded a company in action both in France and in Mesopotamia. I had been well reported on annually by my Colonel when with the regiment, and subsequently by my superior, Sir Percy Cox – himself a Major General of the Indian Army seconded to the Indian Political Service – who, when recruiting officers in Mesopotamia, had given an undertaking that those officers so recruited would not thereby prejudice their professional prospects. But now it seemed a case of being out of sight, out of mind. The new regimental commander had not himself seen any overseas service, either with the regiment or any other, nor had he ever set eyes on me, yet I was to be fobbed off with a 'B'.

I at once protested to the High Commissioner, who in turn took up my case with the Secretary of State for India, who ... immediately saw the injustice of my case and issued instructions to the C-in-C India to safeguard my rights and those of three other officers similarly affected. A copy was sent to me for information and I noticed with glee that another had been sent to the regiment with the necessary order ...[9]

Shortly after consolidating my position in the Indian Army the results of the Major's tour came through in the form of an offer to serve the Iraq government under contract for ten years. Up till then I had been drawing the normal pay of a Captain in the Indian Army – the equivalent of about

£800 per annum plus various allowances for rations, horse maintenance and travelling etc., but the new offer was about to equal £1,200 with yearly increases, and the Iraq government paying the contribution to keep alive my pension rights. Thus while still a Captain I was drawing the equivalent pay of a full Colonel and what was better with much more authority, there being no superior nearer than Baghdad – some 250 miles distant and in time several days distant whether by car, train or boat. In my distant outpost there was little on which to spend money save food, drink and sporting equipment ... [So] I was able to save half my pay.

---

9. Lyon was finally retired from the Indian Army in 1935, but rejoined in 1941: see ch. 12. Due to the uncertainty of the future of Iraq, many other British officials there, mostly on short-term contracts, maintained their links with the armed forces or other British services. Edmonds, for example, remained seconded from the Levant Consular Service, later integrated with the Foreign Service, for thirty years before final retirement.

CHAPTER 4

Sir Henry Dobbs, 1923–24

§ LIFE [in Iraq] was much more interesting than drilling a company in a dusty Indian cantonment and ordering about native officers, some of whom were veterans in frontier warfare before I was born. I began to learn about local personalities, traditions, customs and folk-lore. As there was only one road passable for wheel traffic, most of my inspections were done on horseback; and as touring was considered a most important part of my work, I used to cover about 3,000 miles or more per annum. Unlike the system adopted both in India and Africa, I took little more than a roll of bedding and a briefcase. I fed with the locals and used to put up [for] the night with them, hunt, shoot, ride and walk with them. Under these conditions they would talk freely on subjects they would never dare mention inside a government office. They were relaxed, especially when hunting, shooting or fishing; and it was then that one learned things that might have been perplexing for weeks before.

Sometimes it was difficult to understand what caused a tribal chief to adopt a different line to that agreed upon. At first sight one was apt to put it down to lack of moral courage if not actual double-crossing or treachery. But often enough this was due to pressure in the harem, which I always considered rather unfair, for one could reason with a husband but not with an invisible wife. Because they were out of sight we westerners are inclined to forget about them; but eastern women exercise much greater influence than one would suppose, and all the more because it is behind the shelter of the curtain and not subject to cross-examination. I have seen brave men sneak round corners to avoid the prying eye of a jealous wife. I have known a high-born Kurdish dame to whip out a pistol and shoot a shepherd whom she suspected of being a cheap thief. Like their western sisters they are usually much more imbued than their husbands with the importance of strict observance of all religious practices. A Pasha during the month of Ramadan will be only too glad to seek a few minutes' respite with a British official on any excuse in order to snatch a quiet smoke or drink unobserved by family or public.

In affairs of honour however the difference between the treatment of the sexes is very marked. A man may frequent brothels and contaminate his own women folk without penalty, whereas on the slightest suspicion of a woman's honour her nearest relative, husband or brother, is bound to slay her to preserve the family honour. The act to be effective must be committed openly and openly acknowledged, there being no punishment for it under local custom.

But the greatest curse of Kurdistan is the blood feud or vendetta, and strange to say it is often the women who keep it going from one generation to the next. A young bride may say to her husband, 'How can I sleep with you in peace when the blood of my brother/father/uncle, etc. is still crying for revenge and that so and so who killed him is still strutting around like a cock on a dung hill?' From that moment there is no peace for the bridegroom till he levels the score. But even then his relaxation cannot last long because he immediately becomes the target for the victim's relations. If they are children he may hope for a few years' grace; but when they grow up their mother will drive them on to take revenge. I knew a tribal chief of the Zarari tribe, a small and insignificant group living in the foothills of Arbil. His forebears had all been murdered by a rival section and he told me he expected to go the same way, and he did. One cold winter's night, when he got up to put some brush wood on the fire, his enemy, who had scraped away the wad of straw plugging the ventilation hole at floor level, pushed his rifle through and in the light of flames shot him dead. Everyone knew all about it, but there was no evidence and no prosecution.

Sometimes it is possible to settle a feud by the exchange of a blood mare for a bride, thereby promoting a renewal of social intercourse. The bride's relations go visiting to see how she is getting along and the bridegroom's family return the call to see how the mare is keeping, for by tribal custom they are entitled to share in her progeny. But if this procedure settles the feud, then it is at the expense of the poor girl's rights.

The Kurds claim that Salah-ad-Din was born in Duwin Qala of Kurdish stock; and when one reads of Richard Coeur de Lion wanting to give him his sister in marriage in exchange for services to be rendered it is quite in accord with present-day practice, though the deal did not go through at the time because of her unwillingness to comply. As a people they admire severity provided it is based on justice. There is the story of Khor Pasha who many years ago ruled Ruwandiz with a rod of iron. A merchant in the bazaar, when buying local produce, was in the habit of putting his foot on the scale in addition to the weights, thus cheating the peasants of their rightful dues. This eventually came to the ear of the Pasha, who sent for the merchant. 'I hear that you claim your foot weighs a *"huqqa"* (a local measure of about 3½ pounds).' Witnesses to this effect being called, the Pasha turned to his executioner and said, 'Strike it off and let it be weighed.' That was the end of the merchant's business ...

Like other mountain races the Kurds are not very verbose. One might conclude from the lack of much brisk conversation that a party was missing fire, whereas in reality all are quite satisfied to sit around smoking and drinking endless small glasses of sweet tea with only an occasional remark. Being strict orthodox Moslems they are easy to entertain. All the talking is done over tea and cigarettes before dinner, and as soon as the meal is over they take a cup of coffee and a cigarette, and after that they depart. For it is laid down by the Prophet that one should not dawdle after a meal lest the host be inconvenienced from returning to his women folk.

There was one chief whom I knew called Kerim Khan of the Khailani tribe who were completely nomadic, crossing the frontier to the Persian highlands in spring and returning to the Arbil foothills in autumn. This provided wonderful opportunities for picking up other people's animals in one country and selling them in the next. It was a two-way traffic at which Kerim was an adept. He told me that once, just before moving off to Persia, he was taken ill and, thinking that he was about to die, he sent for his son and told him to pinch the very beautiful mare which Ahmad Pasha had bought from the Shammar Arabs, sell it across the border and spend the money on a funereal feast. This is a bountiful and expensive affair, of which the principal dish is a sheep's belly (stuffed with rice, butter, meat and dried fruit), called a Gipa, and in some respects resembles the Scottish haggis. The son hastened to carry out what he believed to be his father's last wishes; but, as he recovered, the cash was blown just the same on a recovery celebration and he was no better off than before for, although he had stolen much over a long life, he was as penniless as ever while Ahmad Pasha remained rich. 'And now,' said he in conclusion, 'I don't know how I shall get the money to pay the sheep tax which the local collector is insisting should be paid this year before we cross the frontier.' I had a pretty good guess as to how he would raise the cash but I kept it to myself.

But to resume the [narrative]. The occupation of Ruwandiz [April 1923] had produced a general improvement in security throughout the liwa, and for that matter in the whole of the Mosul wilayat; and it being now towards the end of spring, the High Commissioner, Sir Henry Dobbs, thought it a suitable time to have a change from his office work and look at Kurdistan.[1] He was a most distinguished official; a product of Winchester and the Indian Civil Service, he had seen much service in a long career,

---

1. Dobbs succeeded Sir Percy Cox as High Commissioner in May 1923.

lived in Kabul, and risen to be Foreign Secretary to the government of India. He had a quick temper and a severe exterior which in reality concealed a very kindly nature. His instructions were that his tour was to be entirely private and there were to be no official greetings. He would go by train to Sharqat, cross the Tigris by country boat to where his car would meet him and take him to Arbil over a very rough track crossed by many watercourses. Well, orders were orders, so I did not set out to meet him at the liwa boundary, which was at the Tigris crossing, but instead Mr Shepherd the station house officer of the police was sent to inspect the police post there and follow the High Commissioner back to Arbil, thus ensuring against any mishap.

Sir Henry, accompanied only by Vyvyan Holt, his Oriental Secretary,[2] and his servant duly arrived in nice time for tea; and while it was being laid on he had a look round the compound and, being a keen botanist, immediately spotted several tiny wild flowers which took his fancy. These were at once marked with tent pegs and we went in to tea. It was then the first mishap occurred. About a dozen mules had been ordered for the tour; and while we were at tea they arrived for inspection, for it is usual before going on tour with pack animals to inspect their backs, bellies and legs for galls and blemishes and to have a trial loading of tents and camp kit. But when we emerged with trowels and boxes to collect the specimens, not one was to be seen, for the mules had eaten them all. There was nothing we could do about it except to assure Sir Henry that he would find many more and better as he progressed through the mountains, where the spring comes later.

The next morning, having sent the pack animals ahead to await us at Dera, we set off on our pilgrimage after a good breakfast and duly arrived at Dera in time for a Kurdish alfresco lunch of chicken and rice, followed by fruit and coffee under Mejid Agha's shady mulberry tree. The lunch was, of course, provided by Mejid Agha, and Sir Henry, wishing to be polite, asked if he knew Persian. Mejid, seeing his chance of getting on intimate terms with the great one, immediately said yes, though in fact all he knew was a smattering with which he interlaced his Kurdish. Sir Henry unfortunately turned out to be much the same, though in his case it was a little Persian with a very strong Beluchi base, and it wasn't long before they got stuck. We blamed Vyvyan Holt for this for he was a scholar in both Persian and Kurdish, but he had hung back thinking it was best to let Sir Henry have a go if he felt like it. However, we now dug him out and

---

2. The Oriental Secretary in Middle East countries acted as secretary, public relations officer and translator to senior officials, such as the High Commissioner in Iraq. Holt had succeeded Gertrude Bell in this office in Baghdad.

put him in the ring to restore the situation before the temperature rose to flash point. In any case it was time to resume our journey. Sir Henry, being a tall and heavily built man, had been allotted a fine grey stallion by Charles, who usually rode it himself, and he set off. We had not gone more than a few furlongs, however, when Sir Henry remarked that in his experience it was usual for the tribal chief to accompany the guest as he rode through his territory, so Mejid Agha to his delight was summoned into the Presence, cavorting around Sir Henry on his mare, which unfortunately was in season. The stallion was no respecter of persons when he got the sex urge; and before we knew what was happening there was the stallion with Sir Henry gamely hanging on, mounting Mejid's mare, rider and all. It was a terrible moment; but we were saved the worst when an alert policeman, who by the way was our best polo player, dashed up and separated the animals with a hail of blows, after which Mejid Agha was dismissed in disgrace and the caravan moved on. At sundown we arrived in Shaqlawa where we were to spend the night and the next day.

The village of Shaqlawa was one of the choicest in all Kurdistan, perched as it was on the north-east or shady side of the Suffin Dagh, a long ridge some 6,500 feet above sea level, and covered in snow for three or four months in the year. It was famous for its many springs of ice-cold water, reputed to be more than a thousand in number, which nourished the groves of timber, almond, walnut, mulberry, poplar and oak, which surrounded the village. There was fruit galore, grapes, plums, figs, apricots, melons and peaches as large as cricket balls.

It was the seat of Mirani Abdul Qadir Beg, Chief of the Khoshnaw tribe. He was an enormous fat Kurdish replica of our King Henry VIII, head-dress included. Indeed, among ourselves he was always referred to as Henry VIII, so great was the likeness both in body and soul. When annoyed he would push his enormous head-dress down over his brows and rumble like an elephant; when happy he would push it to the back of his head and laugh like Falstaff.[3] His summer diwan was in the woods just below the village and consisted of a pool of water about 3 feet deep and 20 feet square, surrounded by masonry benches covered with quilts and carpets and shaded by a scaffolding of poplar poles supporting grape vines, and close at hand was a pleasant guest house for winter use. A servant was always present dispensing endless locally-grown cigarettes and glasses of sweet tea from a Russian samovar. Even in the absence of host or other guests with whom to engage in polite conversation, one could lounge and doze on the hottest days to the tinkle and rush of the water into and out

---

3. Hamilton, *Road Through Kurdistan*, p. 71, describes 'Shaqlawah' in similar terms and also refers to 'Kadir Beg' as 'Henry the Eighth'.

of the pool and the twittering of the various birds which abounded in the vicinity.

Before a meal was served the host would ask the chief guest if he felt ready; and on receipt of an answer in the affirmative a servant would go the rounds with a jug, soap, basin and towel, after which more servants would appear bearing a vast tray containing a fat tailed sheep, roasted whole, and stuffed with savoury rice and raisins, and perched upon a huge mound of rice cooked in the eastern fashion with boiling butter poured over it. Around this central dish would be smaller dishes of assorted meats and sweet meats: yaprak, or forced meat and rice, served in rolled-up cooked vine leaves, stuffed onions and tomatoes, ochra and eggplant, poached eggs on spinach, roasted chickens and rissoles, mounds of delicious wafer-thin unleavened bread straight from the oven, local cheese made from sheep's butter and interlaced with mountain herbs, dishes of ground rice and milk pudding, a pastry made of flour, butter and honey and cut criss-cross into diamond formation and served on large trays. Yet more pastry [was] in the form of rings and fingers, referred to jokingly in the local tongue as ladies' navel and qadhi's penis. After the sweet came melons, both sweet and water, and fruit in season. In winter preserved fruit or Damascus fruit was served. The whole was washed down with copious draughts of buttermilk served in large wooden bowls and cooled by floating islands of packed snow, and finally coffee and more cigarettes.

The main products of the village were timber, tobacco, fruit and snow. In the winter months the snow was packed into straw-lined caves and all through the summer it was brought down in mule loads by night to be sold in the Arbil market 30-odd miles away, or exchanged for corn or groceries as the case might be.

Part of the village was inhabited by Chaldean Christians who existed under the protection of their over-lord Mirani Abdul Qadir Beg, who was fond of his serfs and reckoned that one of his Christians was as valuable as a good mule. He was truly the incarnation of a feudal baron of the middle ages. These Kurdish chiefs, known as Beg Zada, were said to have come originally from Persia and were of quite a different stock to the Kurdish tribes over whom they ruled. They intermarried among themselves and like squirelings they squatted around in most of the villages. As intermediaries they dealt with government officials, entertained all visitors, paid all fines, reimbursed themselves liberally by private and personal levies on their people, led them in battle and defended them against all aggressors.

On arrival at Shaqlawa we were received in magnificent style by old Henry VIII. Our Sir Henry was both amused by our host and delighted with the surroundings and the sumptuous meal and retired to his couch thoroughly satisfied. In the morning after breakfast he made a tour of the village, inspecting the Christians' church, the dispensary and the school, after which he insisted on taking a ramble solo through the woods where he was hoping to find more specimens for his botanical collection; and as soon as he had gone I had a short session with the local mudir, or sub-district governor, on the normal administrative matters, after which I retired to the diwan where I was joined by Henry VIII, Vyvyan Holt and Charles. We lounged through the rest of the morning in pleasant conversation with our host, his younger and slightly smaller brother Reshid Beg, the mudir and various neighbouring Bagzada who had happened along. All too soon it was time for the midday prayer for which our host now prepared himself; and after that it began to dawn upon us that the High Commissioner had been a long time away and was now overdue. Soon it was lunch time, but of course we could not start without him, and now Holt was getting anxious for his master. But just as we were debating what to do, Sir Henry Dobbs suddenly appeared through the trees. He was dishevelled, furious and closely accompanied by a Kurdish rifleman. 'I was down in the woods enjoying the solitude,' said he, 'when suddenly I was arrested by this brigand. I could not make him understand a word, and he insisted on dragging me back here.'

I then turned to the rifleman, who was dressed in the usual Khoshnaw style with bandolier and dagger complete. He was one of Mirani Abdul Qadir Beg's retainers, so I left the examination to his master, and this is what he said. 'I was down in the forest when whom should I see but the Presence all alone and unattended by a single servant or policeman. I said to myself "He has lost his way!" If anything should happen to him the Royal Air Force might rain bombs down upon us and the whole village might be destroyed. But praise be to Allah I have found him and I will bring him back to the divan of my Chief where he should normally be sitting drinking glasses of sweet tea, smoking cigarettes and giving forth words of wisdom. So I brought him back. I have saved the whole village from tragedy and surely I have earned a generous reward!' Well, what could one do about it? Nothing! So I told Henry VIII to lay on lunch.

After lunch and a soothing siesta the High Commissioner recovered from his morning misadventure, and as the humorous side of it now began to prevail, his kindly nature reasserted itself as he recounted previous experiences during his service.

Among other journeys was one he had accomplished before the 1914–18 war through Syria and Mesopotamia by *kellek* or raft down the Euphrates and then on horseback through Persia to India. His fellow-travellers on the raft were a number of high-spirited young Turkish officers who had just passed out from the military college at Istanbul and were on their way to join their units in Baghdad. All were eager to try out their firearms and what better targets than the occasional Arab on the bank. This was great fun for them, but not for the Arabs, as they were soon to find out. For the great river in the course of its leisurely meanderings across the plain happened to flow round a peninsula, giving the Arabs at the receiving end ample time to collect arms from their village, cut across the narrow isthmus, and give the raft a hearty greeting as it came round the bend, which wounded some of the passengers and punctured several of the inflated sheep skins. After that there was no more shooting practice; but it served to show the contempt of the Turks for the Arabs, a useful item of intelligence which was subsequently exploited to the full by our troops in the 1914–18 war.

Another story he told was about the time when he was in Kabul, the centre of intensive intrigue and rivalry between the British and Russian envoys; for the government of India was always sensitive about Russian ambitions. One day he noticed that the contents of the waste paper basket in his office were attracting over-much attention from the door keeper, and so suspected that he was in the pay of the Afghan government. So, as the Russian military attaché was a thorn in his flesh, he decided on a simple plan to get rid of him. Into the waste paper basket he dropped, torn and crumpled, a part of a faked draft of a despatch warning his government of the intentions of the military attaché to bring off a coup d'état. The bait was swallowed hook, line and sinker, for within a week the Russian military attaché was on his way to Moscow as a persona non grata to the government of Afghanistan.

After the yarn we all retired early, for on the following day [we were to make] a long trek across the Desht-i-Harir and over the Spilik Dagh to the camping ground at the entrance to the gorge beside the swift-flowing waters of the Alana Su. This was the first time I had been across this plain without any shooting and the change I found most enjoyable. On arrival the tents and camp kit were all in order and our faithful Indian cook Abdul Hamed had a good supper under way. Police pickets had been placed in the proper tactical positions around the camp and we enjoyed a very pleasant night.

Next morning we entered the gorge, which so impressed Sir Henry that he quite forgot his original instructions about the unofficial nature of his progress and was quite interested in the deputation that rode out to meet us. For spring was late in this deep and shady gulch where flowers of all sorts bloomed in the rock crannies soaked in the spray of the numerous waterfalls of the three different sources of water that joined in the gorge to form the Balikian Su. Thus it was intriguing for a visitor to enter the gorge following the Alana Su downstream and halfway through to find himself riding upstream though still going in the same direction.

It was here that Sir Henry divulged the fact that he had brought two presentation watches, one of silver and the other of gold; and now he asked me who in my opinion were the most deserving people to receive them. After much thought I replied that these tribesmen lived a wild and precarious existence in this mountainous district still under dispute between ourselves and the Turks. The most prudent of them remained on the political fence: loyalty to either side could not be expected and in fact did not exist. So if he was thinking of the watches as a reward or recognition for loyalty or services rendered, it boiled down to two chaps only – Charles and myself – and we would love to have a watch each with the Royal Arms inscribed on the back. Such a watch would be a constant reminder of the pleasant pilgrimage we had made in his august company. But he wouldn't even consider this and told me to think again. So I then said Saiyid Taha, the governor whom Sir Henry himself had appointed, should get the gold watch, and Mohammed Ali, the Mayor of Ruwandiz, should get the silver one, and let each provide an alfresco banquet at which the presentation could be made. To this he readily agreed.

Next day the site of the banquet chosen by Saiyid Taha was on a small grassy spit beside the river and under the cliff over which the Russian Cossacks had driven the few male inhabitants who had not fled at their approach. The meal was not very choice, rather cold and greasy for it had been cooked in his house half a mile away. However, we waded in and then Sir Henry made the presentation. After that, Ismail Beg got up and made a speech extolling Saiyid Taha.[4] Beginning with his father, martyred by the Turks for his insurrection, he enlarged on the peaceful administration resulting from Sir Henry's choice of such a good governor and had just said, 'And now not a wolf dare take a lamb nor a brigand fire a shot' when there was the crack of a rifle echoing down the gorge accompanied by the ping of a bullet against the overhanging cliff. Whether this was a joke, a mere coincidence, or a warning from Nuri Bawil to Ismail Beg we never knew. The police pickets had seen no one and they were well placed to deal with any intruder, so we paid no attention and treated it as a mere coincidence, possibly some shepherd trying out his rifle, and, the party over, we returned to camp.

Mohammed Ali's party the next day was very much better. His village

---

1. For Ismail Beg's earlier appointment as governor of Ruwandiz in 1920 see Hay, *Two Years in Kurdistan*, ch. 13 and chs 16–18. Nuri Bawil had a blood feud against Ismail, who had allegedly been responsible for the death of two of Nuri's brothers. It was because of this uncertainty that Ismail had been demoted from governor and replaced by Saiyid Taha. Ismail was eventually shot by Nuri and his supporters in 1932: see Hamilton, *Road through Kurdistan*, pp. 306–9 for a detailed account.

was about a mile upstream at the foot of the massive Hendrin Dagh and just above the fast-flowing river. It was named Jindian or, translated, the place of Jinns or spirits. Above his garden was a cave out of which flowed a copious stream of crystal clear and icy-cold water which at times would gurgle and stop, then after a while, perhaps an hour or two, it would suddenly start again. At the mouth of the cave, and across the stream, was laid a door on which a meal was served, the fruit, the melons and the buttermilk being kept cool in the water which had an output of about 8 cubic feet per second and flowed with such speed as to create a cooling breeze in which one sat while dispatching the mayor's excellent victuals. A choicer place for a picnic could hardly be imagined. If during our entertainment the water stopped, a rifleman was sent into the innermost depths of the cave to fire a shot with his rifle pushed up into the orifice in the rock from which the water flowed. This, accompanied by the call to Allah, started the flow once more; and it was this peculiarity that gave the place its name, and it was here that the Jinns were alleged to lurk. A more mundane but likelier explanation was that there was a vast store of water inside the mountain which made its exit in a sort of natural syphon.

This was the turning point of our journey, for the next day we headed back for Koi Sanjaq, which was about two days' journey, situated on the south side of the Haiba Sultan mountain, itself the eastern end of the Suffin Dagh overlooking Shaqlawa. The day's march took us to the springs a few miles short of the pass; and as one of them was sulphurous and very hot, Sir Henry decided to take a medicinal bath, for which we cleared the ground and rigged up a tarpaulin screen to hide the Presence from the gaping villagers. This was a great success and Sir Henry thoroughly enjoyed his dip.

The next day we reached Koi Sanjaq, a town somewhat like Sulaimani though smaller, built on the south-west side of the mountain and subject to very strong dusty winds, set up by sun's rays forming convection currents which sometimes persisted for days on end and known to the Kurds as Reshaba or black wind. On this occasion, however, we were lucky and were able to greet the notables and perambulate the bazaar in the comfort of still air. Like Sulaimani it is a centre for tobacco which, after being checked at the customs khan, is dispatched by pack mule to Taqtaq, about 15 miles away on the Lesser Zab, whence it proceeds to Baghdad by raft. On arrival the tobacco goes to the factories, the raft is dismantled, the poles sold for building timber, the skins deflated, loaded on mules and sent back with the raft crews to the port of origin. This sort of transport must have been in use unaltered from the time of Noah and the great flood.

The notables of Koi Sanjaq had always been friendly towards us in spite of their internecine feuds ... In the 1920 uprising they had escorted their British Political Officer to safety and only a few months previously they had co-operated with me in ousting the Turkish *Chittas*; and now, led by Jamil Agha Howaizi, their local-bred governor, they gave the High Commissioner a warm welcome, which he greatly appreciated.

The next day we rode to Taqtaq which was the parting of the ways, for here Sir Henry was ferried across the Lesser Zab to be met by a police escort from Kirkuk, while Charles and I boarded one of the *kelleks* or native rafts and drifted downriver to Altun Kopru. Sir Henry envied the last stage of our journey, which no doubt aroused memories of former journeys he had made. He thanked us profusely for our services and, accompanied by Captain Holt and his bearer, proceeded on horseback to where Pa Miller awaited him with the cars to take him to Kirkuk.

On return to Arbil what should we find but the first contingent of the newly-formed Iraqi Army arriving from Mosul en route for Sulaimani, which it was proposed to garrison. It was commanded by Ali Rida al-Askari, elder brother of Jafar Pasha al-Askari, and he was one of those who had supported the Amir Faisal in his rebellion against the Turks. Like his brother he was not only big but very stout. This was generally considered hereditary, as his father had been a well-known Persian wrestler. But a roasted sheep was about all dear old Ali Rida could take on with any hopes of success, and his horse must have wished there had been an RSPCA in Iraq for his weight was well over 20 stones. He told me in confidence that his troops were all Arabs from the plains and as such had a natural mistrust of mountains, just as hill men are inclined to feel naked in the plains. They were not at all eager to go to Sulaimani and he would be grateful if we could supply some police pickets to reduce desertion en route. This sounded rather ominous and reminded me of the story of the Jews conscripted, armed and trained by the Turks during the war. When it came finally to marching them off to the front they asked their commander for police protection. However, Charles arranged for the police to keep a discreet eye on them during their passage to Kirkuk.

The next event of interest was a signal from the Director of Agriculture in Baghdad to say that an agricultural officer would arrive with a harvester to demonstrate the advantages of modern machinery as opposed to the local method of reaping corn with a sickle. In due course Alec Kinch turned up with an ordinary horse-drawn mowing machine in the back of a truck. Apparently they had been unable to send a proper reaper but thought a mower might do well enough to impress the locals.

On the following day the notables were assembled outside the Political bungalow to witness the demonstration. Our landlord had been kind enough to offer his cornfield, which surrounded the bungalow, for the great event, together with a pair of Kurdish mules well accustomed to drawing a plough, and these were harnessed to the mowing machine on which Alec Kinch was brave enough to take his seat. Now anyone who has seen such a machine in action would be impressed by the terrific noise made by the various cog wheels which motivate it; but unfortunately these mules had never heard anything like this before, and the first pace forward produced such a clatter that they immediately sprang into top gear and proceeded to the bottom of the field at full gallop, cutting all before them. After a prolonged struggle, pulling first on one rein then on the other, Alec eventually got them turned before they reached the wadi. They had left a track of cut and chewed-up corn as wavy as the braid on the sleeve of an officer in the RNVR or 'Wavy Navy' as it was called. There was no question of the ears being gathered to one side of the swathe and the butts at the other with the stalks lying nicely together in parallel; it was just a complete jumble, defying any attempt at realignment for making sheaves or stooks. But while the audience looked at this in amazement their feelings were soon turned to horror, for though Alec had managed to turn the panic-stricken animals, he had not been able to stop them, and now they were charging straight at us. The notables in their flowing cloaks scattered in all directions, and as for myself I now realized for the first time how the Roman soldiers must have felt when facing Queen Boadacia's chariots armed with sickles on the revolving wheels. At last they reached the top of the field and the road. It was the way to their home and down it they disappeared in a cloud of dust. As a thriller it was a winner, but as an agricultural demonstration it was a ghastly exhibition, and did more to impede the spread of modern machinery than our worst enemy could have dreamt of ...

CHAPTER 5

The Visit of King Faisal and the League of Nations Commission, 1924–25

§ NOW that security had been established [by December 1924] it was considered desirable by the authorities in Baghdad for the King to visit the capitals of the northern liwas – excluding Sulaimani, which up to then had been left out of the Arab fold and was under the direct administration of the High Commissioner.

The city of Mosul, except for the Christian and Jewish quarters, was Arab both by race and speech; it had accepted Faisal and so was chosen as first on the royal pilgrimage. Arbil was a mixture of Kurds and Turkoman; it had accepted him but not without strong encouragement, if not pressure, for which I was to blame, and was next on the tour. Then came Kirkuk, mostly Turkish, which had held out against all Arab blandishments and refused him, but nevertheless was under the Iraqi administration and in any case was situated on the return route to the capital Baghdad.

On the appointed day Ahmad Effendi Usman the governor, Charles Littledale the Police Commander, and myself proceeded to the liwa boundary, which in this case was the ferry over the Greater Zab at Quweir. The governor, with the aid of the police, had whipped up the local inhabitants to parade at the ferry and also back in the main streets of Arbil where, in accordance with Arab custom, a young camel had been slaughtered in the King's path at the entrance to the town. The war demands of the Turkish Army and police along the 36 miles of road in between had proved too much for the villagers, and all the villages along the route were situated some distance from and often out of sight of the main road. This saved us a lot of bother.

The King was accompanied by his household staff and his half brother the Amir Zaid, who displayed little interest in politics and administration and immediately went off bombing fish under the supervision of Charles, who provided the bombs from our somewhat scanty stock. Colonel Cornwallis, the new Adviser to the Minister of Interior who had replaced Philby, was also in the party and he stayed with us while the governor escorted the King and his staff to the villa of Abubeker (Mulla Effendi) which was chosen as the most suitable for the King's privacy and comfort.

It was the first time I had seen him out of his usual setting in the Baghdad Palace and it proved a most interesting study. He had been brought up in the orthodox fashion of Arab Princes in the nineteenth century; the first seven years in the harem or women's quarters, followed by a boyhood among the Beduin tents learning the ways of the Shaikhs and their tribesmen, and finally a finishing course at the Sultan's Court at Istanbul to make him adept at and familiar with all the intrigues which permeated the capital of the old Ottoman empire. His manners were charming and without any apparent effort he could put visitors at ease in next to no time. If one was invited to an interview in his office he would rise from his desk, sit beside one on a bench, and even light a cigarette for his guest, an act symbolical of a servant to his master. Though his tastes were for women rather than wine, when he called on me he invited me on to the roof of my bungalow for privacy, chose a whisky and soda to drink with me, though really to set me at ease, for he hardly took more than a sip or two while he plied me with searching questions about the liwa and its people. He was surfeited with Palace flattery and wanted the plain truth, and he was not disappointed.

With his own subjects he would never refuse an audience, and a scruffy old tribesman could burst in upon him with impunity even during the hour of siesta. By contrast, the Palace officials and servants were a mixed bunch and many of them scamps. Some of the local tribal chiefs invited to the Royal Reception afterwards complained that their cloaks had been stolen.

When, in company with the governor and his staff, the King went in procession to the Great Mosque for the Friday Prayer, he ordered his chamberlain to give the governor 100 rupees for the poor in accordance with the custom of public almsgiving on such occasions. But when Ahmad Effendi opened the bag there was only 50 rupees in it and he, unused to court etiquette, began to argue about the discrepancy, only to be immediately hushed up by the Master of the Royal Household. 'If the King says 100 you must take it as 100,' said he. As the onlookers and the reporters had heard the order there was nothing for it but to make up the balance from municipal funds.

For several years I had tried to get sanction for a new and much larger school, but always the Ministry of Finance had deleted it from the budget. Now that the King had come I saw a way out. In charge of the Public Works Department at Arbil there was an excellent British engineer called [Major W. A.] Pover, whom I consulted. A master at improvisation, he at once drew up plans for the school on the site chosen opposite the government offices; and to crown all he cast a cement tablet on which was inscribed in Arabic, 'This Foundation stone was laid by His Majesty King Faisal the First on the occasion of his visit to Arbil', date, etc., etc.

On the first opportunity I had I asked the King if he would oblige, and, as he was only too pleased, it was agreed to do it the next day.

Ahmad Effendi, knowing that the majority of the children knew about as much Arabic as an English prep school boy knows French, had carefully selected an intelligent Arab boy who came from far-away Hillah [on the Euphrates, south of Baghdad] to make the invitation speech and had it well rehearsed. When the time came for the ceremony there was a great parade of all the children and front seats for the notables. His Majesty was delighted to hear such a good speech in classical Arabic, though I doubt if he was aware that it was quite unintelligible to the multitude, and he performed the ceremony with his usual grace. When the show was over I had the pleasure of writing to the Ministry of Finance telling them of the ceremony and challenging them to cut it out of the budget if they dare. Thus began the official history of the new school, but behind the scenes it was followed by a most unfortunate event.

There was a Christian clerk employed by the Intelligence Officer in Arbil. This clerk had a brother who was slightly mental, especially during the period of full moon, such a period happening just after the King's departure. Stimulated by too much araq he worked himself up into a frenzy, rushed over to the newly-laid foundation stone and, seizing it with the strength of a madman, he uprooted it and hurled it into a nearby ditch shouting the while, 'Who is Faisal, I am Jesus and I'll have no idols here.' He then made off and after three days appeared at the camp of the Assyrian Levy garrison at Kani-Othman opposite the entrance to the Ruwandiz Gorge. There he declared he was a Turkish spy and didn't come to his senses until the commander put him over the mess table to give him six of the best with a polo stick.

The evening before the King's departure for Kirkuk [19 December 1924] the weather broke: the heavens opened, the earth road became a muddy morass and the many un-bridged watercourses turned into raging torrents. For the locals it was good news for it presaged seed germination and so [was] a lucky omen for the King's visit; but for those responsible for getting him over the liwa boundary on his way to Kirkuk it was far from welcome. As a preliminary precaution police with mules and draft tackle were dispatched overnight to stand by at the worst hazards ready to drag out the cars that might founder. All the private cars in town were then impounded to support the King's convoy.

The following morning [20 December 1924] it was still raining and

Cornwallis proposed postponing the King's departure, but I was against this because at that time of the year the first rain was likely to last several days, and so far it had not soaked in, for the ground was dry 6 inches down. But there was another and greater incentive to speed the exodus. During his visit the King had been besieged by the relatives of all prisoners, and of course, in accordance with custom, he had made many remissions. If he stayed much longer there was a prospect of all the brigands so painfully collected being set at liberty to resume their trade. Finally it was pointed out that he had completed his programme, met all the people that mattered, and there was nothing left for him to do, nor much left for his courtiers and servants to consume. Added to these reasons was a firm guarantee that we'd get him along even if we had to man-handle the cars; and that settled it.

It was only about 35 miles to Altun Kopru where at worst there was ample accommodation for the night if he were forced to stay there; and in any case the land beyond was of much lighter soil than the heavy loam of the Arbil Plain: it was also much flatter going.

The convoy started at 9 a.m., and as it ground up the long muddy slopes the engines over heated and the radiators boiled, imposing a halt on the crest before slithering down the other side with little control of direction. Often a car would slide sideways into a ditch or bounce into a watercourse at the bottom of the slope but off the track and so get hopelessly bogged. The occupants of the car, helped by those behind, would then heave and push till finally the wheels were extricated, or the car foundered through gear box, clutch or back axle failure. Soon it was apparent that the heavier [up-market] cars of the King's household would never get through, so he and his staff were transferred into T model Fords whenever there was a failure. Thus after about six hours' relentless struggle, in which he must have ridden in at least six different cars, we handed the King over to the Kirkuk escort at Altun Kopru. Apart from the foundered cars there were no casualties, though later we heard that just outside Kirkuk a traffic policeman directing the convoy across the stream at Yarwali missed his way in the muddy torrent and was drowned.[1]

It was quite useless attempting to return that night, so we made for the nearby village of Bashteppeh and spent the night with Kidhier Beg, the son of Ahmad Pasha. It was a great relief to be on one's own again, but it was not to be for long. Before resuming the tale it would now seem to be a suitable occasion to recapitulate the recent political history of Iraq,

---

1. For the rest of the story and Faisal's visit to Kirkuk, see Edmonds, *Kurds, Turks and Arabs*, pp. 392–4.

the new official name for what was previously the Turkish province of Mesopotamia, referred to by the British Tommies as the Mess Pot.

In October 1918 our troops had completely defeated and captured the Turkish Army at Sharqat and marched on a further 80 miles to the city of Mosul, only to find yet another Turkish Division newly arrived from Anatolia and camped in the main square. By that time an armistice had been declared in Palestine and the Turkish Commander pleaded that we had no right to advance after the armistice and therefore refused to evacuate Mosul. Our GOC-in-C, General [Sir W. R.] Marshall, however, flew up from Baghdad and told him that we had promised to liberate the whole of Mesopotamia including the Mosul Province, and therefore if the Turks did not evacuate the city and province he would resume hostilities and kick them out. On this they left, but they never officially admitted our claim which had now been the subject of wordy dispute in Paris and irregular unreported warfare on the frontier for the past six years.

But at last agreement had been reached to submit to the decision of the League of Nations, who had nominated a Commission to study the problem on the spot and it had now [in January 1925] suddenly arrived in Mosul.[2] It was composed of three members, chief of which and president was a Swede called [E. af] Wirsén, a pompous, unattractive, gruff Germanic type. I don't think anyone ever understood why he was chosen, for whatever qualities he possessed were not obvious to the man in the street and it was hard to believe that Sweden could not produce a better man. The second member was Count [Paul] Teleki, a Hungarian aristocrat who, as Foreign Minister, had rallied his country and saved it from the Communists under Bela Kun. As a result of the Peace Treaty he had lost that part of his estates which lay in Transylvania, including his family chapel and the vaults of his departed ancestors. He was a professor of geography, a great supporter of the Turanian society – an academic body which claimed that the original Hungarians and Turks derived from the same source. The loss of his estates was a very sore point, which gave him a chip on his shoulder to the end of his life; this and his leanings towards Turkey made him a difficult customer. He was also an experienced lover of women. The third member was Colonel [A.] Paulis, a Belgian officer of great experience in the Congo, whose outlook was no different to that of the typical Pukka Sahib of Poona. An officer of great charm.

They were accompanied by interpreters and three Turkish assessors or

---

2. There is a more detailed account of the Commission's members and its work in Edmonds, *Kurds, Turks and Arabs*, chs 26 and 27. There are copies of reports made by Lyon and his colleagues to the High Commissioner in the Edmonds Papers, Box 1, file 2B.

146 · *Kurds, Arabs and Britons*

protagonists, chief of whom was no less than [General] Jewad Pasha, the Turkish Commander-in-Chief who had opposed us in Gallipoli. The second was Nazim Beg, a member of the Naftchizada family in Kirkuk who previously had fled to Turkey after our occupation. The third was Fattah Effendi, a relation of Shaikh Mahmud of Sulaimani, now once more an outlaw on the Persian border.[3]

The arrival of the Commission in Mosul had been unfortunate. The authorities were unprepared and the reception was tactless. The King had sent some Arab officers in plain clothes to raise the Arab rabble [to demonstrate in favour of Iraq's claim to Mosul] and the police had made a clumsy attempt to make a secret search of the Commission's kit, which in any case was qualified for diplomatic immunity. The Commission, of course, found out and were understandably annoyed. Mosul was the Chicago of the Middle East, a city with an easily roused rabble armed and dangerous: altogether the situation was both unfavourable and ominous.

Thus it was that, without any warning, one snowy morning an aeroplane arrived with urgent orders to collect me and take me at once to Baghdad. I lost no time, but the snow came on so heavily that we had to land in Kirkuk where I had lunch with the Squadron while waiting for the weather to clear – a matter of an hour or two. On resuming the flight I was surprised to see the whole country down to Baghdad and beyond under a white mantle of snow. In winter there was usually snow in the north but no one had ever seen it as far as Basra in living memory. We landed safely, and I got into the High Commissioner's car which was waiting and was soon ushered into the office of Bernard Bourdillon [Assistant Secretary to the High Commissioner] who proceeded at once to brief me.[4] He gave me a résumé of the situation up to date. Sir Henry Dobbs had intended to brief me himself, but meanwhile the situation in Mosul had become more serious and he had hurriedly decided to go there himself. He had carefully prepared a speech for delivery to the Commission there, but a bad landing had caused him to bite his tongue and he was unable to speak. He was still there organizing our team.

The Commission, after their first experience in Mosul, decided to split into three, one member to each liwa, investigating all aspects of local life, the people's origins, religions, language, cultivation, trade, transport and finally, and in private, their wishes for future government – Turkish or Iraqi. On completion of their individual studies they would re-form, study

---

3. See Edmonds, *Kurds, Turks and Arabs*, pp. 395–6, for the names of others connected with the Commission.

4. For Bourdillon's career in Iraq, and later as governor of Nigeria, see R. Pearce, *Sir Bernard Bourdillon* (Oxford, 1987).

The Visit of King Faisal · 147

each other's notes, and then revisit each liwa together for a final inquiry before returning to Switzerland to complete their report and recommendations. The Arbil liwa was allotted to Count Teleki, the Mosul liwa to af Wirsén, Kirkuk and Sulaimani to Colonel Paulis. For our side Jardine was picked for Mosul, myself for Arbil and Edmonds for Kirkuk and Sulaimani.[5] In the absence of Sir Henry Dobbs I was received by the Counsellor. Having briefed me on my assignment he took me to his house where I dined and slept and in the morning flew straight back to Arbil.

There was little enough time to prepare for Count Teleki and company. The first thing was accommodation where he and his Dutch interpreter [J. H. Kramers] could have reasonable comfort and privacy, secure from thieves and rowdy demonstrators but approachable by all whom they wished to interview, or who wished for an audience. A smart police guard [was provided] for their protection day and night, carefully picked for intelligence to note all comings and goings for report to the governor and myself, [together with] a couple of messengers to wait on them, and a stock of firewood and oil. They had their own servants and equipment, wine, groceries and bedding so as to be independent.

Indeed if he [Teleki] was to be won over an atmosphere of courtesy and complete and obvious freedom was of first importance. However, for the first night I decided to invite them, Turks and all, to dinner in the hope that, after softening them up with good food and drink, I might get a lead on the best tactics to adopt for the coming contest. Ahmad Effendi, Charles and myself were a close-knit team on the most friendly terms with each other; and though for Charles and myself it provided great fun as well as interest, for Ahmad it was also a most serious matter for it was his home country that was at stake and should we lose the game his chances of survival were distinctly thin. Knowing this I did my best to keep him in good heart and he responded magnificently and soon entered into the fun of it all. He was related to Mulla Effendi, the chief prelate of the liwa, the keeper of the consciences, father confessor and adviser to most of the notables and all the tribal chiefs; so without any obvious preparations or the employment of any pimps or such-like professional spies and double-crossers we could depend on knowing at once what went on in the town, even behind the purdah of the harems.

The first thing we found out was the arrival of several Iraqi Army

---

5. According to Edmonds (*Kurds, Turks and Arabs* and his diary), Jardine was the British Assessor with the Commission. Edmonds was the general liaison officer organizing the whole event. Lyon was the 'local expert' for Arbil liwa, Major H. I. Lloyd for Mosul, Chapman for Sulaimani, and Miller for Kirkuk. Their daily reports to the High Commissioner are in the Edmonds Papers, Box 1, file 2B.

officers in plain clothes. They were summoned to the office and questioned. 'What were they doing in Arbil?' They confessed with pride that they had been sent by the Palace to raise the mob against the Turks, and for a start they proposed to spit in their faces on the first possible occasion. This was quite contrary to our ideas. I felt no good would come of that sort of conduct but on the contrary it was likely to do our cause much harm. So they were told to return at once to Baghdad, as we had sole control of affairs. I heaved a sigh of relief when Charles reported that he had seen them off.

The following day we three went to the Quweir Ferry [over the Great Zab] to greet the Count and his party at the liwa boundary. He was a man of forty-odd, of medium height, spare figure and obviously a well-bred intellectual. Ahmad Effendi was most impressed, especially by the name, for Tilki means fox in Turkish and we all had a good laugh on this when I explained it to the Count. The heartiness of our greeting seemed to surprise him a bit and it was soon obvious how observant he was. He started off by noticing the ornaments worn by the Kurdish tribesmen and remarked how similar they were to those he had seen worn in Turkey on his way over; and what with his observations on one thing and another he gave the impression of having already made his mind up and was only looking for evidence to justify his theories. I thought it best not to argue with him just yet, but let him have his head. He had obviously not got over his recent experience in Mosul, so I contented myself with asking him, his Dutch interpreter and the two Turks, Nazim Beg [Naftchizada] and the General [Jewad Pasha] to dinner that night. The invitation was politely accepted and so we prepared for the political worst while our Indian cook prepared his gastronomical best.

After a good dinner of roast partridges washed down with lashings of good whisky we all sat around the fire talking of this and that – anything except shop. The Count expanded in the warmth and was most interesting. I gathered that he was an aristocrat of the old type with hundreds of serfs, thousands of acres over which to hunt and shoot, and [that] the baronial rights and customs did not stop at that but included practices long since abandoned in England. He had shot chamois in the Alps or Carpathians – I forget which – and was most interested when told of the gazelle and ibex to be had locally. He spoke both English and French; we got on splendidly and I resolved to give him the old school tie snob treatment, for it was evident that class figured highly in his way of life. Before leaving he said he would like to hold a meeting in the morning to lay down procedure and make out a programme for his stay; and I assured him that if there was anything he lacked in the way of comfort, privacy or security to let me know and I would do my best to oblige. We parted on the friendliest terms.

The next morning he held his first session, at which both [assessors], the Turk and myself, appeared and the Count laid down the rules for procedure. He would take a list of notables and tribal chiefs from each side, compare them and decide the order and times for interview. Both assessors could be present or absent, but it must be both together or none. When it came to the point of asking them which government they preferred, both assessors must withdraw as the answers would be confidential. He would like to move freely where and when he liked, to various centres in the liwa to interview people in their own setting, and he invited suggestions from both sides about the most suitable places to visit and the routes to be followed. To this I agreed and offered to provide lists of people, places and routes; but I would like to be given notice so as to be present if the Turk was coming, and in any case to notify the people concerned and arrange [a] police escort compatible with his high office and safety. He could be as free as the wind but his safety was our responsibility. He thanked me for the arrangements made for his comfort and privacy, and that was all for the first day.

The following day I scored my first point over the Turk for he had failed to submit the names of any representatives of the Christians or Jews, whereas I had made a point of including them, and this was not lost on Count Teleki. Soon we had the grape vine about the Turk going round the town electioneering. Ahmad Effendi on the other hand was doing his bit in a much more subtle way. 'What would happen to their religion if the Turks came back?' That made them think a bit! My part was to fortify and encourage those who sought my advice, but otherwise to assume an air of benign but lofty indifference in open court. To those who asked I said, 'Have we not kicked out the Turks by force of arms, and would they not kick us out if they could instead of getting these European Effendis to sort it out for them! It was a foregone conclusion,' etc., etc.

During the tours round the plain I found gazelle and great bustard for him to shoot. He wasn't a very good shot but we got very friendly, and that was the main thing for when the people saw and heard how friendly he was becoming with me they naturally concluded that my band wagon was the one on which to jump. He inquired into all imaginable details about the liwas: the percentage of Arabs, Kurds, Turks, Jews and Christians, their crops, trade routes, imports, system of government languages, of instruction in the schools; and I produced statistics which I invited him to compare with any the Turk could produce. We had good information about the way the Turk was canvassing, and as a contrast we pressed no one but adopted a nonchalant freedom front for we had some very good trump cards.

1. We were in possession, which is nine points of the law in most places but 'nine plus' in the Middle East.
2. The Turks had discarded the Moslem and indeed all religions, whereas with us the Moslem religion was the state religion and the King a descendant of the Prophet. We also allowed freedom of worship for all Christians and Jews.[6]
3. The Turks had just put down a Kurdish rebellion in the eastern province with great cruelty, killing thousands and hanging the saintly Shaikh Said in Diyarbakir. We had put down Shaikh Mahmud's rebellion with hardly any loss of life and had even brought him back for a second chance. All this was well known in the Arbil liwa[7] whose population was 85 per cent Kurdish, and it was easy to remind anyone who had forgotten.
4. The Turks allowed no official language in the courts or schools but Turkish, whereas in Iraq the Kurdish language was recognized in the courts and schools wherever the Kurds predominated, and the same concession applied to those areas where Turkish was spoken.
5. Practically all trade, both import and export, whether by rail, road or river, was with the south. There was a little with Persia and Syria, but practically none with Turkey.

Of all the places visited by Count Teleki's circus the most interesting was Shaqlawa, the home of Mirani Abdul Qadir Beg, paramount chief of the Khoshnaw tribe. There was snow in the village street and much more higher up the mountain, but the old chieftain had a big fire in the guest house and extended the usual hospitality. He had gathered the other chiefs into his diwan or reception hall to have audience of Count Teleki.

The Count went to great trouble to impress the importance of the occasion upon them all, and before he asked them in confidence for their vote, he wanted them to realize that he came to them not as the agent of a single nation but as the representative of fifty-two nations which formed the world's court. To this the old chief responded by asking a simple question, 'How many rifles could Teleki mobilize to enforce their decision?' Of course there was no simple answer to this for the League of Nations had no rifles and Teleki was unable to give a plain answer. He was obviously taken aback, but after a pause compromised with talk about the weight of world opinion and its overpowering influence etc., etc. The old man listened politely for a while but was not impressed. 'In this country,'

---

6. The Turkish Grand National Assembly had abolished the Caliphate in March 1924, so reducing the attraction of Turkey for devout Sunni Moslems.

7. See Robert Olson, *The Emergence of Kurdish Nationalism and the Shaikh Said Rebellion, 1880–1925* (Austin, Texas, 1989) for details of the rebellion and its suppression.

The Visit of King Faisal · 151

said he, 'we count rifles, for without them no one could enjoy his rights.' He had put his finger on the helplessness of the League – as was demonstrated twelve years later [over Ethiopia] – but there was nothing more to be gained by more talk, so I suggested to Teleki that we go up the mountain in search of an ibex. He was very keen, so I got a couple of guides from Qadir Beg and the next morning we started off.

The way up was quite steep in places and as we mounted the deeper lay the snow. Teleki soon began to show signs of stress and the halts for a rest became more frequent as we advanced up the 3,000-odd feet to the summit. By the time we got there he was too exhausted to do much walking in search of ibex. We moved round for about an hour but the only indication of any game was the trail of pug marks of a leopard in the snow, but these disappeared over a bare stretch of windswept rock. The view of the Arbil plain with the city in the distance was magnificent, but Teleki was too done up to take much interest, and I calculated that at this pace it would take us all our time to get down to the village before dark, so we started back downhill. It was a very slow and painful journey as Teleki had to be assisted most of the way. When we reached our quarters he was completely exhausted and he now confessed that he suffered from bladder trouble and was unable to micturate. This was an old complaint dating from his wilder days and evidently not unexpected, for he opened his suitcase and brought forth a catheter which he proceeded to manipulate – a delicate manoeuvre even for trained hands. However when he eventually got it properly home, lo and behold what should come out with the first drops of urine but an earwig! This was most alarming and he asked me what I thought of it. I said I didn't know much about such things, but it could be that there was a nest of them somewhere inside him, and in any event it was a case for professional treatment.[8]

Next morning he was not at all well and, as he had a temperature, I had him taken down by stretcher and relays of carriers the 10 or 12 miles to the edge of the plain where a car awaited him. The RAF, most obliging as usual, had a plane on the Arbil air strip to take him straight to hospital in Baghdad.[9] I sent a code wire to the High Commissioner reporting the

---

8. I suspect that this may have been a practical joke by Lyon.
9. Edmonds, *Kurds, Turks and Arabs*, p. 419, says that Teleki was evacuated by air from Kirkuk, not Arbil. Lyon's forecast was right about Teleki. In a farewell letter to Lyon on his retirement as High Commissioner, Sir Henry Dobbs, when complimenting Lyon on 'the magnificent work' he had done in Arbil and Sulaimani, wrote: 'I have always felt that it was largely due to the impression made by you and your methods upon Count Teleki in 1925 that the International Commission reported in favour of the Mosul Vilayat [sic] being made over to Iraq.' Letter of 29 January 1929 in Lyon Papers.

event and adding that he could rest assured that we would have no more anxiety or trouble from Teleki. Nor did we. When after convalescence he eventually returned with the remaining Commissioners for their final check he was most grateful for all that had been done for him; his pro-Turkish bias had disappeared and when, months afterwards, the results were published they showed that a good majority in the liwa had voted for Iraq and the British Mandate.

There was, however, a sad sequel to Count Teleki. About fifteen years afterwards, when Hitler was expanding his empire, Teleki was again in power – this time as Prime Minister of Hungary. He still had that chip on his shoulder as a result of the loss of his estates in Transylvania and as a result fell to Hitler's blandishments in allowing a German occupation in exchange for the return of Transylvania to Hungary. Too late he realized he had exchanged the bone for the shadow and so let his country down. In such circumstances there was only one thing for an honourable high-born Hungarian gentleman – suicide. He shot himself.

After the departure of the League Commission there was a political lull, and when the decision [by the League Council] in our favour was published [16 December 1925] there was a notable change for the better – at least in the Arbil liwa which enabled me to give more time to the improvement and supervision of the administration and for surveying the situation on the liwa frontiers. It was now that Captain Hamilton started his famous 'Road through Kurdistan' connecting Arbil with Persia by a direct road through the Ruwandiz Gorge, thereby enabling wheel traffic to pass for the first time in history.[10] At the same time [Major W. A.] Pover, the PWD engineer, commenced a programme of new works and buildings, including the consolidation of the road to Altun Kopru and Kirkuk and a bridge over the Greater Zab to take the place of the ferry.

The tribes in general were more amenable, but this was not always the case in the neighbouring liwa of Sulaimani. Here, in spite of the occupation by Assyrian Levies under Colonel [G. G.] Cameron and the addition of Iraqi Army troops, the British Political Officer seemed to be still having heavy weather. Shaikh Mahmud was lurking in the Avroman mountains on the Persian border, unmanageable, undisciplined in spite of his exile in India; he was still imposing taxation on all those too weak to resist, and was as a consequence a focus for all outlaws from neighbouring districts. Kerim-i Fattah Beg, the murderer of Captains Bond and Makant, was still roaming the countryside ... pursued by the Levies and the RAF but as yet

---

10. See A. M. Hamilton, *Road through Kurdistan* (London, 1937), for his own account, plus much else. Hamilton was, in fact, a civilian, not an army officer. He actually began constructing the road in 1928 and completed it in 1932.

without success. The powerful Pizhdar tribe was divided in its allegiance in the manner typical of tribes under political stress, one half supporting the government, the other helping Shaikh Mahmud. In fact Babakr Agha's section of the Pizdhar appeared to be the only useful party supporting the administration, and being paid for it at that. To the man in the street he appeared to be the one and only infallible oracle and guide to the authorities, and this seemed paradoxical to me and a very poor dividend for the efforts so recently crowned with success. So, as the Sulaimani liwa was still a convenient refuge for fugitives from the Arbil police, I was tactless enough to write a memo giving my views on the subject. This brought about repercussions I had little dreamt of at that time, but which were cooking for me on my return from leave in the UK.

It was about four years since I had been home and with the end of spring [of 1925] I went. The journey was now much easier as the Nairn brothers had established a transport service across the Assyrian desert from Baghdad to Damascus and Beirut, by twelve-cylinder Cadillacs, thus cutting out the long voyage from Basra and Bombay ...

CHAPTER 6

Bringing Sulaimani under Iraqi Rule, 1925–26

§ ON return to Arbil [later in 1925] I found things much the same, with the exception of a strip of public land round the base of the Qala which Ahmad Effendi the governor had appropriated and on which he had already built a row of shops. I had held him on a very tight rein and it was natural for him not to let slip an opportunity for increasing his real estate. He had neither robbed nor oppressed anyone and by local standards was exceptionally honest, so I let it pass.

In the neighbouring liwas of Kirkuk and Sulaimani, however, things had been anything but quiet. In the town of Kirkuk there had been a sudden and serious disturbance arising from a simple bazaar squabble.

There was, at the time, a detachment of Assyrian Levies resting in the town while on their way to Sulaimani. These troops, though Christians, were all hill men; sturdy fighters, very different to the cowed and emasculated local Chaldeans who could be insulted with impunity by any Moslem in the bazaar. Indeed, the traditional attitude of the old Turks towards the local Christians was such that it was commonly said if a Turk wished to blow his nose he would use the head-cloth of the nearest Christian, and if of a friendly disposition hand it back after use instead of throwing it away. The local Moslem traders were unused to the Assyrians and a dispute over the price of a few pounds of meat flared up to a fight as soon as the shopkeeper told the soldier, 'When you are gone to Sulaimani your women will be ours.' It spread like a grass fire and eventually the police opened fire. In the light of subsequent inquiry it seems this was a much too impetuous and premature action when prompt use of the baton might have broken up the crowd, but the immediate result was to transform the contest from a stick and stone affair to one of firearms for everyone who owned a rifle, and most of them did. Soon it became a full-scale massacre of the local Christians. The Assyrian soldiers rushed back to their quarters, spread the alarm and seizing their rifles put into practice the emergency drill, which

Bringing Sulaimani under Iraqi Rule · 155

amounted to seizing the strategic points in the town, chief of which was the house of Minas Effendi, a prominent Christian, which happened to be situated on the highest point in the Qala or mound on which the old part of the town was built. From this point they commanded the bridge across the river and the roads going north and south, and proceeded to shoot as many of the locals, armed or otherwise, as came into view.

There were only two British officers with the detachment, the senior sick with fever and unable to do anything, the other had only just arrived in the country and had had no time to learn any local language or even to know his own troops. He was Percy King [later my brother-in-law]. At great personal risk, amid a hail of bullets from friend and foe alike, he went across the bridge and got the troops back to their quarters while the RAF Squadron stationed on the airfield demonstrated overhead. Many a gallantry medal has been won for less, but all he got was the subsequent duty of principal witness defending his native officers on the capital charge. This also he did with the whole-hearted loyalty which with him took first place among all virtues, truth included. He undoubtedly saved their necks.

The regiment of Moslem cavalry stationed in the barracks was not suitable for employment in such an affray and in fact looted the kits of the Assyrians stored in their barracks; so a company of British troops of the King's Own Regiment was flown up from Baghdad and, marching through the streets with fixed bayonets, restored confidence and order. After their arrival the Assyrian troops were marched up the road to Sulaimani. They were set upon by the local tribesmen who got a warm reception and quickly dispersed after suffering heavy losses.

Sir Henry Dobbs then flew up from Baghdad, addressed the notables and promised that order would be restored and justice done. This ended the incident so far as the town was concerned. On such occasions the casualties are difficult to assess as those taking an active part are naturally shy of subsequent police inquiries and so conceal their dead [and] nurse their wounds at home rather than attend hospital; but the most reliable estimate was reckoned at about eighty dead and about 200 injured.

The news of this outbreak of course spread in all directions and triggered off a renewal of activity by the outlawed Hamawand chiefs and by Shaikh Mahmud, who came out of his lair in the Avroman mountains and proceeded to levy taxes in the Shar Bazher district of Sulaimani. This was countered by a column of Assyrian Levies from Sulaimani, who made an assault on the village of Kinaru in which Shaikh Mahmud was reported to be staying; and this, although unsuccessful in its primary object of capturing the Shaikh, certainly checked his activities and was not without its amusing incidents.

The intelligence officer, Flight Lieutenant McGregor, accompanying the column had given strict orders to his interpreter to ride two lengths behind him. The troops advanced; all went well and the objective [was] duly reached; but, as is normal in mountain warfare, the crux came during the retirement, for it is then that the concealed tribesmen make their maximum effort. As the bullets gradually increased, the interpreter's courage began to ebb till finally he could stand it no longer and, digging his spurs into his horse, he galloped ahead, at the same time firing his rifle backwards over his head regardless alike of orders to come back, and of the fact that his bullets were more dangerous to the troops than to the enemy. Thus he disappeared into the distance heading for camp. When the column eventually arrived he was hauled before his officer. 'Did I not tell you to keep two lengths behind me, O Yahia Effendi?' said McGregor. 'And where were you during the withdrawal?' 'Sir,' said Yahia Effendi, 'did you not see me? Alone I fought one thousand tribesmen till all my ammunition was expended!' He was not under King's Regulations and there was nothing one could do to him under civil law. So McGregor gave him the title of 'Roderick the Bold', a name which gave him every satisfaction and stuck to him till the end of his service.

On this occasion, as usual, some of the Pizhdar tribe were supporting Shaikh Mahmud while others were with the government, and as neither section would fire upon the other it is not easy to understand what use they were, as indeed I had pointed out some months previously. But it so happened that while the troops were engaged at Kinaru, Percy King, who was battalion quartermaster at the time, arrived at the camp with rations. Hearing the distant firing he asked the Assyrian officer in the camp who was fighting against whom. 'Sir,' replied he, 'we were fighting Shaikh Mahmud and the Pizhdar tribe.' 'Oh,' said Percy, 'and who are those armed tribesmen I see coming along over there?' 'They are Pizhdar, sir,' said the officer. 'Right,' said Percy, 'then give them five rounds rapid fire.' This they did with great enthusiasm, on which the tribesmen immediately disappeared. But it afterwards turned out that they were a party of the friendly Pizhdar coming in to report to the district governor. All this shows how Gilbertian the use of tribes can be.

Meanwhile a regiment of Kurdish Cavalry under Lieutenant Colonel Laurence, VC, had been detailed to march from Sulaimani to Halabja and remain there as a garrison. Laurence, when a rough riding sergeant in the 18th Hussars, had won the VC in South Africa. As a trainer of horses he was superb; it was a pleasure to ride any horse trained by him, but any native soldier in his unit who brought in his horse with a sore back got a sore back himself on the triangle. Nothing was too good for a horse or too severe for the rider. He had plenty of courage but little time for anyone who disagreed with him and so he had earned the nickname of

'Stuffy'. On the way to Halabja he was set on by the Ruthzadi section of the Jaf tribe and only managed to fight his way through because his men were more afraid of him and his hunting crop than they were of the enemy. Even then he lost his wheel transport, including the treasure chest containing the regimental funds.

It was at this precise date [later 1925] that the order came for me to proceed at once to Sulaimani by aeroplane and assume the duties of Political Officer there. I was not too keen to go having just got the Arbil liwa into a state of peace and progress and was looking forward to more leisure and sport. But I realized I had brought about the transfer by my criticism [of the administration of Sulaimani: see Chapter 5]; so with a kit bag, a roll of bedding, and my dogs I got into the waiting plane and waved goodbye to Arbil ...

I had been instructed to make recommendations for restoration of law and order in the liwa; but before I could look round I got an urgent call from Colonel Laurence to visit Halabja and sort out the many problems with which he was confronted. This was not so simple as it seems for there was no security on any of the roads and it was only about a week since he had to fight his way through the Jaf, and the airfield at Halabja was not yet fit for planes. So, as there were no properly trained mounted police such as I had used in Arbil, I applied to Colonel Cameron for an escort. Now it so happened that, attached to his Assyrian Battalion, there was a number of assorted Assyrian volunteers, in all thirty-nine. They were dressed in miscellaneous garments from frock coats to complete native costume, but armed with rifles and mounted on ponies they had acquired in the course of their wanderings. They were commanded by an Assyrian Rab Emma, or lieutenant, called Maksoot, with a second in command called Raoul. They were all ages but very keen, their main interest being loot. If they thought an opponent had anything worth having they would follow him to the death. Getting them back was not so easy. These Cameron made over to me and I accordingly christened them the 39th Irregular Horse (Lyon's Own). They were just what I wanted as they could move faster than infantry and their absence from HQ made no inroads on the garrison's strength or duties. So it was arranged with 'Stuffy' [Laurence] to send a squadron to meet me half way the next day and I set off with my hearties who duly handed me over to Laurence's squadron, then commanded by Captain [S.] Fosdick.

On arrival at Halabja I found the Colonel installed in one of the large houses belonging to the late Usman Pasha and his late wife Adila Khan, the Queen of Halabja. He had already caught a deserter, court-martialled him, sentenced him to death and shot him, even before receipt of the official confirmation from headquarters. He was now engaged on a programme of pie dog extermination. The dogs were quick to realize their danger, as I soon discovered. The first morning, while sleeping on the roof, I was aroused by a rifle shot, and from the perimeter could be seen scores of pie dogs streaming out of the town in all directions. I calculated that canine cunning was of such a high order that it would take months before extermination was complete, and whether by then some alternative form of garbage collection could be set up was of no immediate importance. More urgent was the provision of labour for reconditioning the airfield, the sole link with headquarters for replenishment of equipment and canteen stores. Old Stuffy's indent for replacement of gear lost by enemy action was so high that a wireless query came through asking how the unit had managed to arrive without so many saddles and bridles, etc. However, he needed local supplies and cash from the local treasury, information about the location of the various sections of the nomadic Jaf tribe, the names of the local mudirs or sub-district governors and their location in case their assistance might be needed, [and] general instructions on how to deal with the local governor and with any civilians arrested by his troops. I had also to study local conditions with the qaimmaqam or district governor and brief him on all matters affecting the troops; how to deal with their fire-eating Colonel and the necessity for providing him with timely warning of any tribal movement affecting security.

The qaimmaqam was Hamid Beg, a nephew of the late Queen of Halabja. He had a local reputation for being close-fisted with his tenants, but I found him intelligent, courageous, and a great sportsman with whom I afterwards enjoyed many a good day's shoot. He kept half a dozen hounds and a tame wolf with which he hunted the wild pig, and he so admired the field work of my spaniel that I bred and trained a pup for him. This gave him immense pleasure for, when out shooting partridge with his relations, it mattered not who shot the bird, for as soon as it fell the dog would bring it to him and to no one else. He had several wives and a vast number of children, one of which afterwards became Iraqi Ambassador in Spain.

Having done what I could for the time being in Halabja I returned to Sulaimani by the same means as before and without incident, the 39th coming to meet me half way along the 50-mile track. For the next month or two I was kept busy with callers; many of them time-wasters, but all had to be received with the usual cup of coffee [and] cigarette, and listened to with patience if I was to get to know them and their problems well enough to make recommendations for the restitution of law and order.

Up to date Sulaimani had been a special province under the direct supervision of the High Commissioner and not under the jurisdiction of

Bringing Sulaimani under Iraqi Rule · 159

the government of Iraq, for this was the centre of Kurdish nationalism and although attempts had been made to set up a Kurdish enclave they had proved unsuccessful. And now it was hoping for too much to make a Kurdish Switzerland [i.e. Kurdistan as proposed in the Sèvres draft treaty of 1920] so far from the sea: moreover, the fact that the Kurdish people overflowed the boundaries of Persia, Turkey, Russia and Syria made it all too complicated now that peace with Turkey had at last been signed. The British government were no longer prepared to make expensive and embarrassing experiments, however deserving the cause. Thus Sulaimani must be treated as a normal liwa of Iraq with, of course, safeguards for the Kurdish language in the schools and courts wherever the Kurdish people predominated. [My assessment of the measures necessary was as follows.]

There must be regular police, mounted and foot, properly trained in the use of arms, and there must be all the other standard departments of the administration of a normal Iraqi liwa.

As, in all departments, it was weaker than the neighbouring liwas of Arbil and Kirkuk, an effort should be made to lighten the burden of administration by the temporary transfer of the districts of Chamchemal and Ranya to Kirkuk and Arbil respectively. Chamchemal district was geographically cut off from Sulaimani by the Qara Dagh range of mountains through which there were only three passes in its 100-odd miles, and only one of these fit for wheel traffic. Ranya was separated by the unbridged Lesser Zab river.

The insecurity on the roads had choked off normal trade and caravans could only proceed at set times and under armed escort. So it was essential to build police forts sited at strategic points along the principal roads from which the police could signal to each other, and so to headquarters by helio during hours of daylight and by Aldous lamp during darkness. Sanction for all trained signallers to get an extra allowance [had] to be obtained from the Directorate of Police, also iron rations and water tanks to enable the garrison to withstand any attack until relief arrived. Caravans could seek shelter at such posts along their route in the event of a sudden raid.

The main road from Kirkuk to Sulaimani was so bad that in heavy weather a motorized convoy had been known to take six days over the journey of 70 miles. Bridges, culverts and general consolidation of this road was a first priority. Similar protection [had] to be arranged next on the route southwards to Halabja, and afterwards to the Penjwin sub-district on the Persian frontier to the east and to Surdash and Shar Bazher on the north.

The programme of checking Shaikh Mahmud and the Hamawand raiders with planes and Levies would, of course, continue, but the provision of a network of posts would constrict their movements, reduce their chances of success, and provide much earlier information on which to mount a pursuit.

In addition the government should officially sequestrate all Shaikh Mahmud's property and make sure that the rents and taxes were collected as a first priority so that, even if the Shaikh tried collection, the tenants would be able to claim they had already paid up.

These measures took some time to think up, longer to get sanctioned, and still longer to put into effect; but implemented they were, and before I left [Sulaimani] some four years later [1929] I was officially congratulated on having one of the most peaceful liwas in the country. This was not accomplished without many a skirmish; but gradually, as the administration tightened its grip, the outlaws weakened until it became obvious to them that the game was not worth the candle.

To succeed in pacification the confidence of the people must be won, for without it no evidence is forthcoming and the process of law is thwarted. So police must be friendly as well as competent, an attitude altogether foreign to the peoples of the east, and therefore by no means so easy to teach as to verify. I remember on one occasion I noticed that when a party of tribesmen rode into a village the chickens would gather round in the hope that some of the horses would lift their tails and release some succulent half-digested grains of barley in their droppings. But when a posse of uniformed police rode up the chickens would retreat to their underground refuge. Doubtless they had seen the fate which had overtaken some of their number on previous occasions. Thus an adequate ration allowance for man and horse at any rate removed the excuse for battening on the countryside.

Life in Sulaimani for the next couple of years [1925–27] presented a picture of variegated colours and shades, an occasional foray or perhaps an occasional disappointment punctuating a gradual change for the better but always full of interest ...

The favourite relaxation of the local Kurds was to sit on benches outside the café exchanging gossip ... while drinking endless glasses of sweet tea ... There was also gramophone music purveyed from old-fashioned machines with wide trumpet-shaped horns. Across the mouth of the horns was a string net adorned with screwed up pieces of paper which attracted my attention, and on further investigation the following explanation was given. When gramophones first made their appearance in Kurdistan the mullahs of the orthodox Moslem religion at once perceived that this new invention would encourage the people to stay around the tea shops instead, as was customary, of spending most of their time in the courtyards of the mosques. For in those days the mosque was the centre of culture, information and learning, and it was common practice for the mullahs, who had the latest information on the bazaar, to advise the ignorant peasant to go with one of the mosque servants to one of their own agents, where they were told they would get an honest deal instead of going to the open market where they would be victimized. This practice brought in good pickings for the Holy Men, though sometimes, when the peasant returned home with a wretched piece of short measure cloth, he would get a wigging, if not worse, from a long-suffering and over-worked wife.

So the mullahs issued a 'fatwah' or ban on the new machines on the plea that they gave forth undesirable infidel music and culture. But the mullahs' union was not a completely closed shop, and one or two junior and less affluent clerics saw their chance. For a reasonable fee they wrote out some verses of the Koran, and these, when hung at the mouth of the gramophone, would act as a filter and all sounds passing through would be disinfected, pure, sanitary and inoffensive to the ears of all true believers ...

The RAF bombing squadrons in the north of Iraq were stationed one each at Kirkuk and Mosul, while at Sulaimani there was a flight of single-seater 'Snipes' which were handy little machines for liaison with [military] columns. They were fitted locally for dropping small supplies and had boxes with sliding bottoms for releasing live poultry. It was interesting to note that chickens on release fell to the ground like stones, their wings bent up and stayed up till they hit the ground, but ducks were able to volplane down to the ground and land uninjured.

There was also a wireless station on the airfield manned by RAF staff who must have found life rather dreary on such an isolated post. One day, when riding past the entrance to the Great Mosque, I saw what was unmistakably a BOR [British other ranks] dog – a type of mixed breed which invariably attach themselves to the British soldier. He was sitting patiently at the entrance to the outer courtyard. No Moslem's dog or any pie dog would be tolerated in such a place, so I dismounted to make further investigation. Sure enough at the next entrance to the inner courtyard was a second dog of a similar type and there, sitting at the edge of the ablution pool, were two British servicemen, happily angling for the tame carp. They were blissfully ignorant of the holy nature of their surroundings or of the fact that each fish was supposed to represent the soul of some holy pilgrim who had passed on, yet not a single protest had been made by any of the faithful. The men of course were quite unaware of the fact that dogs were not welcome in a mosque compound and that the fish were tame and hand-fed. I trembled to think of what would have happened had they committed the same outrage in a mosque of the Shia sect where infidels before now had been murdered by fanatics for merely going into a mosque to take photos ... I asked the mosque servant or sacristan why he had not intervened. He replied that he didn't know any English and if he had tried to prevent them he would not have been understood and it might have led to a disturbance for which he would have been blamed. The airmen were of course apologetic as soon as they understood, and it was settled that I would one day show them better sport out in the country ...

As winter drew near we began to look for some recreation that would take the place of polo, and if possible include the local Kurdish gentry; for anything that would serve to bring them into the society of British officers would help towards gaining their confidence, friendship and support. I recalled that after the Armistice the 110th Transport Company of the Indian Army had founded a pack of hounds with such success that it remained and flourished long after their return to India and eventually was incorporated in the royal stables. It was called the Exodus Hunt, after the Hindustani *ex sao das*, meaning 110, and as such provided sport for troops, RAF and civilians in Baghdad. So my suggestion to start a local pack was at once agreed upon.

The first thing, of course, was to find the hounds; and as there were no fox hounds available we had to be content with what was known in India as a Bobery Pack. This in our case consisted of cross breeds between the Saluki and the fierce types of Kurdish sheep dog. They were very fast, very fierce and hunted on sight. A circular was sent round to the various notables and tribal chiefs setting out the proposal, inviting them to join and help by providing whatever hounds they could spare. They would be welcome to join in the sport and there would be no subscription for them. In practice we could feed them on battalion waste, augmented when necessary by a small subscription from the officers.

The response was good and in no time we had about six couple of the fiercest types which would chase everything that ran away on their approach. The kennels were built with local labour and a young and keen officer of the HLI [Highland Light Infantry], who went by the name of Brassneck, was unanimously elected as Master. This cognomen he won on a very alcoholic night by diving into what he thought was a swimming pool, but was in fact dry concrete. He luckily suffered no serious ill effects, and what more stout-hearted a chap could be wished for as MFH. The pack was called the Sulaimani Vale, and in the first season killed a wolf, seventeen jackals, three foxes, a cow and an old woman, who actually died of fright. Shaikh Qadir, brother of Shaikh Mahmud, and a number of the locals used to turn out and enjoyed the fun, till eventually after the third season the pack was infected with rabies and had to be destroyed.

Of course life was not all fun; there was plenty of administrative work, in addition to the building and servicing of the administrative machine which was designed to enforce law and order. Occasionally on information received there was a foray to intercept reported raiders, and though they nearly always escaped, it was good practice for the troops. All the time, however, the police were being recruited and trained, the forts built and the roads consolidated. Thus passed the following two years [1925–26] before my next spell of home leave.

CHAPTER 7

Sulaimani: Shaikh Mahmud and Local Society, 1926–29

§ [ON leave in 1926 Lyon met and became engaged to Vera King, sister of the Percy King mentioned in the previous chapter. They were married in the spring of 1927, first by civil marriage in Beirut, then in church in Jerusalem, before returning to Sulaimani.]

... It was soon after [my return in the spring of 1927] that a decision was made to occupy and garrison Penjwin – a sub-district headquarters village on the frontier where it was crossed by the main caravan route to Persia; and as I would have to go on column I arranged to send Vera back to Kirkuk where she could have the company of Mrs Lloyd [wife of Captain H. I. Lloyd, Administrative Inspector, Kirkuk] and Mrs Corner during my absence.

The column pushed off according to plan and reached Penjwin without incident, but for some administrative reason which I cannot now recall, I did not go with it but accompanied the supply column which set out the next day. It consisted of hundreds of hired pack transport animals carrying rations and military stores under the protection of one company of Assyrian Levies, deployed with one section on each side as flank guards and two more sections acting as advance and rearguards. As the track over the Goyzha Pass and onwards was very rough and narrow the convoy was inevitably strung over a long distance in spite of every effort to keep it closed up. However, all went well on the first day; and just before sundown on reaching a suitable spot the animals were halted, unloaded and camped down for the night.

The next day the convoy set out through undulating country covered with scrub oak, in the expectation of getting over the last range and across the open Penjwin plain before nightfall. By afternoon the troops were trudging along with an air of boredom and indifference to their surroundings which frequently called forth the censure of their British

Captain, when suddenly there was a sound of galloping horses and a burst of rifle fire which immediately aroused their interest and completely changed their attitude. To these hill men from the rocky fastnesses of the Tyari district, mountain warfare was an art acquired long before they had enlisted, and it was a heartening revelation to see their speedy reactions. Without waiting for orders from the British commander they immediately seized the ridges on either flank, while the rearguard closed up the straggling convoy into a depression where the animals would be sheltered from all but long range indirect fire.

The attack was typical of the methods used by the Hamawand, galloping up from a flank and firing from the saddle into the brown in the hope of stampeding the animals and their drivers. However, the speedy action of the flank guard had given them an unexpected shock and they turned about, hotly pursued by the troops nearest to them.

The close range firing was soon over and if I had any criticism to offer it was that they were over-keen in pursuit, for these Assyrians were loth to turn back from their quarry so long as there was any chance of loot. Apart from a few wounded donkeys the convoy had suffered no casualties, but the troops had made a creditable bag and we loaded up a few corpses for the purpose of identification when we reached our destination. Unfortunately the action and subsequent delay caused by the tardy return of these over-keen troops made it too late for the caravan to attempt the last pass before nightfall. As it was pretty steep, covered with scrub and over 5,000 feet high, it was decided to stop and bivouac at the first suitable spot where water was available. This we did, sending a wireless signal to Penjwin explaining the cause of our delay. And as there was a possibility of another attack the following day, the Penjwin Force sent out a party to picket the last pass, thus enabling us to complete the journey without further interference. Thus after installing a garrison and sub-district governor, we returned to Sulaimani where the bodies were identified by the police as Hamawandis from the section of the outlaw Kerim-i Fattah Beg, whose son Saber had been leading the party of raiders.

This was the turning point in the activities of the Hamawand raiders so far as Sulaimani liwa was concerned, for the programme for erection of police block-houses was now nearing completion and many of them [were] already occupied. Raiders' movements could be quickly reported, caravans warned and interception arranged. The main road to Kirkuk had been improved with bridges and culverts, making it passable for wheel traffic in all but the worst weather. Funds were sanctioned for a wheel road to Halabja with a branch to Penjwin. Gradually law and order was restored and native taxis from Kirkuk began to use the roads, and some took up residence in Sulaimani. Their penetration into the hills had a most civilizing effect; their mere presence was a token of government strength, and tribal leaders, who previously never travelled without a troop of mounted riflemen, found they could come to town by car quicker, and in greater comfort with less expense. Large raiding parties were on their way out and with the growth of public confidence the police were able to look after the smaller fry.

Thus although Shaikh Mahmud still lurked in the fastnesses of the Avroman mountains, sometimes on one side of the Persian frontier, sometimes on the other, his movements were now restricted as he was cut off from most sources of support. The Hamawand outlaws whose homes were in the Chamchemal district were obliged to pass through an area of close police supervision, with posts or block-houses at all the main passes through the Qara Dagh range, which separated it from the remainder of the Sulaimani liwa. The Shaikh's agents found it increasingly difficult to squeeze rents and taxes out of his sequestrated villages from which the government had already made a collection, and his prestige and claim to Kurdish kingship gradually dimmed and faded. Finally he sent in a letter that he was once more willing to make submission, and in earnest of his good intentions sent his second son, Baba Ali, with his Chief of Staff, Majid Beg, to meet me at Penjwin, where I at once went by plane to bring them in and make suitable arrangements for the Shaikh's reception.

Shaikh Mahmud's father, Shaikh Said, had been the leader of the Barzinja Saiyids, claiming descent from the Prophet and therefore distantly related to King Faisal. But there the connection ended, for he was first and last a fire-eating if short-sighted Kurdish patriot whereas Faisal had been the spear-head of Arab independence.

Shaikh Said had been slain in Mosul by the Hester Sowars – Turkish riot police – who, mounted on mules, were used by the Turks much as the Cossacks were used by the Czars of Russia and were just as ruthless. He was buried in the Great Mosque in Sulaimani and was locally revered as a saintly patriot second to none. Shaikh Mahmud was a small boy at the time of his father's death and escaped concealed under the voluminous garments of a Mosul woman, but from that moment he had a chip on his shoulder and was a nuisance to the Turkish administration.

He was physically very strong but lacked the gentle manners of King Faisal. More outspoken and doric in speech, he had a touch of Shakespeare's Falstaff. On more than one occasion I heard him joking about the thunder box, the use of which he had learned during his convalescence and exile in India. But, for all his shortcomings as a ruler, he was a courageous and clean fighter, and for this he earned the respect of all British officers against whom he fought. One of his tricks was to keep a few British bullets in his pocket and when under fire he would pull one out and show his men how it had failed to penetrate his heavenly protected body. Strange to relate many of them believed him in spite of the fact that he had previously been shot in the liver and would have undoubtedly died but for British military surgery.

It was the first of many meetings when he came to tea after his arrival in Sulaimani and my wife was delighted to entertain him.

His eldest son had not much personality and afterwards became a Deputy in the Baghdad parliament. The second son, Baba Ali, had great charm. He went to the Victoria College for sons of Middle East aristocrats which was then in Alexandria, and afterwards he went to a university in the USA.[1] The third son, Shaikh Latif, at that time no taller than his rifle, was a chip off the old block and was to be a thorn in the side of the Iraq government for the rest of his life.[2]

I was naturally pleased at the Shaikh's submission for I had made security a priority since my arrival in Sulaimani, but it was not long before I felt a tinge of regret for him, and at a public dinner attended by the senior officers of all services in the garrison, RAF, Levies, Iraqi Army, Police and Civil officials, I proposed a toast to the health of Shaikh Mahmud. At first the Arab officers were taken aback and I could see consternation in many faces before I explained to them the old proverb, 'When the fox is caught the hunt is ended', and its significance to all of us. For, had he not been responsible for improving our military efficiency in keeping us up to the mark by periodical forays? And for that matter, I added, 'How many of us would be unemployed but for the Shaikh?' They soon saw the joke and all joined in the toast.[3]

But there was still much to do in the way of implementing what was called 'The Forward Policy' previously decided at a conference in the High Commissioner's office in Baghdad and still on the list; and the last area still under complete tribal control was the Pizhdar country. This tribe was spread over both sides of the Persian frontier which their chiefs completely ignored, as indeed any attempt by either the Persian or Iraqi government to assert its authority over them. Only a year before they had captured

---

1. Baba Ali later entered Iraqi politics and served in several ministries in the 1940s.

2. For details on Latif's later career see D. McDowall, *A Modern History of the Kurds* (London and New York, 1997), pp. 289, 294, 296, 317.

3. After his submission Mahmud was exiled to Persia. He returned to head a rising in 1930 but was defeated by RAF action. He was then exiled to the Lower Euphrates and his properties sequestered. They were returned to him in 1938. In 1941 he escaped from Baghdad and offered to raise forces to fight on the British side against the revolutionary forces led by Rashid Ali. But from the later 1920s the Barzan family became the main Kurdish dissident force in Iraq.

about sixty Persian soldiers and sent them in to Sulaimani, from which they had been duly returned to Kermanshaw via Khanaqin by the Iraqi authorities.

Like most frontier tribes their policy was for one section to treat with the government while the other remained in opposition. Each section had a young chief as a mudir or sub-district governor, drawing pay and allowance from the government but paying it nothing but lip-service. I have no doubt they collected what they could from the wretched cultivators but it never got as far as the treasury. But now that Shaikh Mahmud was out of the way I deemed it a suitable opportunity to make a move which would imply their recognition of government authority; and the simplest way was to demand sheep tax. Accordingly I notified the authorities in Baghdad and proceeded with the plan. About a month afterwards, when reading a copy of a Political Report from the High Commissioner's Office to the Colonial Office, the government and C-in-C of India, and the various agencies in the Persian Gulf, I spotted a paragraph criticizing the Political Officer in Sulaimani for rashly proposing taxation of the Pizhdar tribe, thereby hazarding the newly formed and untried Iraq Army in a trial of strength with the proud Pizhdar. This got my goat and I immediately asked permission to go to Baghdad for an interview. I was received by [Major B. H.] Bourdillon, who was the Counsellor, and there to hear my complaints. I pointed out that I had notified the authorities – High Commissioner's Office and the Iraq Ministry of Interior – and no one had told me to hold my horses. The proposal was within the scope of 'The Forward Policy' and the widespread criticism was therefore unwarranted and damaging to my career as an officer of the Indian Army. What was more, the tax had been collected and was now in the Sulaimani treasury without involving any troops, and so I wanted an apology. He said he quite sympathized with me but it was impossible to expect an apology from the High Commissioner who represented our King. He would explain it to the High Commissioner and I could go in afterwards, provided I promised not to be cheeky, and he would arrange for the next report to contain a paragraph stating that the tax had been duly collected without any trouble.

Sir Henry, though a kindly man at heart, was inclined to be quick tempered. It was commonly said that he vented his wrath on the gardener on Sunday mornings and on one occasion Lady Dobbs had intervened saying, 'Beat the gardener, Henry, if you must but why throw the flower pots off the parapet into the Tigris?' So, duly warned, I entered the Presence and was graciously received. Indeed, he congratulated me on my work and so after that I could not well kick up a dust. He had always been very kind to me, sending a car to the aerodrome whenever he had occasion to summon me to Baghdad. As soon as I arrived he would greet me himself and, if his wife was not in residence, he would personally conduct me to my room, show me the bed on the roof if it were in the hot weather, indicate the books that might interest me and the ice chest where a cool beer could be obtained without ringing for a servant. I had often heard of the Winchester School motto ['Manners makyth man'] and Sir Henry certainly lived up to it. Lady Dobbs was equally charming and staying there was like having a weekend with a favourite uncle.

From now onwards there were fewer alarms and excursions and I could settle down to the normal routine of administration ...

I had now [by the spring of 1929] accumulated about eight months' leave to my credit, [my wife was pregnant], and as there was no necessity for hurry we could draw the equivalent of two first-class fares and wend our way home at our leisure by any route we pleased ...

CHAPTER 8
. . . .
Kirkuk: People and Locusts, 1929–30

§ FOR the return to Iraq I booked [the family, now including a baby daughter] on a cargo boat of the Strick Line sailing direct from Manchester to Basra ... As for myself, I returned by the quicker route via Marseilles and Beirut to Baghdad, for I was being transferred to Kirkuk and it was essential to go ahead and get the new house ready for the family. I had served four years in Sulaimani; I was sorry to leave it, but I had done most of what I had set out to do, and anyway four years was quite long enough in one place on foreign service.

There was nothing much new to me in Kirkuk, where I had served before, except the Iraq Petroleum Company – then known as the Turkish Petroleum Company[1] – which had struck the first gusher at Baba Gurgur [in 1927] and was now setting up field headquarters on the ridge just outside Kirkuk, for which it revived the original Assyrian name of Arrapha.

The official change-over at Kirkuk was brief and terminated by taking over the keys of the office safe in which the cypher book was kept. My colleague had kindly added two bottles of cold beer and two glasses with which we ended the ceremony.

The governor [mutasarrif] of Kirkuk at that time was Umar Nazmi Beg, a native of Kifri and a graduate of the law school, who had previously served as a judge. He was an able official and good company, though there were times when he got very cross, especially when the government failed to sanction his suggestions, which I am bound to say in my opinion generally seemed sound and reasonable. He suspected that they had not been given adequate consideration and that the Minister was little more than a political rubber stamp, signing letters that were probably drafted by a junior clerk. On such occasions I would coax him along to have a beer with me in the local club, after which he was able to look on life a little

---

1. It was renamed Iraq Petroleum Company in 1929.

more objectively, and I would write to my Chief pointing out the advisability of influencing the Minister to reconsider the matter.

In general the Iraqi governors were very human and obliging if one could gain their confidence, though of course there were exceptions. Many of them were married to very religious women who ruled their homes. In the month of Ramadan no Moslem would dare to smoke or drink coffee in public or even in their homes during the hours of daylight, though for the remaining eleven months it is customary to have coffee and cigarettes on tap all day in government and commercial offices ... But my house and office were always a safe refuge for those who could not repress their yearning for a cigarette during the sacred month, and the number of notables and senior officials from the governor downwards who found some excuse to visit me was unbelievable; the smoke fumes could always be attributed to myself by those who strictly kept the fast. In a way I suppose this could be classified as a mild type of friendly blackmail, but any gesture to win the confidence and friendship of those in authority was well worthwhile, both from an official and personal point of view.

The officials and notables of Kirkuk were most friendly: I always enjoyed their company and they relished a good story or joke even when against themselves. For instance one day, when rounding a corner in my car, I found myself in the midst of a stone-throwing battle between the children of two quarters of the city, and suddenly a stone crashed through the windscreen. I naturally reported this to the governor, emphasizing the danger of losing an eye through broken glass, and the unlikelihood of the boy responsible being able to pay adequate compensation. But he shrugged off my complaint, saying that it was an accident: the stone was not thrown purposely at my car, it was just child's play. I didn't press the matter further, but within a week he got a large stone through the windscreen of his own car, whereupon he issued an order fining every house in that quarter one rupee. I though this a bit too good in the way of business, so when I congratulated him on his good fortune in escaping personal damage, he gave me a sermon on how dangerous it was and how necessary it was to take disciplinary action. I then reminded him of my own experience, which I shrugged off as child's play, and pleaded for mercy. He was quick to see the point and we had a good laugh over it; but I noticed that for a long time afterwards he kept a very agile policeman armed with a cane in the front seat of the car and I heard of no further incidents.

The Mayor of Kirkuk was the younger of two brothers who could hardly have been more unlike each other. The elder was a senator, ponderous, solemn and devout; the younger agile both in mind and body, efficient, and agnostic. He delighted in a joke, could mimic everybody and loved parties. To illustrate how unstable was public opinion he told me the following story. From some cause or other, which now escapes my memory, the administration was on tenterhooks over an unexpected rising of the Talabani tribe who were reported as massing for a march on the city. All the gossip in the tea shops was about the prospect of loot by the tribesmen, and cowering in their offices the officials were discussing means of effecting their safety and that of their families. Then, when the political temperature was at its zenith and a single stray shot might have started a riot, the news suddenly broke that one of the pupils in the secondary school had committed a homosexual assault upon his teacher. This sensational news ran like wild fire through the city and out to the uttermost ends of the province, to the exclusion of all else. When at length it reached the Talabani chief he immediately sent in word that, though up till then he had always regarded government school education as suspect, he had now changed his mind; and since the tables had been turned on the teacher he would see that in future his sons would attend the school. The projected coup d'état was forgotten and life both in the country and city resumed its normal rhythm.

There were four main families of notables in Kirkuk – the Naftchizadas, Qirdars, Aouchis and Ya'qubizadas. The first, headed by Husain Beg, were an old Turkish family which had the local oil concession. The Qirdars, headed by Haji Jemil, a much revered and astute old gentleman, were wealthy merchants, cousins of the Mayor of Istanbul. Haji Hassan Effendi Aouchi, head of his family, an ex-mudir and a keen farmer, had spent a large fortune making an irrigation canal on his land in the Hawija plain bordering the Lesser Zab river. His sons were great sportsmen and fully upheld the family name Aouchi, which in Turkish means hunter. The Ya'qubizadas were municipal officials with considerable property in the city. They had retreated from Kirkuk with the British and so cast in their lot on our side and Mejid Effendi was Mayor of the city. All four families were solid reliable Turkish stock, and after the war their leadership and support was a most stabilizing factor in local government.

There were also two clerics of great influence: Saiyid Ahmad-i Khanaqah, a wealthy divine who presided over a Moslem guest house where food and lodgings were provided to the needy who attended prayers in his mosque; and the Chaldean Archbishop, who presided over the Christian flock and had the distinction of being one of the rare clerics to hold services in Aramaic – the language of our Lord. I never quite understood why he had such an exalted rank. It certainly was not justified by the size of his flock, though his personal qualities were of the best and commanded universal respect. The Jewish Rabbi was a very poor third.

The riot and massacre of a few years before had lowered the local blood pressure, the arrival of the railway and the growth of the oil industry provided ample employment, so that it was probably the most peaceful and prosperous period in the province's existence before and since ...[2]

The Kirkuk liwa or province was bounded on the north by the Lesser Zab river, on the west by the Lesser Zab and Tigris, on the south by the Jabal Hamrin or Brown mountain and the Diyala river, and on the east by the Kurdish hills. Thus the eastern edge was all foothills inhabited by Kurds, the centre strip was steppe country dotted by ancient Assyrian tumuli characteristic of all the cultivated lands of the north, intersected by streams flowing westwards and inhabited by a mixture of Turkomen and Kurdish cultivators. The western strip was quite flat and inhabited only by two Arab tribes; the Obeid, a shepherd tribe which had originally come from the high desert beyond the Euphrates, and Jibbur, who were riverian cultivators; a miserable lot heavily infected with a disease called Bijil, unsightly to behold but a non-contagious type of syphilis. There was a mud road down the centre as far as the Diyala which was passable for wheel transport in dry weather but anywhere else could be traversed only by pack transport ...

In the steppe country along the banks of the streams there were plenty of francolin or black partridge, and in the flat plain bordering the Zab and Tigris more gazelle, bustard, demoiselle crane and sand grouse in countless packs. This area, known as the Hawija, was completely uncultivated at that time and in the spring was dotted with black tents, camels and thousands of sheep and goats. It was then that the sheep were counted for tax – eight annas each for sheep and goats and twelve annas for camels – lambs excepted. It was then that the inhabitants of nearly all the villages in the adjacent steppe country vacated their houses to escape from the plague of spring fleas and took their flocks to the fresh green pastures of the Hawija where they would be out of reach of the ripening corn. For them it was the festive season when the young bloods would exhibit their horsemanship, visiting their neighbours' tents and feasting on lamb and rice or perhaps boiled barley, with truffles and young thistle tops cooked in fresh butter, the whole washed down with copious draughts of buttermilk ...

This flat plain ... was always the first place for the locusts to make their appearance. They usually hatched out in early March or late February, dependent on the weather. At first they are like black fleas, hopping only an inch or two at a time, and at a casual glance look like a strawberry net spread out on the ground. As they grow they advance with ever longer hops till by the end of the month they can do 4 or 5 feet, consuming

---

2. Almost immediately after the family's return they had all to go to Baghdad for two weeks for inoculations against rabies after one of Lyon's dogs was found to be infected. All his dogs were destroyed

everything, even the tent ropes if there is nothing more edible within reach. Behind them there is nothing but black stumps and their own excreta. Driven onwards by insatiable hunger they cover quite a distance during the hours of daylight, those behind leapfrogging those in front, never resting till sunset. There is something inexorable about their progress, which becomes ever faster till at length they get their wings; and then they may be seen in clouds miles long in frontage, darkening the sky with their density and, as if guided by a single commander, marching or flying all in the same direction. They never turn back. They naturally attract all sorts of birds, which feed on them through all their stages of development but yet seem to make no impression on their numbers.

The cultivators beat tins and light fires to protect their crops but they likewise make no impression on the swarms, which merely shift to the next field, leaving the poor cultivators worn out before the next contingent comes to clean up what remains. There is little or no national co-operation between the cultivators; each will strive to save his own crop but shows little interest in the fate of his neighbours, so their efforts are no real answer to the problem which requires international co-operation by all the countries liable to infestation.

The first stage is information about breeding grounds. If near villages the government can offer money to the children for egg collection. Ploughing the infested area exposes the eggs to frost and birds; but the cunning insects often breed in rocky, well-drained soil in ungetatable and unploughable areas which escape treatment. Destruction of the hoppers by spraying with crude oil, poison bait, or by burying them in trenches into which they can be driven as they advance, are all useful methods, though they never effect complete annihilation. Poison bait is unpopular with cultivators as the arsenic oxide is indestructible and causes heavy casualties among the cattle and sheep for years afterwards. Moreover the government issue of large quantities of arsenic oxide seems invariably to be followed by unexplained deaths among the unpopular and unwanted members of the community.

The last act of the locust is to dig a small hole in the ground in which the female inserts her egg bag, about the size of a peanut and containing about thirty eggs which hatch out in suitable weather conditions in the following spring. If perchance there should be an unusual period of warm sunshine in the end of January or thereabouts, followed by drought or frost, the young locusts hatch out and, finding nothing on which to feed, they die where they hatch. This happens once every few years and is, I believe, mainly responsible for the otherwise unexplained absence of locusts after a year in which infestation should have produced plenty of swarms. But always some few escape.

1. RIGHT. Lieut. Col. W.A. Lyon in uniform, *c.* 1939.

2. BELOW. W.A. Lyon, Capt. C.E. Littledale *(left)* and Sir Henry Dobbs, the High Commissioner *(right)* in a characteristically informal pose, mid-1920s.

3. LEFT. Sir Arnold Wilson, 1921, from a portrait by Eric Kennington, after he had left Baghdad.

4. BELOW. Sir F. Humphreys, the High Commissioner, *(seated one from the left)*, Vyvyan Holt, the Oriental Secretary *(standing behind him)* and others, in 1932, just before the end of the mandate.

5. The Cairo Conference, March, 1921, which decided the future of Iraq. Front row: Sir Herbert Samuel (*third from left*), Winston Churchill, (*fourth from left*), Sir Percy Cox (*fifth from left*). Second row: Sir Arnold Wilson (*left*), Gertude Bell (*second from left*), Jafar-al-Askari (*fifth from left*), T.E. Lawrence (*sixth from left*).

6. The Mosul Commission, 1925, which settled the future of Mosul. (*standing, l. to r.*: — Fattah, Badri, Kramers, Charrère, Roddolo, Pourtalès, Weber, Piggot, — *seated, l. to r.*: Nazim, Edmonds, Jewad, Paulis, Wirsén, Teleki, Jardine, Sabih, Kamil)

7. ABOVE. The Mardin Frontier Conference, 1930, described by Lyon, who stands fourth from the right.

8. BELOW. Miss Gertrude Bell *(second from left)* and others, *c.* 1921. She was a dominant influence on Baghdad policy 1918-21 as Oriental Secretary and eventually became an enthusiastic proponent of Faisal as king.

9. Sir K. Cornwallis, the Ambassador, Lord Mountbatten, the Regent Abd al-Illah, and Nuri as-Said, prime minister, in 1941, after the end of the Rashid Ali crisis.

10. King Faisal visiting the Patriarch at Khoun Khyat in 1926, as part of his strategy of assuring non-Muslims of his favour.

11. Mahmud Pasha, chief of the Jaf, and Babakr-i Selim Agha, chief of the Pizhdar, who supported the government loyally throughout the critical period before 1925.

12. The Lady Adila Khan of Halabja, widow of Usman Pasha Jaf, brother of Mahmud Pasha, and another strong supporter of the government.

13. Shaikh 'Mulla' Mustafa Barzani, 1923: a leading Kurdish nationalist and rival of Mahmud Bazanji, who features in Lyon's account as a great warrior.

14. Kurds drinking coffee in a typical Kurdish tent.

15. ABOVE. An RAF plane over the Gara Sind, 1924: typifying the dangers pilots faced when 'pacifying' Kurdish rebels in the early 1920s as part of Churchill's scheme to police Iraq from the air.

16. BELOW. Shaikh Mahmud Barzinja *(fourth from left)* in exile in 1942, taken by Freya Stark, who sympathized with him.

The first spring after my arrival in Kirkuk [1930] proved just such freak weather when the appointment of a local locust control officer was under consideration. As there wasn't a locust or even the report of one anywhere about, the provincial governor considered it unnecessary to fill the appointment, which was claimed by a certain Abdul Wahab. He was well known for his past exploits, running the blockade during the war, and afterwards evading the duty on tobacco caravans, which he slipped through the hills and round the checkpoints by night. However, after much palaver, it was agreed to give him a chance on probation, provided he could find the locusts. So the brave Abdul mounted his steed and went forth in search of the locusts and the justification for his appointment. For days he quartered all the likely breeding grounds in the province without success. To all his inquiries the fellahin replied, 'Last year there were many but this year "Praise be to Allah" there are none.' After about ten days' fruitless search he was returning a disappointed man, when nearing the irrigated gardens outside the city he spied a tea shop. He dismounted for a 'cuppa' and as he sat drinking, he heard that unmistakable rustling noise made by a grasshopper rubbing its hind legs together. He leapt up, caught it, kissed it, pinned it to his headcloth like a soldier's cap badge, and mounting his horse entered the city in triumph. It passed muster at a casual inspection and, supported by a fictitious and tendentious report, got him the job. As the spring advanced there were a few minor swarms, but Abdul failed to display the same energy in their extermination; and, questioned by a friend, he admitted that locusts in large numbers were a pest, yet Allah had sent them for some reason as yet undisclosed, and anyway where was the sense in doing himself out of a job for the next year? And didn't the Arabs eat them?

The city of Kirkuk must have been one of the oldest in the world, and the bazaar was typical of the Middle East, each trade having its own street or corner to the exclusion of all others. There were the sellers of fruit and vegetables, cloth, butchers, bakers, dyers, potters, coppersmiths, silversmiths, blacksmiths and leather workers, all in their own groups. There were barbers, who still practised the art of bleeding, and some would also draw teeth. At the entrance of the shop the patient could be seen sitting in a chair with the blood spouting out in a fountain from his arm, to be caught in a special basin, in the rim of which was cut a semicircle large enough to hold the upper arm when used for bleeding or the neck when giving a shampoo.

The local dentistry was very crude, as I noticed one day when I was attracted by some heartrending shrieks coming from a barber's shop. The patient's head was pressed firmly into the jamb of the door while the 'dentist' proceeded to hammer a two-pronged gauge under the root of a molar tooth. On my approach and noticing my amazement the 'dentist' assured me with a quick confident grin that there was no cause for alarm: the situation was well in hand and with a few more blows the tooth would come out. He was as good as his word and finished the job while I waited. The patient seemed quite satisfied and went on his way.

Kirkuk city was not without its culture – Turkish and proud of it. At Ruwandiz in the Arbil Province there was Sayed Hussein who was not only a Kurdish poet but also a craftsman who could make wood cuts, and published a newspaper which he printed in a hand-operated press. In Sulaimani, likewise, there was Haji Piramerd who published his own Kurdish poetry and newspaper in another hand-operated press. And now here in Kirkuk was a local poet called Hijri Effendi, who performed in Turkish. No state occasion was complete without him and his endless poems. They were all specially composed for each occasion and followed the same pattern: flattery for the distinguished guest, praise for the governor, a few quips on local topics followed by a description of the boundless wealth now available from the oil wells – always referred to as streams of black gold and in contrast to the poverty of poor Hijri. It was a plain hint for a state subsidy which never came his way.

On one occasion, when King Faisal came to open an oil well, he was obliged to listen to the first twenty stanzas, after which, seeing that old Hijri had enough manuscript to contain another 200, he quietly told his ADC to step forward and accept the poem on his behalf. Either he was well accustomed to poems of this type or else he had been tipped off by the governor. On another occasion, when the Fields Manager of the oil company was the guest of honour at an official tea party in the municipal garden, I asked him what he thought of the poem being recited in his honour. I thought his reply very apt. Said he, 'Not knowing Turkish I wouldn't know whether his poem was good or bad, but I feel something should be done about it. That poor little old man should not be allowed to go on. Either he should be richly rewarded or else taken away and shot!' I expect the King must have felt the same, and as he wasn't shot I hope he was suitably rewarded.

All three poets were popular in their own localities but received little encouragement from the Iraqi authorities in Baghdad. Indeed, they were barely tolerated, official patronage being available only for the poets who used Arabic. Both Kurdish and Turkish were suspect as liable to encourage a separatist movement. The Kurdish struggle for independence had been a constant source of trouble in Turkey and Persia and the conservative Turkish culture of Kirkuk was likewise suspect in Iraq, a country newly torn out of the old Turkish empire. Indeed, on one occasion when a party of Turkish troops passed through, en route to some official celebration in

Baghdad, the population in their enthusiasm turned out to a man. They slew a young camel at the entrance to the city – the highest honour that can be paid in the Near East – and so many people ran after the first car load that they failed to notice those that were following and several were run over ...

My predecessor was an officer who could sit, talk, smoke cigarettes and drink endless glasses of sweet tea for hours on end. He also had a liking for good food and drink, qualities greatly appreciated by the local gentry, who preferred the stool or couch to the saddle, and privately considered most British officials unnecessarily energetic. So highly was he esteemed by one sub-district governor that, to show his respect, he embellished the latrine seat in the guest wing of his headquarters with a ring-shaped cushion for the honourable posterior. Looking back over the years I have failed to find such a touching personal tribute in my own experiences or those recorded by the many travellers in the Middle East. If there is one thing in which these people are supreme it is their hospitality. Even the poorest hastens to bring forth his samovar and tiny store of tea and sugar that would otherwise be probably kept for the annual festival. They are all brought up in the tradition of Hatim Tai, who when camped in some far desert alone with his wife was visited by a stranger. Rather than send him away hungry he is said to have slain his one and only animal and means of transport – his riding camel – to provide a meal for the unbidden guest.

Among such people one cannot but be happy, and altogether life during this period in the Kirkuk Province was very pleasant and not nearly so tough as in Sulaimani. But suddenly, after about a year, I was detailed to move off to Mosul and take over from a colleague who had been ill for some weeks and was now due for combined sick leave and furlough in the United Kingdom ...

CHAPTER 9

Mosul: The Frontier Commission and the End of the Mandate, 1930–32

§ BEFORE going to Mosul I had received special instructions from my Chief in Baghdad about handling the new governor [Tahsin Ali], who was new to the job. I was to ride him with a very light rein as he had no previous experience in administration. He was a political firebrand who had belonged to T. E. Lawrence's outfit in Palestine and owed his appointment to the King. I promised to put up a kindly and helpful front, but as soon as I met him I could not help noticing a striking resemblance to Ben Tillett, at that time a notorious rabble rouser in British dockland.[1]

I stayed in my colleague's house, and as he was still ill in bed his wife asked me to escort her on the usual round of farewell calls. I was thus able to meet all the people who mattered, both British and local Iraqis, without any further formalities. I already knew most of the British officers in the garrison, RAF, Iraq Levies and Iraqi Army, having accompanied them on numerous expeditions in the Kurdish mountains of Arbil and Sulaimani. Foremost among them I found my brother-in-law, Percy King, now serving as Special Service Officer in the RAF, and Captain John Redding of the Guides, a very close friend and now serving with the British Military Mission. Apart from the elderly notables and some of the senior officials the younger generation of Iraqi officials had grown up during the twelve years since I had served in Mosul under Colonel Leachman, and so were new to me ...

Soon after my arrival in Mosul I was told that the Frontier Commission, of which I was a member, was due to go to Mardin, the capital of the

---

1. Ben Tillett (1860–1943) was a British labour leader who formed the Dockers' Union in 1887 and led the London dock strike of 1889. He later became a leading member of the Trades Union Council and was a member of parliament 1917–24 and 1929–31.

adjacent Turkish province, and the date fixed was two days later.[2] The arrangement between the two governments was for the Frontier Commission to meet in Mosul and Mardin in alternate years to deal with any frontier complaints outstanding. According to the regulations then in force the Frontier Control demanded certificates of vaccination and inoculation for smallpox, typhoid, plague and cholera; and when I mentioned this to Tahsin Ali,[3] suggesting that the date be postponed till all these formalities were completed, he pooh-poohed the idea, saying that if we did not turn up on the day on which we were expected the whole party would be dislocated, and there was now no time to give adequate warning, as communications with Turkey were so haphazard and unreliable.

I said I was sure the civil surgeon – at that time a British doctor – would never consent to giving us all these inoculations at once even if they were procurable, and even then I for one would not stand for it. 'There is no necessity to bother Dr McLeod,' said Tahsin Ali, and summoning his secretary told him to send up the most junior doctor in the local health service; and on his arrival commanded him to get from the secretary the names of all proceeding on the Commission and issue certificates to each for each of the diseases mentioned in the regulations. The young Iraqi doctor bowed and took his leave without a murmur. As soon as he had gone Tahsin Ali remarked, 'This is a silly formality but we must comply with it – all we need is a handful of certificates to show at the checkpoint.' The next day all the certificates were ready; and ever since I have wondered what credence can be put in the thousands of such certificates presented annually to our British authorities by visitors from the Near and Middle East.

The Commission was made up of Tahsin Ali, myself, the governors of the two frontier districts, a secretary, a typist, a couple of orderlies and the car drivers. We pushed off in good spirits and harboured for the night in the tents of Shaikh Ajil al-Yawir, the Shaikh-ma-Shaikh (or Shaikh of Shaikhs) of the Shammar tribe. He was chief of all the numerous sections of the Shammar who wandered about in what the Arabs called Al Jezira (i.e. the island), which included all the country lying between the Tigris and Euphrates rivers, and at this time he was camped close to the Turkish border opposite Nisibin. He was a most imposing figure, about 6 foot in

---

2. The standing Frontier Commission was set up in 1926 following the treaty which settled the Mosul question. Initially it met six-monthly to settle any Turko-Iraqi disputes over frontier matters; but in later years, as these diminished, it met infrequently.

3. The original has 'Ben Tillett' here and throughout this section. I have replaced it by Tahsin Ali.

height with a soft voice, a handsome face and a grand manner. The food was ample but simple and no drinks were provided other than coffee, water and buttermilk. First a large mat of gazelle skins was laid on the floor, then four slaves came in with a huge tray, about 6 feet in diameter, on which was a vast pile of rice surmounted by the carcasses of three or four roasted sheep. Another slave came around with a jug of water, a basin and towel to each guest in turn to enable him to wash his right hand, which is always used for eating, whereas the left hand is used for cleansing the posterior, either with water if available and if not with pebbles. I have often wondered if this had a connection with the biblical reference about 'not letting the right hand know what the left hand doeth'. On the Shaikh's invitation the guests squat round the tray sitting sideways with the right shoulder towards the centre. To each is given a round of unleavened bread about the size of a soup plate, and then each guest eats by hand as much as he can and then rises to wash his hand and mouth while someone else takes his place. After the seniors the juniors, and after them the servants; and finally the remains go to the women's quarters behind a reed screen at the other end of the tent, which was about 60 yards long. After the women and children have eaten, the remainder, if any, is given to the dogs and nothing is ever left over. Everybody gets a chance when the Shaikh entertains: nobody waits for anybody else and so one eats quickly on such occasions. After the meal coffee and cigarettes are provided in an unceasing stream, and on this occasion the talk went on far into the night. Not as one might suppose about the various frontier cases to be dealt with at Mardin, but about cases of Turkish raqi or araq, considered much superior to the Mosul booze, and how many could be brought back customs free on this diplomatic mission. There was also a good prospect of picking up some good French booze cheaply when we called on the French post commander on our way through. Tahsin Ali was a thorough libertine and didn't intend to let any chance of pleasure pass him by.

Next morning we set forth in high spirits, partly in anticipation of enjoyment yet to come and partly because no liquor had been provided by the Shaikh. It was a case of no liquor no carry over. The French Chef de Brigade was away on tour so we left our cards at his headquarters and proceeded onwards to Nisibin.

At the entrance to the town we were greeted by the Turkish district governor and a guard of honour. It happened to be shortly after Mustafa Kemal's edict for the emancipation of women and the compulsory wearing of European hats by all men, and as yet the people in such a remote province had evidently had some difficulty in adjusting themselves to the new fashions. The Turks, however, are a simple and primitive people who, for want of a directive, left the enforcement to the local police who simply tore off the offending headgear. In the case of the women's veils (yashmak) they justified their action by the supposition that they were worn only by members of the oldest profession. In the case of the men the eastern headgear was roughly confiscated and any protest was promptly rewarded with a beating. Thus it so happened that, as we were inspecting the guard of honour, there arrived an Arab arrayed in the usual nightshirt-like garment and the usual Arab head-cloth and 'agal' – a woollen rope-like ring used for keeping the head-cloth in position. He carried the usual little cane and was perched upon his camel. So far so good: there was nothing unusual in such a costume, but to comply with the new regulations he had superimposed a bowler hat on his native headgear, which altered the whole picture. There he sat on his camel with the bowler hat crowning a completely eastern costume, and with his little camel cane he bore an unmistakable resemblance to Charlie Chaplin. I had never seen such a ridiculous sight in my life and was quite unable to restrain my laughter. The rest of the mission, from Tahsin Ali downwards, joined in, and to make it worse the poor camel man began to laugh back at us.

In a trice the Turkish police, at a sign from the governor, dragged him off his camel and under a hail of blows into the fort, from whence his shrieks could be plainly heard as the police continued the treatment. I am sure the poor fellow was quite innocent of any intention to ridicule the Turkish law, and no doubt if we had not been there his attempt to comply with the regulations might easily have passed muster, for the local police in matters of European headgear were probably as ignorant as himself. We pleaded with the governor to spare him, but I fear in vain: in any case he had had a terrible beating already, so we hastily completed formalities, bade him farewell and resumed our journey to Mardin, which was about 30 miles distant.

The city of Mardin lies at the foot of the Turkish hills and is built on a slope facing southwards towards the Jabal Sinjar, an isolated mountain due west of Mosul. In origin Mardin is, like Aleppo, really much more Arab than Turkish, but the Turks had done all they could to suppress both Arabic language and culture. Like Mosul it used to have quite a sizeable minority of Christians, but they had also been greatly reduced in numbers by the harsh treatment of the Turkish government, which had always regarded them as potential fifth columnists, and on one pretext or another had liquidated most of them by massacres, both red and white. The red variety is a bloody affair though comparatively quick: the white takes longer as it amounts to marching the victims around the country without provision of food or clothing till one by one they collapse and die on the roadside. This was the favourite method of dealing with Armenians, who of all classes were hated most. During the war many Christians had fled across the plain to seek refuge with the Yezidi tribesmen in the Sinjar mountain fastnesses. These wild worshippers of Tauz Malik the Peacock King, quite unfairly known and referred to as devil worshippers, had always sheltered the fleeing Christians and though often their villages had been pillaged by the pursuing Turks, they had never surrendered a refugee.

After the formalities of greeting usual to such occasions, we were installed in a wing of the vali's (governor's) house and found it furnished with the barest necessities. The food and drink [were] no better nor more European than what any Iraqi governor could put up, and we slept in our own camp beds, several to each room.

The next day our formal talks started: they were confined to agreement on a programme and ended before lunch. After lunch I felt like taking a stroll round the city, but to my amazement I found the suggestion frowned upon by the Turkish Liaison Officer, who made all sorts of excuses against my going. I found this most annoying and asked him if their security was shaky; and when he denied this, as he was bound to do, I asked him if we were guests or prisoners. That finished the argument. I was then provided with a Turkish Captain to escort me, and off we went for a tour of the bazaar. This proved rather disappointing, with nothing to show any better than what could be seen in Mosul or Kirkuk, very little as good and everything from food to jewellery more expensive. The few shopkeepers I addressed in Arabic cringed as soon as they saw my escort, and very soon I came to the conclusion that it was best to leave them alone as they might be suspected of Arab sympathies and subjected to a severe police grilling as soon as I had gone. There was no prospect of seeing the prison or hospital, but I was told that the vali had planned for us an excursion into the country to visit the monastery of Deir-al-Zafferan, about 10 miles distant behind the hills.

The next day the talks began. They were all concerned with claims over frontier infringements, ranging from alleged over-flying by our planes to raiding of camels and cattle. The vali was an intelligent lawyer who shortly afterwards was appointed Director General of the Turkish Police. He could coo like a dove, growl like a bear or raise his hands in a saintly innocence to suit every occasion according to whether the claim under discussion was his or ours. Tahsin Ali was no match for him and I soon concluded that we had little hope of getting any of our claims met and so had better concentrate on giving nothing away. Two or three sessions of this can be very wearisome and I was glad when the vali proposed the promised excursion one afternoon.

We all bundled into motor cars and, though the road was rough, the drive through the foothills was very enjoyable. The monastery had of course been warned and the priests had prepared tea for us. The building, like those of Mosul, was of juss[4] and in poor repair. It had little of architectural interest that I could see but they had one treasure. It was an ancient testament, hand-written on gazelle skin and with the capital letters illuminated in much the same style as the Book of Kells in Trinity College, Dublin.

Having slipped our Turkish shadow for a few minutes I pointed out to the Superior what a valuable treasure it was and how, if kept much longer in his mouldy monastery, it would soon disintegrate. If he would let me have it on an official receipt I would send it to the British Museum where it would be in safe hands. I was sure our experts and church dignitaries would be very interested. If he wished to sell I was sure it would raise quite enough cash to give the monastery a new lease of life. And if he didn't want to sell we would send it back. Knowing Dr Barsum of Kirkuk, whose brother was His Beatitude of Antioch and head of their church, I was sure there would be no difficulty about it. The Superior toyed with the idea for a while but finally told me he was frightened to part with it as the Turks made a periodical inspection, and if the Testament was not on view they would all be thrown into prison. I returned empty-handed.

The last night of our stay was chosen by the vali for a state dance. It was held in a barn-like hall with the cobbles peeping through the newly cemented floor. Not the happiest choice for a dance but then the Turks were tough. The orchestra was a local scratch lot which did their best, though at European music they were obvious beginners. Nor did the guests seem familiar with it but made up with enthusiastic support for native songs, the most popular of which was called Choban (the Shepherd). This must have been one of the first occasions on which the women were allowed out for they all clustered together at one end of the hall like a flock of sheep in the presence of a dog. At the other end of the hall were the vali, Tahsin Ali, and their respective followings drinking raki – the only alcoholic drink available. The vali turned to me saying, 'Behold the music has started. Why are you not dancing?' To which I replied that, according to European etiquette, the head of the Mission, Tahsin Ali, should lead off with the vali's wife, whereupon the rest would follow. But Ali said he couldn't dance, and as he had no wife with him for the vali to dance with, it was up to me. So I went over to the other end of the hall and invited the vali's wife to dance. She was a tall woman and very fat, at a guess I'd say all of 16 stone. No, she wouldn't dance, so I made my bow

---

4. Juss: a coarse type of plaster of Paris that dried as soon as it was mixed and enabled the masons to build domed ceilings without the need for timber and steel girders.

and returned to the drinkers, well satisfied with my escape. However, the vali immediately asked why I wasn't dancing so I told him that I had invited his wife but she hadn't accepted. On this he went straight over to her and after a few sharp words returned saying, 'She will be honoured to dance with you.' So there was nothing for it but to have a go. I was never any good at dancing, but at least I could get around without falling, provided I had an average partner. But the vali's lady was like a massive meat mountain. Perhaps Victor Sylvester[5] might have moved her, but all I could do was gyrate around her till the band stopped. The truth was she couldn't dance and was honest enough to say so in the first place but was over-ruled by her husband. I had done my duty and earned a respite.

I think the invitations must have been restricted to government wives, civil and military, for the country was still in the stage where non-official ladies were shy of availing themselves of the liberties offered by Mustafa Kemal, and so it was left to the official ladies to set an example. Nor were there any young unmarried women there so far as I could see. The best of the bunch was the young wife of the local judge and I did my best with her for most of the evening.

The following morning, with splitting headaches, we packed up and returned to Mosul. Tahsin Ali and Co. had forgotten all their plans for bringing back contraband booze, and anyway it didn't matter as the vali had given each of us a case of raki to take home as a souvenir, though as far as I was concerned the mere sight of it was enough to make me wish I had joined the Salvation Army. I never inquired about what happened to my case and was glad to forget it.

A few days later who should arrive in Mosul but Jamil al-Midfai (Jamil the Gunner) who had just been appointed Minister of Interior. He had been one of T. E. Lawrence's 'braves' in Palestine and was a bosom pal of Tahsin Ali. As for myself I had not forgotten that he was the chief instigator of the Tal Afar rising in the spring of 1920 in which all the British personnel, officers and men, had been brutally murdered and for which his name had been on our wanted list right up to the time of Faisal's arrival in Iraq.[6] So it was with mixed feelings I received a message to see him in the governor's office. On the one hand I would be delighted to see him hanged, on the other I knew that we were now on a new leaf of history; he had been brought over by the King by whom he had now been appointed as Minister of Interior; and as an Iraq official I was bound to accept him.

---

5. Victor Sylvester was a popular dance-band leader in Britain in the 1930s.

6. Tahsin Ali had also been one of the leaders of the force that attacked Tal Afar. See E. Tauber, *The Formation of Modern Syria and Iraq* (Ilford, Essex and Portland, Oregon, 1995), pp. 246–57 for details.

I had barely greeted him and taken a seat when he and Tahsin Ali opened up on me. Apparently Percy [King] had been using a minor revenue official in the Aqra district as an intelligence agent and Tahsin Ali had intercepted a letter in the post from him to Percy. Both the Minister and Tahsin Ali seemed outraged at the idea of employing an Iraq official as a spy. What did I know about it? I told them the answer was 'absolutely nothing'. 'Was he not my brother-in-law? Can you deny that?' 'He is certainly my brother-in-law but I am not his keeper. He is a Special Service Officer, seconded from the British Army to the Royal Air Force, and he is responsible to his Commander at the AHQ. If you have any complaints to make they should go through the proper channel, and although this is the first I have heard of it, I consider that, as the Royal Air Force are responsible for the defence of Iraq, there is nothing heinous in getting the co-operation of an Iraq official.' Having said this I then asked if there was any further subject for discussion and, there being none, I bowed and left.

They were both furious and soon it was evident they had taken the matter up with my Chief, Sir K. Cornwallis [Adviser to the Minister of Interior], who wrote asking me to come to Baghdad and stay with him. But I heard from Percy that his Chief had been on to him about it. Percy had asked for an interview with Cornwallis and been refused. So I replied that I had nothing to add and no connection with the whole affair. If he wanted me to go to Baghdad I would of course do so, but as he had refused an interview to my brother-in-law I would not stay with him: blood was thicker than water in our family. What was all the fuss about anyway? Didn't he well know that [Captain J. F.] Wilkins, the Chief of CID, had filled the King's palace with paid informers? At most it could be said that Percy or his agent had been clumsy to be found out by a couple of ... [Arabs] like Tahsin Ali and Jamil al-Midfai. I was not going to be brow-beaten by anyone, least of all by them. If I wasn't wanted I'd prefer to return to my regiment in India. Well that ended the incident so far as I was concerned and I didn't have any more lip from Tahsin Ali. It always pays to have a spare string to one's bow or fiddle ...

In those days there was no decent hotel in Mosul and any European visitors who were not in the services usually stayed with us. While there, among others, we entertained General Ironside, who at that time commanded, in India, the division earmarked for dealing with any trouble in Iraq. He had come to make a personal inspection of the country, especially the communications along the frontier and the local resources available in case of need. Freya Stark also stayed a while with us, and so did Rosita Forbes. I well remember the Air Marshal calling on us at tea time when Rosita was with us. She was in a class by herself for vamping the male sex, and could go anywhere and do anything she liked without visa or permit. As long as they were men it mattered not whether they were British, French, Arab or Turkish officials, she always got her way with them.

One day Sir Hilton Young – afterwards Lord Kennet – came along. When it was time to dress for dinner it suddenly occurred to me that, with only one arm, he would have trouble with his tie. I didn't like to risk asking him, for people with a disability are often offended if notice is taken of it. So I told Mohammed [my servant] to go up to his room and ask discreetly if he could be of any assistance. When he returned I asked him how he got on. 'The Pasha said he didn't need any help so I went outside and looked through the keyhole.' 'How did he manage his tie?' I asked. 'He held one end in his teeth, Sahib,' said Mohammed, giving a life-like imitation.

Of all the personalities who visited Mosul during my service there, [there was] only one [who] was the cause of any commotion. It was the King's son, Prince Ghazi. Being an only son he was of course spoiled in the harem. Then followed a sudden change to Harrow School where, as a junior, he was understandably unhappy, soon to be snatched away before he became senior enough to understand and enjoy what it was all about. Then in the Iraq Military Academy as a cadet, [he was] pampered by Iraqi ADCs who, to say the least, were far from desirable in the qualities required for teaching the higher discipline so necessary for eastern kingship.

His visit was, of course, a great occasion for the newly formed Iraq Army garrison, the majority of whose officers were only too anxious to advance their prospects by obsequious behaviour. With them was their instructor, Captain Redding of the Guides Infantry. He was dressed in his regimental uniform and conducted himself with the correct precision of a guardsman. For the Guides, like my own regiment, were of the Punjab Frontier Force, which had much the same standing in the Indian Army as the Guards have in the British. It appears that during the inspection the Iraqi officers, led by their Commander, kept on leaping to attention and saluting every time Ghazi asked a question, turned or even looked their way. There was nothing steady about them; they were like a lot of monkeys on hot bricks. It was altogether a childish performance, and when it was all over the Iraqi Commander, supported by Nettlefold and Tahsin Ali, raised a complaint against John Redding: (1) he was improperly dressed in that he wore chaplis – the sandal worn by mountain troops of the India Army; (2) that he was slack in saluting Ghazi. It smelt very like a frame-up. Nettlefold did not get on well with Redding and was not the most popular officer among the British community. It was said he was the most senior Major in the British Army, having spent most of the 1914–18 war at some base camp. As for Tahsin Ali, nothing he could do would surprise me; so when John Redding told me about it I advised him to stick up for his rights, which he did; and as a result Jafar al-Askari, the Minister of War, came up to inquire into the case. His decision was that John Redding was a Captain in the Guides holding the temporary rank of Major in the Iraqi Army, in which Ghazi was only a cadet, and therefore not entitled to any salute. Nevertheless Redding had courteously saluted him on first greeting, and again on his departure, which was all that was necessary, even if it had been his father the King. He was wearing 'chaplis' (Frontier Force sandals), which were the correct dress of his regiment, just as a kilt to a Scot. John Redding was lucky for Jafar Pasha was an exceptional personality, honorary Colonel of the British Yeomanry regiment which captured him in the Suez Canal in 1915, and subsequently called to the English Bar. Few of the Iraqi ministers were anywhere near his class.

There was an occasion when King Faisal was due to hold the first big review of his newly established army in Baghdad. The Minister of War at the time thought it a good opportunity for showing himself off to the gathered multitude by taking a Royal Salute himself before the King's arrival on parade. But the commander of the [Iraqi] troops said he'd be damned if he gave him a Royal Salute. So they indulged in a public slanging match, at which they were both pretty expert, and finally agreed to seek out the British Major General who was head of the British Military Mission. He had not become a General for nothing, and his verdict was not unlike the Judgment of Solomon: 'In the British Army the Royal Salute is given once only on parade and only for Royalty, but in your army you may do what the hell you like.'

On completion of my tour of duty in Mosul I returned once more to Kirkuk, which now had a new governor. He was Tahsin al-Askari, youngest of three brothers of which the most famous was Jafar Pasha, who had held many Cabinet portfolios, including that of Prime Minister, but whose favourite choice was Iraqi Ambassador at the Court of St James. The father had been a professional wrestler who came from the village of Askar in the district of Chamchemal, halfway between Kirkuk and Sulaimani, and it was from this village that the family name was taken. Jafar was a very large and powerful man: his brother Ali Rida Beg too was very large and in addition very fat. He was a Brigadier in the Iraqi Army, and his Sam Browne belt was as long as a horse's surcingle.[7] Presumably they both took after their father. The third brother, Tahsin al-Askari, was tall but not overweight. His twin sister was married to Nuri Pasha, whose sister in turn was married to Jafar. These two intermarried families were the pillars of Faisal's throne, and they were the founders of the Iraqi Army by whom,

---

7. Surcingle: an elasticated band round the girth area of a horse to hold a blanket.

188 · *Kurds, Arabs and Britons*

alas, both Jafar [October 1936] and Nuri [1958] were eventually murdered. Ali Rida was broken-hearted at the death of his brother and committed suicide [in 1936], and Tahsin was the only one to die of natural causes.

They were all very westernized and their wives mixed freely with the British community, though they were in purdah to all Iraqis whose wives were in purdah. Tahsin al-Askari was not over-endowed with good health or intelligence but he was very courageous, charming, fond of a party and working with him was a pleasure after Tahsin Ali. He was also a bridge player and the time passed all too quickly during his tenure of office. By this time, however, what with one thing and another, the British staff in the Iraqi government were getting less and less, so I had to supervise the Arbil Province once more in addition to that of Kirkuk; and it was while I was in double harness that, at the request of the Iraqi government, Sir Ernest Dowson came to study the land tenure in Iraq [1932]. He had wide experience of the subject and a high reputation in Egypt where he had put land tenure in order. He had also put into operation the Land Settlement in Palestine.

Iraq, being one of the most far-away provinces of the old Turkish empire, had never been properly surveyed, and the few land records in existence were extremely vague and bore little resemblance to the lands therein described. For example, as the Turkish land clerk could claim a fee for each title deed issued, he could and often did issue, say, 100 documents each, say, for 10 acres, instead of one document for 1,000 acres. No official might have ever visited the spot, much less surveyed it, and the boundaries recorded were generally fictitious and for purposes of identification practically useless, though for exploitation of a grossly exaggerated claim ideal. There were other deeds with boundaries from the river Tigris to the Persian mountains, presumably enclosing half a province.

In the past a Turkish official of exceptional zeal [Midhat Pasha, vali of Baghdad 1869–72] had done his best to found a land registry [in accordance with the Ottoman Land Code of 1858]; but Sultan Abdulhamid II, no doubt misinformed by some of his many spies, came to the conclusion that Nadhim Pasha [as vali of Baghdad 1910–11] was giving away crown lands and so had him waylaid and murdered on his return from leave in Istanbul.[8] The land register in Iraq was thus in a ghastly mess. Insoluble disputes cluttering up the courts, often leading to murder and its sequel of blood feuds, were of everyday occurrence. As the people had little or no

---

8. General Husain Nadhim Pasha was a Turkish military commander of great ability who was acting vali of Baghdad in 1907 and vali 1910–11. He was disliked by Sultan Abdul Hamid but was recalled in 1911 by the Young Turk CUP government and murdered in Istanbul in 1913, on the orders of Enver Pasha, not of the Sultan.

security of land tenure, other than their ability to defend it with their rifles, it can easily be understood what little progress had been made in agriculture. For who will dig a well, excavate an irrigation channel, plant a tree or build a decent house on land from which he may be evicted at the whim of any local tyrant?

Iraq was now [1932] almost at the end of the Mandatory period and it was obvious that the Iraqis would soon no longer tolerate British administrative officials. Technical officers only would be required in future.[9] It was also obvious that, with the growth of railways, roads and irrigation projects now possible from oil royalties, something drastic must be done to clear up the mess, enable compensation to be paid to the right owners, and provide security of tenure for all occupied land.

Sir Ernest sent round a complicated questionnaire to each province; and, after we had produced the answers and he had studied them, he followed up with a tour of each province where he investigated any outstanding items affecting any particular district. He then produced a scheme for land settlement, including definitions of various categories of land rights, legal sanctions and technical recommendations for survey. This was quickly incorporated in a new Law and it was decided to start field work in the autumn with three land settlement 'Lyjnas' or Commissions. The work would entail living in tents, and often in tribal areas riddled with blood feuds. For Iraqi officials it was a very [unattractive prospect], so volunteers were called for from British officers still serving; and that is how I became President [as a Land Settlement Officer] of No. 1 Land Settlement Commission.

I was due for leave in the coming summer and it was arranged for me to spend about three weeks on my way back in Palestine studying the working of the Land Settlement there before taking the field in autumn. I had served nearly three years since my last leave, and as [my wife] was expecting another child, I lost no time in sending her home in advance. This proved to be a wise precaution for just before then [in 1931] Shaikh Ahmad Barzani showed his resentment of the Arab Army in his country and drove them out.[10] There were times when he seemed to be moonstricken, renouncing the Moslem faith and eating pig like the Assyrian Christians. The Assyrian Levies had in the past been used by the government, or rather the British who were the Mandatory Power, to deal with

---

9. Details of the reduction of British staff are in Longrigg, *Iraq 1900–1950*, ch. 6. The number of British Administrative Inspectors was reduced from twenty-four in 1923 to ten in 1933. Longrigg lost his own job in 1931 after sixteen years in Iraq. Lyon's administrative post was transferred to an Iraqi national in 1932.

10. For details see McDowall, *A Modern History of Iraq*, pp. 178–80.

Kurdish uprisings; but they could not be used against the Shaikh of Barzan for they had once sheltered his brother from the wrath of the Turks; and, though he was subsequently caught and hanged, there remained a brotherhood between the Barzanis and Assyrians which made their employment undesirable. The Barzanis all wore red and black turbans and, though their loyalty towards Shaikh Ahmad was on religious ground, it was Mulla Mustafa his brother who was their leader in battle. There was nothing moon-stricken about him. He was one of those very few men who delight in battle for its own sake, and, as he afterwards confessed to me, he would much rather shoot Arab soldiers than either ibex or chikoor.

However, the government had decided [after the defeat of an Iraqi force in December 1931] to occupy Barzan and Bira Kapra, which was on the left bank of the Greater Zab on the direct track from Mosul and Aqra to Barzan. To approach this route, however, would entail a very steep climb in single file up the Aqra Dagh and then the Piris Dagh – both over 6,000 feet – and finally crossing the Greater Zab at Bira Kapra by ferry or raft, three formidable obstacles even if undefended. Instead the column assembled at Ruwandiz [in the spring of 1932] and marched up the Baradust sub-district through the Margasur (red meadow) valley, thus avoiding the two mountain staircases and the hazardous river crossing. The column was composed of Iraqi Army infantry and cavalry commanded by an Iraqi General and accompanied by two British Staff Officers of the Military Mission, Major Allfrey and Captain Mansergh, both of whom subsequently attained the rank of General in the Second World War. With them was Flight Lieutenant Pelly, the Special Service Officer, who afterwards became an Air Chief Marshal. Before they reached the boundary of the Mosul Province, however, Mulla Mustafa came down to meet them. From the heights on each side of the Margasur valley he subjected the column to a withering fire which caused confusion and panic. Practically all the transport carrying food, ammunition and blankets loaded on mules, was stampeded, and the morale of the troops broken. Had the Mulla and his men so wished they could have killed or captured most of the column, but with tribesmen it's the loot that matters; so they broke off the engagement and went home loaded with loot beyond their wildest dreams.

As soon as the news reached Baghdad, General Rowan Robinson, Chief of the Military Mission, immediately flew up from Baghdad to Ruwandiz and thence [went] by horse to join the column. Colonel Headlam, Chief Instructor of the Military College, and a close relation of the Bishop of Gloucester, was dispatched to Advanced Headquarters at Ruwandiz and a plane was sent from Baghdad to collect me. There I was appointed Political Officer of the column, with orders to report on the situation and make recommendations for the occupation of Barzan. Jafar Pasha, who was

Minister of Defence at the time, asked me what rank I would like to have while so employed. I replied that there was no rank in his army high enough for me, and if he would agree I would go in mufti, with the authority I had always had on various columns with British and Indian troops. In any case I was well known to both the troops and the Mulla so I anticipated no difficulty. To this he laughingly agreed.

When I reached Ruwandiz, however, Colonel Headlam took a very poor view of my old tweed coat and jodhpurs, so I had to remind him that I was talking to him as department to department and not as pip to pip [i.e. by army rank] – for I was then only a Captain though I had sixteen years' commissioned service; in any case on the present form of the Iraqi Army no one but a fool would accompany them in a decent suit.

On the way up to Margasur whom should I meet but General Rowan Robinson, popularly known as Row Row: a dear old gentleman and a very gallant officer. He had already been shot in the foot and was on his way back to hospital for treatment. This is how it happened. The troops were bogged down in action and he had tried to get them to advance. 'When I blow my whistle,' said he to the nearest Iraqi officer, 'we will all advance. So please pass the word along to all the men.' 'But, sir,' said the officer, 'it is very dangerous and if we advance we will be shot.' 'Never mind that,' said Row Row, 'just tell your men to advance when they hear the whistle.' After that Row Row blew his whistle and advanced. He was the only one to do so and had gone only a few paces when he was shot in the ankle. As the sole target he had drawn the enemy fire. When he had crawled back the officer said, 'There, sir, what did I tell you? It's far too dangerous.'

After greeting Row Row I went ahead and reached Margasur village, and there I dropped Hurmez, my Chaldean servant who had succeeded Mohammed. He wept for me as I went on with a couple of mounted police and my kit on a pack mule for there was the sound of distant firing. A few miles on I met the cavalry regiment in brisk retreat with a few distant snipers speeding them on their way. They had been sent back as unsuitable in such hilly country. Later I came up with the column, which had dug in for the night. The two Britishers told me that the reverse was due to the failure of a flank guard on the high ground, which resulted in the Mulla's men cutting the tail off the column, thus getting away with most of the transport and stores. The rearguard had likewise failed to react. It is well known in military circles that, without special training, plainsmen tend to get scared in the mountains, just as mountaineers feel naked in the plain, and this was a typical example. It had been decided to push on again as soon as adequate supplies had been dropped by the RAF, to use a troop of the well-trained Arbil mounted police as advance guard, and to march only under continuous air cover.

In the middle of the night I was awakened by much rifle and machine-gun fire. It was early spring, and we were at a fairly high altitude and I was very cold. Neither I nor the two British officers could hear any hostile bullets coming in, and so they went around the position trying to stop the firing while I went to visit the police. It was the same old trick as practised in the North West Frontier of India. A couple of snipers sent for the purpose of disturbing the whole camp by firing an occasional shot and thereby getting unsteady troops to fire back, depriving everybody of sleep and wasting precious ammunition. I found the police in good heart under their inspector. Many of them had been in escapades with me before and they gave me a good welcome.

As soon as the troops were re-equipped the column proceeded onwards and [in June 1932] reached its objective without further opposition. The RAF kept a continuous air umbrella over the marching column, and in addition dropped many bombs – some of them of the delayed action kind – in the Barzani village, making life so difficult that in the end the Shaikh came in to make his submission.[11]

My next job was to site and organize the building of police posts by contractors in suitable positions within hello and Aldous lamp communication of each other, and for this purpose I moved about independently with a small escort of about one section of mounted police, though the troops never went out in less than one company strength and then always with air cover.

While I was engaged in these operations the government brought out its own notes and coinage to take the place of Indian rupees which up to then had been current in Iraq. Instead we now had a dinar, based on the pound sterling and of equivalent value, but divisible by 1,000, the units of which were called fils. This was of course an excellent idea for the government, but the people had now been used to rupee notes and coinage for about nineteen years and country people are very conservative, especially in outposts of Kurdistan, where advance notification had not as yet penetrated. As a result the hired transport employed by the troops refused

---

11. McDowall, *A Modern History of Iraq*, p.179, says that Shaikh Ahmad surrendered to Turkish troops on the frontier. Mulla Mustafa continued to fight until June 1933, when he submitted after the RAF had destroyed most of the Barzani villages. Both brothers were then exiled within Iraq. There was a further Barzani rising in 1934–35 led by Khalil Khushawi, which demonstrated the inability of the Iraqi Army to deal with tribal risings without the help of the RAF. In 1943 Mulla Mustafa re-entered Barzan and raised a revolt, demanding the fulfilment of earlier Iraqi pledges to the Kurds. After two years of negotiations he was eventually defeated by the Iraqi Army in 1945, after which he moved to Iran to establish the Mahabad Republic. He remained a leader of Kurdish nationalism until his death in the 1970s.

payment in the new money and threatened to strike unless paid in rupees – a procedure which would hamstring the whole operation. I therefore hastened down to Advance Headquarters in Ruwandiz and called a meeting. Among the hired caravan drivers were some who had been on the column with me in 1924 and who had ended up well in the money and with fair compensation for casualties to man, mule and camel when I paid them off at Altun Kopru. So I addressed myself to them in particular and asked if they had a fair deal that time. Of course they knew me well and readily agreed; whereupon I explained the new coinage to them: how it was guaranteed by the British Treasury and how I was being paid in it, as indeed were all British officers in Iraq. After that they accepted, provided I handled the money as they hadn't all that much confidence in Iraqi officers paying out. So I was compelled to ask the Iraqi Commandant to hand over the pay rolls and cash and spent the next day settling all claims.

My task on the column was now completed; and as a telegram arrived with the news of [the birth of my elder son in July 1932] I lost no time in getting to Baghdad, where the government were still struggling to get the new currency accepted. Then to Beirut where I caught a boat home.

The first night out when, arrayed in my dinner jacket, I was enjoying a couple of drinks in the first-class bar, preparatory to dinner, whom should I meet but Colonel Headlam. He was in a very seedy old suit in which he had crossed the desert and looked it. 'Good evening, Colonel,' said I. 'Are you going home steerage on the cheap? Come and join me in a drink, and if the steward makes a fuss I'll say you are my guest.' The Colonel lost no time in telling me that he was travelling first-class, but his kit had been mislaid by the travel agents and he had nothing but the suit he was now wearing. The wheel of fortune had turned full circle. I could afford to be generous with him and we were quite friendly for the rest of the voyage.

CHAPTER 10

Baghdad: Land Settlement in Kut and Kirkuk, 1932–33

§ MY leave passed all too quickly for I never took the full amount to which I was entitled but took the cash instead ... I arranged for [my wife] and family to return by boat while I went ahead to do a course in Land Settlement in Palestine before returning to Iraq ... On arrival at Jerusalem I presented my official introduction to the Director of Land Settlement who kindly organized my course, which covered surveying in the field, law court procedure and land registration. I visited a number of Jewish settlements and studied their way of life which for the majority was communal ...

On arrival at Baghdad I leased a house in the Rakhaita suburb from Muzahim al-Pachachi. It was a newly built house about half a mile south of the Alwieh Club, which was the centre of Baghdad society with rose gardens, tennis and squash courts, billiards, bar, ballroom, and a limited number of residential chambers. It was convenient for the family, and the house was on the road to Kut and so enabled me to reach the scene of my new work without having to pass through the city. Our landlord, though his name derived from the word, 'sheep's trotter seller', was a cultivated lawyer who had previously been Iraqi Minister in London. He was a great advocate of free speech and told me how he often went to Hyde Park on Sundays, sometimes taking his own soap box and performing in English. He was much impressed by the courtesy of the London police and the London crowds in general, and so far as we were concerned he was a satisfactory landlord.

There is no point in describing here the technicalities of land settlement, including as it does cadastral maps, Moslem laws of land tenure and inheritance, the legal categories of land, and such like. There were three commissions headed by [Captain A. H.] Ditchburn, [Captain C. C.] Aston and myself, each provided with an assistant, a land registry clerk, a court clerk, a typist and a survey party.[1] The other two commissions were on the right bank of the Tigris and we lived in tents for about nine months of the year. For the other three months we hired a house in Baghdad to complete all paperwork, for during that period the heat was so intense that it was impossible to make any survey fixing except for about an hour or so after dawn, and office work in tents was so uncomfortable as not to be worthwhile. All work, including correspondence, was in Arabic and before we set forth the Minister gave us a lecture on the new Law and told us to be generous in our interpretation of it. Friday was the official holiday and usually I left one clerk in charge for that day and took as many of the staff as my car would hold to Baghdad for the weekend.

The sub-district allotted to me was Aziziya on the left bank of the Tigris about half way to Kut-al-Amara, the scene of our defeat in 1916. I had been there before for a short time with my regiment in early 1918 when we were constructing a railway line from Kut to Baghdad, but this had since been taken up after the Armistice and the only place I could recall was the ancient arch of Ctesiphon and the derelict Nahrwan Canal about 3 miles east of the river where I used to shoot ducks for our officers' mess.

Now, however, I had to make a detailed study of the Arabs living there, their mode of life and cultivation, and above all the way of the river Tigris, without which there would have been nothing at all. Up till now I had always supposed that rivers flowed in the lowest part of a valley but to a certain extent the Tigris was an exception to the rule. The Tigris valley is completely composed of alluvial soil carried down from the mountains since the world began. There isn't a single pebble to be seen nearer than the foothills which form the Persian frontier. After rain, and especially when the snow melts on the mountains, the Tigris comes down like thick brown pea soup and, as the water reaches the flat area south of the Jabal Hamrin, its speed slackens and the silt is dropped raising the river bed ever higher every year. When it is about to overflow its banks the cultivators and city dwellers frantically work to strengthen the banks. Sometimes it overflows and forms a marsh, but again dropping its silt and leaving the bed of the marsh higher when the spate is over. Then the cultivators and city dwellers repair the breach; and so it goes on year after year, resulting in the Tigris flowing on top of a low self-made ridge instead of in the lowest ground, which might be as much as three miles from the river bank. The river is thus in a state of unstable equilibrium and a

---

1. Longrigg, *Iraq 1900–1950*, p. 214, says that R. F. Jardine was a fourth Land Settlement Officer, and Lyon later (p. 211) also mentions that there were four officers. All had been Political Officers and Administrative Advisers.

potential danger during every flood season. As an example, during the flood season our house, though a quarter of a mile from the Tigris, had 4 feet of water in the cellar. Had the dyke given way we would have had 15 feet of water over our garden and the city would have been submerged. So far as this affected the rights of land tenure there was a clash of purpose between the city dwellers and modern cultivators on the one hand and the original inhabitants of the area ... The rainfall south of the Jabal Hamrin was never enough to grow a crop except in occasional depressions where the water might collect and provide enough moisture for a very sketchy crop of barley. But with the advent of fuel oil at less than two pence a gallon the alert citizens of the towns, seizing an opportunity to get rich quick, invested in power pumps and erected them all along the banks of the river. There were hundreds of them, of horse power ranging from 50 hp to 300 hp, so many in fact that it was a wonder any water was left in the Tigris, and I doubt if there would have been but for seepage back underground. Once the water had been pumped over the bank it flowed gently along the distribution channels of the irrigation system back to about 3 miles from the bank. This cultivation was the basis of the land claims by the pump owners, and it was in their interests to keep the dykes intact, else their crops would be inundated, their distribution channels ruined.[2]

But before all this had happened there were the local inhabitants to consider. In Aziziya they were an off-shoot of the Beduin Shammar, who had crossed the Tigris more than a hundred years before and lived a precarious existence between the Tigris and the Persian foothills. They were called Shammar Toga. Originally a nomadic shepherd tribe, they had by degrees indulged in a little cultivation of a sort. Their first efforts, not yet superseded, probably dated from Noah's time. Without plough or even mattock they sprinkled seed in the mud cracks at the edge of a marsh, went on their way and returned when the barley crop was ripe. They liked marshes for they were invaluable obstacles to police, government sheep counters, revenue collectors and such like unwelcome intruders, and they proved even more efficient in holding up wheel traffic. So from their point of view a breach in the dyke was most welcome, indeed they were frequently guilty of making one.

In addition to this haphazard cultivation, called '*chibbis*', they occasionally erected a water lift, constructed from a couple of palm tree trunks with a cross-piece for axle and a wheel over which was a rope and a sheepskin bucket, powered by a camel, donkey, or even a woman if the

---

2. On the introduction of pumps and their economic and social effects, see S. Haj, *The Making of Iraq 1900–1963* (Albany, NY, 1997) esp. pp. 47–8.

owner were very poor. Some of them had a wooden plough drawn by a single pony, or even by a donkey and a woman yoked together – an offence against the Mosaic law even graver than that of yoking an ox with an ass. Such a contraption would serve not more than half an acre of millet at most, and usually much less, and they seldom chose the same spot twice. That was about the best any of them could do on his own: the remainder helped out their nomadic existence by working on the pump owners' location for a small share in the harvest. Nevertheless there was no denying they were the original inhabitants and loudly they clamoured for their rights in the whole area which, with a very few exceptions, was state land as yet unalienated, and now within my power to allocate.

This was indeed a problem requiring much patient inquiry if injustice was to be avoided, for it couldn't be denied that the 'wide boys' from the city with their power pumps were vastly increasing the productivity of the area. I could not forget the absentee landlords, the land hunger of the people, and the cruelty to man and beast that resulted from boycotting in Ireland when I was ... a boy. True the Shammar Toga were very poor types and expert liars, and whatever one did was open to criticism, but a decision had to be made. That was what I was there for.

So I kept in mind the Minister's advice; and after hearing all the evidence I allocated to each who had anything approaching a bona fide claim about five times as much as he was capable of cultivating in any one year, situated on the river bank approximately where they had previously cultivated. Where this fell in an area now under power pump I rewarded the pump owner with an extra amount of equivalent area at the tails of his holding. The remainder I registered in the name of the government. This enabled the Shammar Toga to continue with their primitive methods with reasonable room for expansion if they so desired, though I was pretty certain that in spite of my warning they would sell their birth rights for a mess of pottage after I had passed on.

I gave all judgments on the spot and offered to advise and help any who wished to appeal. Strange to relate, however, they all took it well – from the wealthy Mayor of Baghdad, who had a big holding, down to the poorest pair of brothers who had established a claim ... When the first of these brothers made his application, claiming for himself and his brother, I told him to go and fetch his brother so that both could put their thumb marks on the document. He replied that he was unable to bring him. When I asked why he said, 'We have only one "dish dash" [an ankle-length shirt] between us and I am now wearing it. But I will go and give it to him and he will then come and put his mark.'

In this, my first assignment as a Land Settlement Officer, I was very fortunate, for afterwards another officer, settling the next sub-district, was so overcome with the Arabs' tumult that he only issued his decisions in the comparative calm and safety of a Baghdad office after he had completed all the cases and withdrawn from the area. Among the few who had title deeds to be investigated was Daud Daghistani. He was a handsome Circassian gentleman with fair complexion, a steely blue eye and a white lambskin kalpak, the traditional headgear of Circassians. He was a very prominent racehorse owner and his father, famous for his physical strength and courage, had been killed by a British shell as a General while besieging General Townshend's force in Kut-al-Amara. This was one of the places I had to visit during the course of my work as Aziziya lay in the Kut Province.

It was most depressing to see the extensive British military cemetery just outside the town. Nearly all [were] youngsters of the Devons, Dorsets, Oxford and Bucks Regiments, cut off in the flower of their youth. Close by stood the memorial to their opponent, General Daghistani. I am glad to record, however, that when I eventually left Iraq in 1944 his grandson, true to type, was a most promising young General in the Iraqi Army.

... I finished all the field work by the end of June [1933], packed up the camp and withdrew to an office in Baghdad shared by the three of us, and there completed the paperwork for the season in which the sub-district of about thirty-odd villages or centres contained an area of about 130 square miles.

Seeing that I was engaged in this work for the next eight years I [will] mention the various successive stages in which the work was carried out.

1. Passing of the Land Settlement Act [1932].
2. Notification by the Minister in the Gazette, and in local government offices affected, of the sub-districts in which the law was to be implemented.
3. Survey of astronomical points in the area as a base for the cadastral maps.
4. Notification by President of the Commission to each successive mukhtar or village headman that the cadastral survey would commence on a fixed date, and all claimants to be instructed to accompany the surveyor and indicate the boundaries of plots claimed by them.
5. On completion of survey of claims the headman is notified of the day on which inspection and hearing of claims will commence.
6. All village boundaries investigated and proved.
7. All boundary disputes of plots are investigated and settled.
8. All legal disputes investigated and settled.
9. Maps with all plots numbered sent to Survey Office for reproduction.
10. Results published on noticeboard and in all local government offices.

11. After [a] forty-day period for submission of appeals to the High Court the land is registered.
12. Title deeds and maps available for sale at a nominal fee from the Land Registry Office in Baghdad. Apart from small stamp duty on all documents submitted, the proceedings from start to finish were free.[3]

During that summer of 1933 there was a massacre of men, women and children, all Assyrians, in the village of Simel [Simayl] about 40 miles north-east of Mosul. This unprovoked attack was carried out by the Iraqi Army, and soon afterwards about 800 Assyrians attacked the Iraq Army camp on the slopes of the neighbouring mountain south-east of the junction of the Tigris and Kharbur rivers. It was unsuccessful; and so the Assyrians, once more on the march, collected their goods and chattels, crossed the Tigris and went across the Syrian frontier to Hassech, where the French settled them. It was a dreadful thing to happen in the first year of Iraqi Independence, though worse was to follow. King Faisal was in Switzerland at the time undergoing a health cure when he died suddenly in September. His body was flown to Baghdad airport, and among other officials I had to go to his funeral. It was a very hot day, the arrangements were muddled, the cortège late, and the river being low, there was a steep slope down to the boat bridge, where the gun carriage took charge, ran over and killed an Iraqi Major and all but jettisoned the coffin into the Tigris.

Along the 3-mile route to the Royal Tomb at Adhamieh the roofs were lined with wailing women, the streets thick with dust and flies. After a stop and start endurance of about two hours I found myself suddenly amid the Kurdish chiefs of Arbil. They said they had had enough of it and were going off for a cool drink. There was no knowing when it would end as we had made so little progress, and in such a disorganized mob I didn't see how I could be missed; so with them I slipped off down a side street and eventually reached home. This was to signal the end of another era ...

Having completed my task in the Kut Province I was now appointed to investigate and clarify all land rights in the oil fields of Kirkuk. The oil was now coming into production and the company were all the time probing further and further, building more roads, well-heads and camps all over the place and required definition of land rights in order to know whom to compensate. My sympathies were always with the Kurds and I was glad to leave a flat uninteresting country populated by a miserable lot of Shammar Toga ...

---

3. See Haj, *The Making of Iraq 1900–1963*, pp. 49–51 for a critique of the land settlement policy of the 1932–58 period.

Back in Kirkuk I was on my home ground and had a warm welcome alike from the notables and Petroleum Company officials. The Mayor at once found me a house; it was the same one in which all the Political Officers, including myself, had formerly lived and now I was back again full circle ...

At that time the proved oil field extended from Baba Gurgur – site of the first well – to the Lesser Zab, though afterwards it spread north-westwards half way to the Greater Zab, and south-eastwards to the foot-hills of Qarahassan; and I pitched my camp 25 miles out on the river bank and worked inwards towards the city. For what more definite boundary could one wish for than a swift river running through rocky gorges, with excellent fishing, and a plentiful variety of wild fowl and game birds? ...

This was a district having enough rainfall for wheat and barley crops without any irrigation. The cultivation was done with mule-drawn ploughs and of a much better standard than in the Kut Province. Most of the land was unalienated but with pockets here and there covered by old Turkish title deeds, and all except the steepest hilltops was under the plough. There was no fortification of the soil with manure, chemical or natural; instead, after the harvest, the stubble was ploughed in and left to fallow for a year or two. In villages adjacent to the river animal manure was used to grow melons, elsewhere it was used as fuel. The Company had made an excellent road by which I could get home for the weekends ...

This tour passed very pleasantly. I was no longer concerned in probing the administration, bullying or cajoling Iraqi governors into following an honest and impartial procedure now that the Mandate had run its course. I was quite free from the contamination of politics and the accompanying intrigue. Indeed, now that I was no longer vested with administrative authority, I found myself not infrequently consulted by governors with whom I had previously worked. There was nothing secret or confidential about my work. I had a definite and positive objective. It was to clear the land of all disputes and to grant official recognition to all cultivators who had earned it by their labour, and thereby give them legal security of tenure which could not be upset at the whim of any tyrant great or small. I was well known to all the people, impatient for the coming of my commission, and there were always representatives from neighbouring villages and districts watching the proceedings against the time when it would be their turn. Though I had no police the bitterest blood feuds over land and water rights presented no personal menace for they knew I could not be bribed, and I had a rule against all litigants and their supporters bearing arms in my presence. This was easy to enforce for, on the slightest sign of contempt of court – even though held in the open field round a plane table – I would threaten to pack up and move on to the next village, leaving them to brawl to their hearts' content. This invariably brought them to heel, for to be left out when everyone else was getting free title deeds was more than they could bear.

Usually I would pitch our tents at a central village from which the surveyors would map the surrounding villages; and as the claims were completed on the map, I would visit, clear all disputes, register all bona fide claims in the name of their occupiers and the remainder in the name of the government. There might be anything up to 500 or 600 plots in a village and in a season anything up to fifty villages might be completed. Sometimes there was a lot of arithmetic in working out the shares in land inherited from a grandparent, especially when, as was customary among Moslem farmers, they had a full quota of wives. In such cases the lowest common denominator might run to six figures to enable every descendant to receive his or her correct share.

Usually the camp would be in one village for at least a month, during which time one got to know everyone and all about them down to the most intimate details of their lives, such as the bride price of each unmarried maiden. I had a radio set which could get all the world news in Arabic from the BBC. This was a great attraction to the locals who were always free to listen. I also taught some of the clerical staff and the surveyors how to play bridge, and on occasions, with the help of [my wife], we played a team of the Oil Company. The people I found most friendly, my staff gave of their best and never grumbled at long hours if I considered it advisable to complete a village rather than come again another day for only an hour's work. We were a happy team ...

[In the summer of 1934 Lyon and his family returned to England on leave, now with a third child.]

CHAPTER II

Kirkuk: The Army Coup and Revolution, 1934–41

§ ON the expiry of my leave [late in 1934] I returned to Iraq and my task of land settlement ... I had rented a house in the Sarikahia quarter of Kirkuk, though, except for the three hottest months in the year, I lived out in camp and only came home at weekends, taking with me any of the staff who wanted to rejoin their families. They were now in proper training and carried out their various duties without the fuss and confusion so common to those who are unused to camp life with its hazards and periodic changes of scene. We were a happy team and the work progressed without a hitch. Altogether the next two years [1934–36] were among the most peaceful during my service, away from all administrative responsibility and political intrigue ...

I had not been long in Kirkuk when [in 1936] I got an order from the Minister of Justice to proceed with my staff to Diwanya – 100 miles south of Baghdad on the Euphrates river. This was both unexpected and unwelcome for I had been detailed to clear all disputes and issue title deeds to holders of all lands in the oil fields area, which by now had expanded to Chamchemal in the Sulaimani province and across the Lesser Zab into the Arbil province. I also knew that Diwanya was at that time the most lawless area in Iraq as well as being climatically the most unpleasant in which to live or work. The inhabitants were all Arabs of the ... Shia sect and the country all round was a veritable dust bowl. The lands were irrigated from the Euphrates and their rights, present and future, had been promised by successive ministers first to one faction and then to another. It was rather like Palestine, as the rival factions hated each other almost as much as the Arabs hated the Jews. There was an Iraqi Army garrison in the town, which at that time dared not move outside in less than battalion strength. As for police they could not go out at all. Under such conditions of insecurity it was obviously impossible to send forth my court messengers and surveyors to prepare the people for the advent of my Land Settlement Commission, so I decided to go ahead to Baghdad and ask the Minister for an explanation of his order which I considered impossible to carry out.

He was a Shia from these parts and was only too well aware of local conditions: he was also a very frightened little man. I asked him why he had picked on me rather than Ditchburn, who had lived there for years as a Political Officer and afterwards as Administrative Inspector, or even Aston, who had also great experience of these people, having served for years in the Euphrates area. But all the Minister would say was that it was a direct order from the Prime Minister, Yasin Pasha al-Hashimi, so off I went to see him.

Now Yasin Pasha had fought against us to the end as a Brigadier in the Turkish Army. He was no supporter of King Faisal, as were Jafar Pasha, Nuri Pasha and Jamil al-Midfai, who had all deserted the Turkish cause and joined in the Arab revolt under Faisal. I had not met him till 1933, when his farm in the Aziziya sub-district was among those I settled. He was not in power at that time but I had found him very reasonable and, unlike most of the Arab officials, he had the unmistakable manner and bearing of an army officer. So now I decided to make a direct approach, asking his reasons without making any of the preliminary passes which are usual in such interviews. He was quite frank, explaining how he had picked on me as a disciplined military officer trained to carry out orders. The fact that I knew none of these people would be all the better as a surprise and shock to them. He knew I could accomplish no real or honest settlement of their tangled affairs under the conditions at present prevailing in the area. He confessed that he was being chased and pestered by these warring factions and, to get respite, was often driven to seek refuge in the Alwieh Club, a British-founded club of which he was a member. For among the Arabs there was no such things as being 'Not at Home', which was an English convention and a polite way of saying one was not receiving visitors. 'And now,' said he, 'please go to Diwaniya. Publish all the official notifications about Land Settlement. Make a diversion there and keep them off my back! I can assure you that your professional reputation will not suffer. I know well you can't really do any settlement. You will only have to stay there a very short time I can assure you.' I could see he was hard pressed, but I little knew just how hard when I agreed and took my leave.

That same day by chance I met Vyvyan Holt, the Oriental Secretary to the British Ambassador [Sir Archibald Clark Kerr],[1] We had known each

---

1. From 1932 and the end of the Mandate the High Commissioner was replaced by an Ambassador, though he remained in the Residency and continued to have considerable influence.

other for years from the time when [H. A.] Goldsmith was Political Officer in Sulaimani in 1921. He [Holt] pressed me to come and have lunch as he considered the Ambassador ought to meet someone who was in daily contact with the people, especially as there was great unrest on the Euphrates. I reminded him that he knew quite well my views on the succession of Ambassadors we had had – one and all preceded by press advertisement and all subsequently proved uninterested in either the Iraqis or the British community outside their very restricted circle of toadies.[2] I had long since ceased to be impressed by their state functions and I'd rather not come. However, he told me there would be no one but himself and HE at lunch and insisted on my coming, so to please him I agreed. During the lunch Vyvyan brought the conversation round to local politics, which at that time were very unstable. I asked the Ambassador how he found the Iraqi politicians, and to my surprise he replied that, as he found Yasin Pasha the PM and Nuri Pasha, the Minister of Interior, were playing ball with him, he didn't bother about anyone else. To this I remarked that on past performance since Iraq [became] independent, political changes were apt to be frequent and sudden, but there were about two dozen prominent men in the country out of which all future Cabinets could be formed, irrespective of party, and by knowing these one would be familiar with any Cabinet that could govern the country.[3] The conversation then turned to chikoor shooting, which the Ambassador wished to try out in the Kurdish Hills; and that is roughly what I remember of the lunch talk. I made my adieu, collected my staff and office and camp furniture, and boarded the train for Diwaniya.

On arrival [20 October 1936] I leased an office in the town, camped in the garden with my staff and proceeded to issue the usual proclamations to all concerned. This was something quite new to the locals, and soon some of the faction leaders came cavorting in to find out all about it. I took care to explain the procedure and emphasized how important it was for all those seeking to establish their land rights to appear when called and to submit all the documents they had in support of their claims. They

---

2. Longrigg, *Iraq 1900–1950*, p. 226 lists the Ambassadors from 1932 to 1951. Only one, Sir Kinahan Cornwallis (1941–45), had any previous direct experience in Iraq, and one, Sir Basil Newton (1939–41), had no experience of any part of the Middle East. The crisis of 1941 might have been averted if he had been more knowledgeable and had acted more effectively.

3. For a list of Iraq's short-lived ministries from 1920 to 1958 see M. Khadduri, *Independent Iraq 1932–1958. A Study in Iraqi Politics* (London, 1951; 2nd rev. edn, London, 1960) pp. 370–2. Lyon's comment on the small political class and the brevity of their tenure of office is fully supported by M. A. Tarbush, *The Role of the Military in Politics: A Case Study of Iraq to 1941* (London, 1982), ch. 3.

would also be obliged to accompany the surveyors and mark out their claims.

In fact, however, I found the situation even worse than I expected and I had no intention of sending out any surveyors to get shot, still less of going myself. However I made a brave show with all the preliminary paperwork and had the satisfaction of knowing that I was at any rate keeping the litigants away from Baghdad and off the Prime Minister's doorstep. He had promised me it would not be for long, nor was it.

Only about ten days after my arrival in Diwaniya news came of a military coup d'état [on 30 October 1936] by General Bakr Sidqi, who had marched to Baghdad with his division of troops and taken over the city after the [Iraqi] Air Force had dropped bombs on the serai, or government headquarter offices. Yasin Pasha the PM had fled to Damascus, where he died the following year, and Nuri Pasha had taken refuge with the RAF at their base in Habbaniyah, from whence he flew to Jordan. His brother-in-law Jafar Pasha, founder of the Iraqi Army and now Minister of Defence, had gone out to meet the troops on the road to Baquba and reason with them, but he was murdered for his pains. His brother, Brigadier Ali Rida, on hearing the news, committed suicide; and neither the British Military Mission nor the British Ambassador had an inkling of what was afoot. I have often since wondered what he thought when the two Ministers who played ball so well with him that he didn't bother about any others had fled the country.

This was a serious state of affairs, but it was not without its amusing side. [C. J.] Edmonds, who was then Adviser to the Minister of Interior, on hearing the bombs drop around his office in the serai, got into his car and proceeded homewards. But just before he got to the serai gate whom should he see but the poor pedlar of matches, cigarettes and sweets. He was lying on the ground and the blood was spurting out from an artery which had been cut by a bomb splinter. Like a good Samaritan he pulled up, dumped him in the car and delivered him at the hospital, which was close by, and resumed his journey. Had he not acted swiftly the poor man would have died, and Edmonds naturally thought he had done a good act and that the man would be grateful. But to his dismay he found that the man had adopted him as a father. From then onwards he was held responsible for every misfortune that overtook the pedlar, and there were many, for he was a poor salesman, a worse husband and a prolific and feckless father. In fact he became a nuisance to Edmonds until the end of his service.[4]

---

4. There is a detailed account of the coup and his own experiences in October 1936 in Edmonds's diary. See Edmonds Papers, Box 27/1 pp. 555-67. But there is no mention there of this anecdote. For detailed analysis of the coup see Tarbush, *The Role of the Military*, ch. 6.

For a day or two there was chaos with the accompanying disorder and looting of the Jews before Bakr Sidqi set up Hikmat Sulayman as Prime Minister. As Yasin Pasha had fled there was no longer any reason for me to distract the Diwaniya tribal leaders, so I packed up my outfit and returned with them to Kirkuk, where I reported to the new Minister of Justice that I had resumed my former task in the oil fields.

From now it was obvious that whoever had the army's support would rule the country. The young officers were impatient for power; and although agriculture and trade were prospering, increasing oil revenues prudently controlled, and funds earmarked for vast irrigation projects, yet the government never again had the same air of security, though [this] did not directly affect my work. No doubt the government lacked the skilful diplomacy of King Faisal, now dead, and his British advisers sacked by his son King Ghazi, who was of a very different type. King Faisal had been brought up among the Beduin of the Hijaz and educated at the Court of the Sultan of Turkey. He knew his Arabs and treated them always with patience and respect. With his British advisers he was a skilful and courteous diplomat. By contrast the young King ... lacked his father's manners, patience and understanding of the Arab tribesmen, discarding the Iraqi officials who had served his father in favour of his young military favourites. Indeed it was a mercy he did not survive till the outbreak of the 1939 war: had he done so history might have been quite different and certainly worse for the Allies.

But I must not anticipate: suffice it to say that the administration carried on uneasily till the following August 1937, when Bakr Sidqi was murdered in the officers' mess in the Iraqi Air Force station at Mosul. The assassin was never brought to justice and it was common knowledge that it was in revenge for the murder of Jafar Pasha. This was the signal for a second military coup d'état. Hikmat Sulaiman's Cabinet fell [16 August 1937] and Jamil al-Midfai reigned in his stead [until 25 December 1938]. From now onwards Iraq was in a state of political instability. From the beginning the elections had always been cooked and there was no way of changing the government other than by revolution. It soon became apparent that the army was the decisive factor and whoever had its support would be political boss.

For my part I was thankful to be out of it all and living in camp as I did, doing work which was most popular and beneficial to the people. I soon found how friendly they were. I was welcomed in all their discussions whether on affairs of the family, economies or politics; and of the latter one thing was very certain: it was the growing influence of the German Minister [Dr Grobba], at the expense of our own. He was a proficient Arabic scholar, spared no expense in entertaining the politically important members of Baghdad society, and gave German trade such a boost that Krupp Harvesters became the index of local status. A religious shaikh, who previously was never seen out of his flowing robes, was now adorned in a boilersuit supplied with his Harvester, from which he proudly greeted all comers. It was the same with many other imports from Germany, not excluding their propaganda and culture. By 1938 Jamil al-Midfai's administration lost its popularity, and yet another military coup put Nuri Pasha into power as Prime Minister [25 December 1938] with Rashid Ali al-Gaylani as Palace Minister. My work was, however, free from political interference, and by now I had covered four sub-districts in Kirkuk and had started yet another across the Zab in the Arbil Province, to where the oil field now extended, so I went on leave during the summer of 1938 ...

[My wife] kept pressing me to buy a house in Cheltenham, to break away from my job and get employment at home. Thus the rest of my leave was spent between house-hunting – a sport which has never appealed to me – and job-hunting which was still more depressing.[5] In the end I bought a house [in Cheltenham] ... but jobs for my type [of person] I found most difficult to get. There is nothing more humiliating than to go round touting for a job, and my experiences of it completely eclipsed the joy of summer leave with my family at the seaside. The best I could land was a promise as a photographic officer in the RAF. It would mean living in some remote airfield in England at the lowest rank of pay, less British taxation, which up till then I had escaped, and without any married accommodation. This did not compare with my pay in Iraq, then over £2,000 plus army pension; and [I had] the knowledge that if war came, as seemed likely, then I could get recalled to the Indian Army [which I had left in 1935] with its higher rank, pay and allowances, offset only by much lower taxation at the Indian rate. There was also a reasonable if not good expectation that my long service and knowledge of conditions in the Middle East would make me of much more value to the army than if I started from scratch in the RAF, and in any case I knew very little about aerial photography. Thus after much deliberation I gave up the idea of living at home, bought a second-hand 8-cylinder Ford saloon in good condition for a little over £100, said goodbye to the family, and embarked with it on a ship bound for Haifa.

The voyage was uneventful but not the disembarkation, for this was when the Arab hatred of the Jewish immigration, controlled as it was by

---

5. Among the few surviving Lyon personal papers are a number of copies of references he had apparently obtained for these applications. All gave him the highest praise for his work in Iraq, for which he had been awarded an OBE.

the British authorities, was at its zenith.⁶ My car was dumped on the dockside, but there were no officials to deal with the usual formalities; and on inquiry I was told they were all Jews and had fled. There was the sound of distant rifle fire in the bazaar, but as there was no one in sight I couldn't be bothered to wait around indefinitely, so I got into the car and drove off to a hotel where I had frequently stayed on former visits. From there I telephoned George Dunkley, the general manager of the Iraq Petroleum Company, and asked him what it was all about, he being the best authority on intelligence, seeing that the Arabs in those days made a practice of blowing up the pipeline to show their disapproval of our policy. He said it was nothing to worry about. One of his staff would be grateful for a lift to Kirkuk, and would I come to dinner and arrange details? I accepted, being grateful for the company on such a long drive – about 700 miles – and after spending an enjoyable evening at the Dunkleys' house I started off at dawn the next morning. The Company's officer ... was familiar with the route, which was just as well for it was completely deserted except for a British Armoured Car patrol which we passed about 20 miles out. All normal traffic had apparently been scared off the road, so we batted along as fast as the car would go till we got to the bridge over the Jordan river. After that we did not expect to meet any landmines or ambushes and so cruised along for the rest of the day along the pipeline, reporting in at each pumping station passed, till we got to K3, where we spent the night in the Company's guest house. Next day we continued our journey into Iraq and, crossing both the Euphrates and Tigris by ferry, arrived in Kirkuk without incident.

In the absence of my family I invited the Survey Officer to live with me and thus share expenses. He was seconded from the British Army to instruct Iraqi surveyors, and he was now engaged in fixing the astronomical points on which the cadastral maps of [the] Land Settlement Commission would be based. His work being thus linked with mine, we lived in harmony and most of our weekends (Thursday night to Saturday morning) were spent together, shooting or fishing according to the season ...

It was when I was camped at Altun Kopru, with the work progressing smoothly, the crops ripening nicely and the people happy, that suddenly the news broke that the young King Ghazi was dead [3 April 1939]. The manner of his sudden death was not published for several days, which I now feel was a mistake, for in countries where mass hysteria is common it is better to publish the truth at once, however unpalatable, than to allow time for false rumours by holding it back. In fact, when very drunk, he

---

6. In 1938 there was intense Arab opposition to the proposal of the Peel Commission of 1937 for the partition of Palestine and the creation of a small Jewish state.

had got into his car with his black slave and driven it full tilt at speed into an electric power standard.

The next thing I heard was that the Mosul rabble had attacked the British Consulate and stoned the Consul to death. I was shocked at this news; and as the next day was Friday I decided to go at once to Mosul instead of Kirkuk. My staff tried to dissuade me, I believe from genuine anxiety about my safety, and the local notables joined in, though I was not quite so sure whether their interest lay in the fact that I had not quite completed the settlement of all their land disputes. However, disregarding them all, I set off that evening and arriving in Mosul without incident, stayed with the RAF Intelligence Officer whose house was not more than 50 yards from the scene of the crime.

It had all started as a result of a rumour put out by the German Minister in Baghdad [Dr Grobba] that the British were responsible for the young King's death. His agent in Mosul had whipped up a crowd of coolies working on the railway to a fanatical fury and [they] marched down to the Consulate, which was one of several isolated houses in open ground about half a mile south of the city. The Consul, Mr Monk Mason, was an elderly and kindly man, respected by his Arab neighbours for allowing all and sundry to draw water from the tap in his back yard. Being quite unaware of what was afoot he came down to meet them. He was immediately set upon and ... stoned to death. The telephone line had been disconnected and none of his British neighbours was able to get in touch with the police, who must have been well aware of what was happening and no doubt had been bribed to delay action till it was too late. The ground was still littered with paper out of the looted Consulate; and as I surveyed the scene my thoughts went back twenty years when an anti-racial riot started in Mosul – in this case against the Assyrians – and station house officer Mullroy, ex-sergeant of the Liverpool Dock Police, went forth single-handed and, with fists large as legs of mutton, cleared everybody off the street except for those whom he left knocked out in the gutter.

How our prestige must have fallen in those twenty years! It was obviously a put-up show and boded ill for the future. We were to have further proof of the German Minister's machinations in the defection of Rashid Ali the following year ... The Iraqi government, of course, made all the diplomatic apologies required of them, including £20,000 compensation to the Consul's widow; but Hitler's propaganda was both unceasing and increasing and, ably supported by the German Minister, was not without its reactions on the extreme Nationalists who wished to make a complete break with the British connection. Yet our Embassy was apparently indifferent to what was going on. Thus the uneasy months passed till the outbreak of war [3 September 1939] when I naturally applied to return to the Indian Army. But then the British Embassy intervened, and as a result orders were received that all officers should remain at their posts where it was considered they would be of most use to the war effort: Nuri Pasha [Prime Minister], under British pressure, broke off relations with Germany, and though few if any thought that Iraq would be even remotely involved, it was considered a friendly gesture suitable to Iraq's status as an ally.

After the Polish campaign hostilities went off the boil: the Western Front settled down to a passive sort of defensive trench warfare which was labelled by the Americans the 'Phoney War', with the French in the Maginot line and our forces covering the left flanks from where it ended at the Belgian frontier to the sea. As for me, there was nothing for it but to stick to my job and [my wife] courageously came out with the two boys by the Simplon Orient express. Life went on as usual ... till the beginning of the hot weather in 1940 when I took all the local leave due to me and went with the family to Lebanon to find a cool refuge for the children.

It was just about then [May 1940] that the Germans broke through; and on reaching Rutba – the last post in Iraq – we heard that the Italians had declared war [11 June 1940]. We pushed on, but at the first checkpoint in Syria the French arrested our driver. This was most awkward for there we were, about twenty-five people and a few children, in the desert without a driver for our coach: but after considerable delay and much heated argument they brought him back and let us proceed to Beirut with a gendarme by his side. From Beirut we took a taxi to Ainzehalta where we stayed in the Hotel Victoria. The hotel was comfortable, the food, service, mountain scenery and cool breezes were all satisfactory, but every day the news got worse till the French surrendered [22 June 1940]. The situation in the Middle East had now completely changed for the Grande Armée de l'Orient, with headquarters at Beirut, on which such great hopes were based, became completely disorganized. In the crowded cafés of Beirut the officers could be seen gesticulating like Arabs as they debated among themselves what to do, and in the end the vast majority opted for Vichy. The only troops to maintain any semblance of military bearing were the Moroccan Spahis, who still carried out their duties in a smart and soldierly manner.

For us too the situation had changed, for England was now in danger and, with [my daughter] at home, [my wife] determined to join her. And now that the front had crumbled I had no great confidence in the stability of Iraq, so I had perforce to agree. The Simplon Orient line was now out of action and all my efforts to get a passage home for her and the [children] from Beirut either by air or sea were fruitless. I could not stay on indefinitely in the Lebanon, so arranged for the British Consul to keep in touch with [my wife] and I returned to Baghdad, where I renewed my efforts to get passages from Basra. In the end I succeeded in getting them places on a Strick cargo boat sailing on August 28. By then the situation at home had become much worse, with the Luftwaffe trying to knock out our RAF as a preliminary to invasion, but [my wife] was determined to go and she was quite right ...

On my return to Kirkuk I found the house so silent now that [my wife] and the children had gone, that, for company, I invited John Brady, a young educational officer, to come and share it. He was the son of an Ulster parson and an excellent mess-mate whose companionship did much to dispel my loneliness;[7] and so the months went by till in the new year [1941] I had yet another demand on my services. I was to become a sort of fire brigade. My colleague [on Land Settlement] Henry Ditchburn had been working up the right bank of the Tigris as far as Mosul and had now crossed to the left bank and started in the sub-district of Tall Kayf. But on the dismissal of Sir K. Cornwallis as Adviser to the Ministry of Interior [in 1935], his assistant Edmonds had taken his place, and now Ditchburn had been recalled to assist Edmonds. I should mention here that since the implementation of the Land Settlement Law by four British officers there were now only two left, i.e. Aston and myself. The government had appointed about six Iraqi Presidents of the Commission to keep it going, but a parliamentary inquiry had revealed that the two British officers had settled twice as much land per annum as the six Iraqis, and the reason for this was not far to seek. It was that the Iraqi lawyers were adverse to field work, the hazards of camp life and the responsibility for making decisions in cases which were often tribal or political dynamite. Thus when it came to Tall Kayf none of them was willing to face the racial and religious tension that had been worked up over it, for it contained the village of Tall Kayf, inhabited by over 10,000 Christians of the Chaldean sect, by far the largest of its kind in the whole country, the cradle of many bishops and priests as well as of the Chaldean communities in Mosul, Kirkuk, Baghdad, Basra and many cities in the United States. And now the tenant right, as well as the rent of its extensive lands, was being claimed by the trustees of the Great Mosque in Mosul, whose tall and slender spire rivalled the leaning Tower of Pisa in its disregard for the perpendicular. Already there were fiery articles in the Baghdad papers supporting the Moslem against the Christian claims which, in a land where massacres were recent, had scared

---

7. See John Brady, *Eastern Encounters. Memoirs of a Decade 1937–1946* (Braunton, Devon, 1992), chs 16–18, for an account of their experiences in 1940–41; see also the Appendix to this chapter for an extract on their imprisonment in May 1941.

my Moslem colleagues, none of whom was willing to deal with the case. So once again the Minister of Justice asked me to take it on. To this I replied that I considered the publication of such articles to be Contempt of Court, and as such I called on them to put a stop to them. Subject to this condition I would take it on, but if any more of such articles were published I would down tools and walk out. To this he agreed, telling me in confidence that it was only a question of cutting the Gordian Knot by getting a judgment in this one village which was holding up the work, and after that I would hand over to an Iraqi and return to my stint in the oil fields, leaving the parties concerned to appeal should they so desire.

I was approaching the end of my second contract with the Iraqi government, after which I would be free to please myself; and anyway I was getting tired of these diversions. But, having agreed, I went to Mosul and pushed on with the case, which I finished in about three weeks' intensive work; and having given the lawyers on both sides a copy of the judgment for purposes of appeal, I returned to Kirkuk and resumed work on my original stint. I never knew whether my decision was appealed or not for shortly afterwards circumstances intervened which ended my service with the Iraqi government.

In the spring of 1940 [22 February 1940] the army had once more taken a hand in politics and put Nuri Pasha in as Prime Minister, only to replace him a month later [31 March 1940] by Rashid Ali, who was supported by four generals known as the Golden Square, none of them in harmony with the Regent Abd al-Ilah, who endeavoured to return to the policy of his late uncle King Faisal with the co-operation of the British. Thus the political situation was getting more difficult as the months succeeded each other, with successive Prime Ministers increasingly favourable to the triumphant Axis.[8] Rashid Ali refused to break off relations with the Italians, whose Embassy was now a centre of Axis conspiracy and propaganda; and there was reason to believe that he was intriguing with Von Papen [the German Minister] in Turkey. The government had agreed to the passage of British troops [in line with the Anglo-Iraqi Treaty] but restricted the numbers on Iraqi soil at any one time. Finally the Regent called on Rashid Ali to resign; and when the latter called on the Generals to intervene once more, he withdrew from the capital to Basra, thus making normal government impossible.

---

8. Nuri as-Said was PM from 25 December 1938 to 31 March 1940, with three different Cabinets. Rashid Ali was PM from 31 March 1940 to 31 January 1941, followed briefly by Taha al-Hashimi from 1 February to 1 April 1941. Rashid Ali returned to office as PM on 12 April 1941.

The Army Coup and Revolution · 213

Now at last the British Foreign Office listened to the pleas of the Regent, supported by Nuri Pasha and the informed British community in Iraq. The British Ambassador [Sir Basil Newton] was recalled and Sir Kinahan Cornwallis was appointed in his stead.

As soon as he arrived in Baghdad [4 April 1941] I went to see him. I explained how the political situation had degenerated: how the army now ruled the country under the premiership of Rashid Ali – all of them traitors and only waiting the chance to come out in the open on the side of the Axis. He told me in confidence that his first act was to call for British troops from India and that on the morrow a General was arriving by air to make arrangements for their reception. To this I replied that I had now earned enough leave to cover the remainder of my contract, and I could therefore leave without breaking any agreement; so I would like to offer my services as Political Officer to the force. It was thereupon arranged that I should wait till he had interviewed the General, after which he would see me again. Next day the General arrived, and in due course I was ushered in. He had already been briefed by the Ambassador on my experiences as Political Officer to numerous columns in the past; and after a short interview he told me that the authorities in Delhi contemplated appointing an ex-officer who had served in Iraq during the 1920 rebellion, but being now in his seventies, the General considered him too old. So on the Ambassador's advice he would recommend me for the appointment. I was delighted and wanted to hand in my resignation to the Iraq government and start for Basra straight away. But the Ambassador said 'No'. A signal was being sent to Delhi and I was to return to Kirkuk and not move out of it till I got a signal from him; meanwhile the whole affair was to be regarded as Top Secret. This was a disappointment; but knowing the red-taped procedure of the Indian Army, there was nothing for it but to comply. After all it would, I thought, only be a matter of a few days before the signal came.

Back in Kirkuk there were all sorts of increasingly sinister rumours, and soon the Petroleum Company got orders to evacuate all women and children; after they had left communications were cut. I could easily have escaped to the hills on the Persian frontier beyond the reach of the Iraqi Army and Police, but I had been ordered to stay put; and stay I did while the net slowly closed with me waiting for a signal that never came. I little knew at the time that the British Embassy was cut off and the RAF station at Habbaniyah was under siege by the Iraqi Army. The story of these events is now history, so I will confine my story to my own experiences."

---

9. For a more detailed account of Lyon's experiences with Brady, see the Appendix to this chapter. For a vivid account of the experiences of the British Embassy in Baghdad see Freya Stark (then Oriental Secretary) in *Dust in the Lion's Paw. Autobiography*

The Police Inspector arrived and ordered John Brady and myself to go to the IPC Club with him, 'for our protection', he said. There we found all the men ... of the station rounded up under military guard. After a day or two there, I was weeded out from the rest and taken to a small fort half way along the ridge which was the spine of the oil field, where I was under close military guard for about three days before being taken to the main fort-like building of the KI pumping station, where I also found Haji Green, Chapman, Squadron Leader Johnston, the Intelligence Officer from Sulaimani, and several RAF officers who had been captured after having been forced or shot down, some of them wounded. Here we were sometimes inspected by German officers – a most humiliating ordeal – and on the Iraqi Army officers' receiving-set next door we overheard the Arabic broadcast about the triumphant Iraqi Army's siege of the RAF station, and how [Sir John] Glubb [of the Arab Legion] had attempted to intervene but had been killed. This latter item I'm glad to say was afterwards found to be wishful thinking. From the RAF officers we learned that some of them had landed in the wrong places, and that owing to artillery fire there was only one runway in action in Habbaniyah. Some of them, having just arrived from service in Greece and Crete, had scanty briefing and no previous experience in Iraq or its landing grounds.

It was my first experience as a prisoner and I was so furious at the whole affair that I'm sure I could not have endured confinement for long; but luckily for me I didn't have to, for in under three weeks the German aircraft took off and we were free. The Iraqi Army had been defeated by a small column from Palestine and Transjordan composed of the Household Cavalry, a few guns, and Glubb with his Arab Legion. The Assyrian Levies, supported by the Essex Regiment, had fought valiantly in defence of the RAF camp and on the approach of the relief column had driven the Iraqi Army off the high ground commanding the station. We had won, but it was by a very narrow margin: a little more or a little sooner support by the Axis and we might have lost the oil field.

As soon as we got out I went with John Brady to Baghdad and stayed with Judge Pritchard who kindly put us up. After what had happened there was no holding Brady. He went straight to India, joined up and finished the war in Burma as a Captain of the Gurkhas. The RAF gave me a lift to Basra where I waited on General E. P. Quinan, the Force Commander, to whom I presented my credentials. I did not know then, or indeed till after reading his obituary several years afterwards, that his initials stood for Edward Pellew, which I think could hardly have been a co-

---

1939–1946 (London, 1961), ch. 7. See also Edmonds's diary, Edmonds Papers, Box 27/3, paras 312–490.

incidence, for that was the name of the first Viscount of Exmouth, whose daughter was my great-grandmother. Perhaps we had a common ancestor.

On returning to Baghdad I was gazetted to an intelligence unit of the Indian Army, and thus commenced the penultimate phase of my working life.

The Regent returned from Jordan accompanied by Nuri Pasha. Rashid Ali escaped to Germany and the four Generals of the Golden Square were caught, tried and hanged.[10] Iraq was saved from the Axis but not from itself.

Appendix: Wallace Lyon and John Brady in detention, May 1941, by John Brady[11]

[Brady had worked in Iraq from 1937 to 1939 in education under contract with the Iraq government and had returned there after war started for a similar job in Baghdad. Late in 1940 he was posted to Kirkuk, where Lyon was then based, and they became close friends. He was there when the Rashid Ali political coup occurred in April 1941, leading to the declaration of war on Britain and negotiations with Germany for support.]

Wallace and I were away from the centre of things, but it was fairly evident what turn events were taking. We discussed the matter one evening, and Wallace proposed going out on tour the next day, taking me with him. We would strike out south-west along the pipeline which ran to Haifa, and get as near the Transjordan border as we could. There would be no special preparations as that would arouse suspicion.

But it was already too late. Early next morning an Iraqi police officer appeared with two assistants, and asked us, very politely, to accompany him to the oil company camp, where we would be requested to remain till further notice, 'for our own safety'. Wallace protested indignantly and demanded to see the Mutaserrrif, with whom he was on friendly terms, but the Mutaserrif was in no position to help, even if the demand had been granted. And so began our internment in Kirkuk. This was the 30th April 1941, two days before the attack on [the RAF base at] Habbaniyyah and the declaration of war on Great Britain.

---

10. In fact Rashid Ali and others of his supporters were tried and condemned in absentia and the Golden Square officers were eventually tried and executed. Rashid Ali went to Germany via Iran, together with the Grand Mufti of Jerusalem, who had been a major fomenter of anti-British fervour in Iraq, and engaged in anti-Allied propaganda. After 1945 Rashid Ali took refuge in Saudi Arabia and the Mufti in Egypt. Rashid Ali was welcomed back to Iraq after the revolution of 1958.

11. Taken, with the author's permission, from Brady, *Eastern Encounters*, ch. 18, pp. 68–70. Spellings as in the original.

There were several vacant bungalows in the I[raq] P[etroleum] C[ompany] Compound, all fully furnished, and Wallace asked if we might occupy one of these together. The whole area was fenced with barbed wire, and sentry posts equipped with machine-guns and searchlights had been placed at strategic points on the low hills around the perimeter. Thus the compound could be kept under close guard night and day. But life within the enclosure was to all outward appearances normal. The club bar was well stocked and well patronized, payment being by IOU. Most of the oil company personnel were therefore content to let things be. Not so Wallace or I. Wallace especially had a horror of imprisonment; a brother[12] of his had been a prisoner of the Germans in the First World War and the memory of it preyed on his mind. Although he was a six-footer, he weighed no more than six stone when he was freed. 'We must make a getaway,' he would repeat. 'Roll, bowl, spin, split or burst, we must get out.' ...

[Lyon and Brady made detailed plans for three days, intending to climb over the barbed wire on a dark night.]

What happened subsequently I cannot account for with certainty. Iraqi police had come into the camp to check our documents, which included our Iraqi residence permits. On this occasion Wallace Lyon had expressed himself forcefully on the worthlessness of such documents, and indeed of all such papers bearing Iraqi official stamps. That may have been a cause of offence. Or there may have been something suspicious in our behaviour, or even an informer, though we had not breathed a word of our plan to anyone. Whatever the reason, on the very day on which our plan was to have been carried into effect, a police officer appeared and told us that we (Wallace Lyon and I) were to be moved to another 'camp'. When we protested that we were quite content where we were he reassured us that we would be just as comfortable, adding that in any case he was only carrying out orders. We were allowed ten minutes to collect any small personal belongs we wished to take with us and ushered into an army truck, where we found two other internees in the same category: Godfrey, a civil surveyor, and a senior irrigation officer, whose name I do not now remember. Why were we being segregated from the others? Because we knew too much of the countryside and the language? The four of us were driven off into the desert, the dust and the restricted view preventing identification of our direction. At last we stopped at our new place of internment, which we recognized immediately. It was a fort on the pipeline to Haifa, known as 'H1'.

We had not been taken in by the assurances of our escort, and the move

---

12. In fact, it was his brother-in-law Percy King.

had upset our escape plan, but we were not prepared for the deterioration in our treatment, for up to this point it had been a gentlemanly style of internment. It must be remembered, however, that the behaviour of the Iraqis changed from time to time in accordance with the tide of war, and events were far from favourable to us at that time. The fort consisted of one fairly large shed in which we were lodged, and a walled enclosure with heavy iron gates. Outside was desert all around as far as the eye could see. May in Iraq can be very hot, and in such conditions it was extremely oppressive. There was a water tap for the guard and ourselves, but, at least for the first day and a half, there was no food. Then a raw cabbage appeared from somewhere. Of course we complained to the guard, even threatened them at times with the retribution which would overtake them when we got out, as we surely would, but they remained sullen and unhelpful, obviously awaiting further instructions from some superior, on the extent to which it would be safe to ill-treat us ...

Our irrigation engineer ... had brought with him a small portable typewriter, and he set to work to compose an official protest. The Geneva Convention was being contravened in a number of ways: we were not provided with adequate food or accommodation; we had insufficient means of physical exercise; and we claimed that the guard should contain at least one officer of equivalent rank to us ... This epistle was duly delivered to the guard for onward transmission, with an appropriate warning that they would eventually be held responsible if it did not reach the higher authority to whom it was addressed ...

Whether the 'Geneva Convention' letter was ever delivered to the proper authority will never be known, but it is possible that it was bandied about, and even studied by someone superior to the guard. At all events the Iraqis seemed to become more careful about the rules. Food was provided; it was not plentiful or tasty, but it was probably no worse than the guards themselves had. Then there was another development. The inevitable police officer paid a visit and announced that, as Wallace Lyon was a military officer, he was to be removed for separate internment elsewhere.[13] This was a blow to me personally but there could be no argument.

[The tide then turned in Britain's favour in Iraq, with the failure of the attack on the Habbaniyah airbase.]

---

13. C. J. Edmonds noted in his diary for 4 June 1941 that 'Lyon, Godfrey and Brady (schoolmaster) arrived from Kirkuk. It seems that Lyon, Chapman & Johnson were singled out for particularly harsh treatment.' Chapman, like Lyon, was a Land Settlement Officer and an ex-army officer. If this is Captain E. J. Johnson, he was also an ex-army officer, then a police officer.

These were events we knew nothing of at the time, for we were cut off from all news of the outside world: but we began to notice a pronounced improvement in the manners of our guards; they became polite, almost friendly. They confided that we were to be moved back to Kirkuk to join the other internees. They had not been badly treated, but they had not been allowed to remain in their bungalows. On 30 May Rashid Ali, seeing his cause was lost, grabbed as much of the State Treasury as he could get his hands on, and fled to Persia, where he was welcomed by the Shah. On 31st we were at liberty again.[14]

---

14. Brady then disobeyed orders from the Ambassador to remain in Iraq, got himself to Bombay, joined the army and had a distinguished career fighting in Burma. After the war he was appointed to an educational job in the Aden Protectorate

CHAPTER 12

Political Adviser to the Indian Army in Iraq and the End of Service, 1941–44

§ THE area over which I was to function as Political Adviser was from and including the Diyala Province in the south to the Turkish frontier in the north, and from the Syrian frontier in the west to the Persian frontier in the east – in short, the top half of Iraq which a British Corps and the Polish Army were subsequently to occupy. My duties were: to keep close liaison with the military commanders, reporting any subversive activities to the Ambassador and the General Officer Commanding-in-Chief; to provide all commanders with information on local communications and resources, advising and assisting them in all matters involving the natives of the country, settling all claims for compensation and leaving them free to devote their undivided attention to training and defence; and to advise and assist the five local provincial governors in restoring stable government, public morale, friendship and support for the Allies, and confidence in ultimate victory.

I was allowed to recruit four British officers and the necessary local staff and transport for the job; and in addition three specialists were seconded to me for training. These were officers specially trained in the use of explosives who, in the event of the enemy driving over the Caucasus and occupying Iraq, would stay behind in command of guerrilla bands to disrupt their organization and lines of communication. While under my care they were to learn Kurdish and make friends with the various tribal chiefs whose co-operation would be needed in the event of a British withdrawal.

Some of my property had been looted by the police during my confinement. For this I claimed compensation, and disposed of the remainder for what I could get, for I was determined not to hazard it again. I opened up an office in Kirkuk and set up two more, one at Mosul and the other at Khanaqin.

My first act [in Kirkuk] was to call on Saiyid Ahmad-i Khanaqah, the Moslem high priest, but for whose intervention I would have been whisked away by the German Air Force to a German prison camp. They had marked me down as a key man, for my knowledge of the country and its people would prove embarrassing in the event of a future attack. The old priest had always been friendly to me and now I asked him what he would like in return for his kindness. What about a decoration, say a CMG: I had the Ambassador's authority to offer it? No thanks! Well then what about a nice new car? They were so scarce now that imports had stopped, even my own car which I had bought in Cheltenham second hand for £100 and used over the roughest country for three years now fetched £300. A new one would be worth £1,000 at prices then ruling. But no! What then would you like and how can I show my gratitude? 'I would like you to come and see me sometimes for a friendly chat,' said he, 'just as you used to do.' Well I thought this very noble and dignified of him and in my new appointment it would prove most useful, for nothing went on that he did not know of, even in the planning stage, so I thanked him profusely and told him it would be a pleasure.

On the defeat of the Iraqi Army at the RAF base of Habbaniyah and the relief of the Embassy at Baghdad, the Axis elements retired in their planes to Syria, taking with them some of their Iraqi agents, chief of whom was Rashid Ali al-Gaylani. Here they and their Vichy French supporters were now defeated after some sharp and bitter engagements – bitter because the Free French were also employed against them. Some of the Iraqi rebels had found refuge in Persia and they and their Axis supporters could obviously not be left there to plot fresh trouble. There was the usual dithering about what should be done, and no doubt the exchange of despatches between Ambassadors and Whitehall, with the usual quota of precedent and protocol, might have lasted weeks had not the Russians moved. That of course over-ruled everything. Persia was once again to be over-run as in 1914–18, only this time the Turks were out of it. It was just a race between the British and the Russians for Teheran. The Royal Navy overwhelmed the Persians in the Gulf just as the Russians did on the Caspian Sea, while the respective army columns surged across the frontier heading unopposed for the Persian capital. It was indeed a glorious though almost bloodless victory. Reza Shah was arrested and deported, all objectives were made good, and the Iraqi Kurds, seeing what was happening, followed suit by taking every Persian army and police post along the whole length of the frontier. For them it was a real bonanza; crates of Czech rifles and ammunitions, some of them still packed in grease, were the prizes of war. The Herki chief even offered me a very useful mountain gun as a mark of his respect, which I regretfully had to refuse. The British didn't want it and the Iraqi Army could not be trusted with it, so I told him to bury it. Perhaps it might some day come in handy for the guerrillas.

At this time the Germans had penetrated as far as the Caucasian mountains and were hammering away at Stalingrad. Were they to succeed, there was practically nothing to stop them driving south through Persia to Iraq. Already the oil wells were being cemented and the plant prepared for demolition. The Polish Army captured in 1939 by the Russians was now evacuated through Persia, re-formed under General Anders at Khanaqin, and re-equipped by the British. These troops, both officers and men, had been in Russian prison camps since 1939; now for the first time they got pay and clothing. Owing to their poor condition they were also given one and a half the British soldier's ration and, confronted with such plenty, they quickly indulged in prodigal expenditure. Never had they seen so much food and cash. One of the British officers attached to them told me that in pre-war Poland one could hire a man and boy with horse and cart for about fivepence a day. Now private soldiers were holding out an Iraqi dinar note – equivalent of one English pound – for a local chicken worth one shilling. They had no idea of the value of money and I soon saw that, unless they were checked, the cost of living would go up like a rocket. I therefore approached their General with a suggestion for keeping back some of their pay and reserving it in a fund for their post-war welfare.

In their search for and consumption of alcohol in all its forms they were second to none, while in matters of culture they showed great interest and artistic ability. When they decided on giving a show all the props for the concert, opera or ballet, from musical instruments and scenery to artistically printed programmes, would miraculously appear from nowhere and their performances were of a very high standard. As soldiers they were keen and courageous, but so embittered by their treatment in Russia that they would have much preferred to fight against the Russians than against the Axis. So far as I was concerned with them, in their conduct with the local inhabitants they were much more ruthless than the British troops, and consequently caused more friction; but their commanders were always co-operative and one could not but discount much of their shortcomings in consideration of their experiences since 1939. The Kurds around Khanaqin and Ruwandiz could still remember the harsh treatment they had received at the hands of the Russian Cossacks in 1917, and by comparison the Poles were very much better.

The Polish headquarters was sited at Khanaqin, a town on the main Baghdad–Teheran road just outside the Persian border. The edges of the Diyala river and the neighbouring swamps provided an ideal breeding ground for mosquitoes, as a result of which the town was riddled with malaria. This the British Army Medical Authorities decided to clean up, and clean it up they did. Not only were all the stagnant pools drained and sprayed with oil, but sanitary squads combed every house in the town, flitting everything and everybody with pyrethrum solution. Such an intrusion into Moslem harems had never before been heard of, still less attempted, and was certainly beyond the capacity of any civilian authority to enforce; but with the whole-hearted co-operation of Ramzi Beg, the Kurdish district governor, the operation was explained to the religious leaders and the local town councillors; local police accompanied each squad and the programme was carried out with little fuss and no complaints. As a result of this operation the incidence of malaria in the town in the following year was reduced by about 75 per cent and if ever the British Army did a fine job this was it. It was one of the few occasions when overawing the civil population with the presence of force proved to be justified.

In Kirkuk the first troops to arrive were a battalion of Gurkhas, who, before they had been there long, began to suffer from the usual attentions of pilferers. So the Colonel decided to give them a sharp lesson, and every night a soldier armed only with his kookri crouched in every truck. As soon as a hand appeared in the gloom down came the kookri and in the morning the soldier paraded at the battalion office and claimed his reward – a rupee for each finger. They were all volunteers, for it was just the sort of sport that appealed to [a] Gurkha, and the pilfering ceased.

Soon the British troops began to arrive till their strength went up to two divisions. As the Germans had not as yet been defeated at Stalingrad and some forward units had penetrated as far as the Caucasus, hasty preparations were now made for the defence of northern Iraq.

In the 1914–18 war I had seen how rich a comparatively few contractors – mostly Armenians – had become while the people were exploited and left poorer than ever; and calling this to mind I determined to prevent a repetition and instead bring the inhabitants into the picture. The proposed field fortifications would provide employment where it was most needed, and there is no propaganda better than a full belly. Moreover, if suitably handled, these same people might afterwards prove most useful in providing shelter for the Special Officers leading guerrilla forces in the event of a withdrawal. The plan was approved by the C-in-C and I then gathered the Kurdish tribal chiefs from all over the countryside and explained it to them. They all knew me well and were quite willing to have a go. Colonel Grand, whom I had known many years before as a Sapper subaltern seconded to the Levies, was now responsible for constructing the field defences, which consisted for the most part of earthworks, trenches, tank traps, strong points, etc. He was a most able and experienced officer who knew the country and people well.

The work was divided into sections and let out to the Kurdish chiefs by contract, each section according to the number of his men on the job. It was laid out, supervised and checked by the Sappers and the chief was paid at once on its completion. There was thus no bother about acquittance rolls, middle men etc., for the workers knew the value of the contract and the usual trouble arising from a contractor swindling his labour was eliminated, for these were the chief's own tribesmen. They were also much better workers than the Arabs and the work proceeded with ever increasing speed; as soon as one section was finished they asked for another.

Among them I posted the Special Officers for purposes of liaison, for what better opportunity could there be for learning the Kurdish language and country [and] making friends with the tribal leaders who might later be called upon to shelter them. These people would remain in their mountain villages when the typical army contractor would have bolted out ahead of a retreating force.

The field fortifications covered a vast area both in width and depth, and in all resulted in over a million pounds finding their way into the pockets of these deserving people. As far as the army was concerned it was excellent value for money while at the same time freeing the troops for the more important work of training. It was the first chance the Kurds had of full employment at a time when the cost of living was rising fast. It was also sound propaganda for the Allied cause, and that reminds me of an incident which may now be mentioned since the principal parties concerned are now all dead.

One day, while all this was going on, I had an urgent summons from the Corps Commander, who told me on arrival at his office that his Military Police had observed certain British soldiers from a nearby battery visiting the house of the provincial governor. The house stood in an isolated position on the circular road between the bridge and the oil cantonment. On interrogation by the Assistant Provost Marshal it turned out that, when the [Iraqi] governor was out of town, his lady, accompanied by another female, used to drive slowly round, pick up and bring home any stray couple of soldiers that they met. The soldiers freely admitted that they enjoyed the hospitality, which included love making, and the entertainment had been quite free. Now the General wanted to know what I thought was best to do about it. I remarked that improvement of friendly relations between the army and the natives was one of my duties and surely this was an unsolicited testimonial to the success of my efforts. The governor was a personal friend and most co-operative in all matters affecting the Army; and his wife, though a purdah lady, seemed to have out-distanced him. I could not possibly break the news to him. He would be expected to kill his wife; he would be broken by local scandal, a cuckold of no further use to us. To issue a written order putting the house out of bounds might likewise have unfavourable repercussions for there was no knowing who might read it and it might easily get back to him. So I suggested that the commander of the unit concerned should issue an order putting that road out of bounds to all troops not on duty and put a military police patrol on to enforce it till the unit could be moved elsewhere. Meanwhile I would consult the Ambassador on my next visit to Baghdad. This I did. Needless to say he was highly amused and approved my suggestions. The governor was delicate: his wife was not.

The sexual urges of armies in foreign lands have always presented a problem to commanders in the field since the dawn of history. There is a tradition among the Moslems that when the Caliph had complaints from the grass widows of the faithful demanding the return of their menfolk he called a meeting of the principal wives and asked them how long they could remain faithful to their husbands. After much consultation they replied that ninety days was the extreme limit, and on that the Caliph issued an order that troops were to be given home leave after serving that period at the front.[1]

My duties frequently involved much travel in smoothing out relations between the troops and the inhabitants. Summer rest camps to give the troops a spell away from the intense summer heat were located in Karind, some 50 miles across the Persian border in the province of Kermanshah, and at Penjwin, on the Persian frontier of the Sulaimani Province ... Another journey took me across the Syrian desert to Deir ez-Zor on the upper reaches of the Euphrates to liaise with Ditchburn, the Political Officer attached to General Spears' mission. [Sir John] Glubb [Commander of the Arab Legion since 1938] had left the Iraqi Service some years previously where, as a desert officer, he had been so successful with the tribes that he had aroused the jealousy of adjacent provincial governors and had to leave. Now, as a result of repeated raids and counter-raids, the claims and counter-claims between Iraqi and Syrian Beduin had mounted to an inextricable tangle affecting the security and trade of both countries. Accordingly a grand tribal gathering was arranged, somewhat on the lines of a Jirga among the Pathans of the North West Frontier of India. All the shaikhs of the Shammar, the Agidat and other tribes were gathered to make a balance-sheet and start afresh. But after several days of argument it became obvious that settlement in kind or money acceptable to both sides was out of the question, for some of the claims seemed to go back to the

---

1. For a modern analogy in Iraq in the 1940s see Stark, *Dust in the Lion's Paw*, p. 160.

days of Abraham. In the end, by keeping the representatives of both sides under duress, they arrived at the only possible solution. The judgment was as short as the claims were long. It consisted of three words only: Harferna-wa-Duffina, which translated means, 'We have dug and we have buried'. This was followed by a gargantuan meal, much rejoicing and dispersal.

On the return journey we stayed the night at Hassech on the Khaber river, where we were entertained by the Free French Colonial Officer Octave Auboire and his wife, who produced a delicious meal from a local fish cooked as only a French lady knows how. He was afterwards my colleague as French Consul in Harar, Ethiopia. While in Hassech I called on Daud Marshimun, the uncle of the Assyrian Patriarch, and chief of the luckless band which had fled from Iraq. The French had given them shelter and allotted them lands on the banks of the Khaber, but these mountaineers were feeling far from happy or secure in this flat country surrounded, as they were, by hostile Arabs. Of all the nations of the world this little remnant of what must once have been a powerful nation have been the most unfortunate. In spite of loyal service to the British in both world wars and in the period between, they were the only people on the winning side to lose their lands and their rights. Yet they kept their language and their religion intact ...[2]

When Cornwallis first came to Iraq in 1921 as the Amir Faisal's Political Agent and subsequently succeeded Philby as Adviser to the Ministry of Interior he wielded great influence over both the unsophisticated government and the newly appointed King. As a Political Officer in Kurdistan I had naturally a great interest and sympathy for the Kurds and their aspirations, but I had never been able to get my Chief to view the situation through Kurdish spectacles. He was a dyed-in-the-wool Arabist; and when eventually Faisal died [and] the young King Ghazi, impatient and intolerant, dismissed him [in 1935], he was succeeded by Edmonds, an official who had always been sympathetic to the Kurdish cause.[3] But by then the post

---

2. Hamilton, *Road through Kurdistan*, ch. 26, made an impassioned statement of the Assyrian case which, in his Foreword to the book, Major-General H. Rowan-Robinson (Lyon's 'Row Row') suggested should 'be read with discrimination' since 'there was not only an Assyrian side but a British and an Iraqi side to this troublesome question'. There is a large literature on the Assyrians in Iraq.

3. Edmonds made repeated attempts to draw the attention of Baghdad politicians and the British officials there to their commitments to the Kurds – in particular his memorandum of June 1929; the minutes of the conference he held in March 1930, at which Lyon and the other senior Administrative Advisers were present, and his paper 'The Kurds in May', reporting on Kurdish reactions to the revolution of May 1941, are all in Edmonds Papers, Box 3/2.

[of Adviser] no longer exercised the same influence. The Arab politicians had by then more experience of power, more confidence in themselves: they had tasted the sweets of office and were in no mood to share them with the Kurds, nor was there any longer a victorious British Army in the country to lend weight to British advice.

But now that Cornwallis had returned as Ambassador on the heels of a new British force and with all the prestige of a British satrap dealing with a naughty nation, I tried once more to get a better deal for the Kurds.[4] Their scanty crops so hardly won from their rocky valleys received no tax allowance, yet the chief source of the country's revenue was derived from the oil in the Kurdish foothills. The great schemes for dams on the Kurdish rivers would not irrigate their lands but those of the Arabs in the plains. At the cost of flooding Kurdish villages in the valleys above the dams the schemes would protect the city of Baghdad from flood. Neither the late King Ghazi nor the young King Faisal the Second had made any effort to learn Kurdish, nor recruited a Kurdish bodyguard after the pattern of the Scots or Welsh Guards, which in their national dress would have given them the prestige and pied à terre at the capital to which they were entitled.[5] For was not the famous Salah-ad-Din a Kurd? And had not the Kurds proved superior fighters to the Arabs in many engagements? Yet they were treated as second-class citizens, to be jeered in the streets of the capital when they appeared in their native costumes, which in reality were both more attractive and more serviceable than the flapping effeminate garments of the Arabs. They were of Aryan and not of Semitic race as

---

4. For example, Lyon wrote to Cornwallis on 19 June 1941 that in the Kurdish areas 'the economic state ... is really tragic. These unfortunate people have literally [next] to nothing between them and starvation ... Everywhere one sees people lying about in an emaciated condition. Their clothes spread out on the hedges to dry show more holes than cloth. They have not even the wherewithal to patch them.' And again, on 4 January 1944, 'there are vast and insalubrious areas [of Kurdistan] completely devoid of all medical services'. Both quoted from Foreign Office documents by D. Silverfarb, *The Twilight of British Ascendancy in the Middle East* (New York, 1994), pp. 40, 41. Lyon's demonstrated sympathies with the Kurds were not always welcome to Edmonds: thus on 4 December 1943 he noted in his diary that reports by two Iraqi officials indicated 'that Lyon is being most indiscreet and thereby doing great harm. P[usho] said that he had said that he did not blame Mulla Mustafa for not trusting Govt. promises as he did not trust them.' Edmonds Papers Box 27/3, diary, para. 284. In September 1944, after Lyon had returned from leave, he noted in his diary that 'Lyon ... had sent in a strongly worded report with warnings of probably trouble if urgent steps were not taken to feed and clothe the people before winter' (ibid., diary, para. 413).

5. This was one of several symbolic concessions to the Kurdish sense of identity pressed for, unsuccessfully, by Edmonds in 1929.

Political Adviser to the Indian Army · 227

were the Arabs, and if the country was to be saved from disunion they should be given a new deal. Now in my new capacity as Political Adviser to the Forces in Northern Iraq (at this time 'Paiforce'), one of my chief duties was to keep the Kurdish tribal leaders sweet and quiet while the war was on. Among them were such people as Shaikh Mahmud, at one time ruler of Kurdistan, Mulla Mustafa, brother of Shaikh Ahmad, Chief of Barzan, the Pizhdar Chief, the Jaf, and many others. These had repeatedly defeated the Iraqi troops and in the past had only been held in check by the threat of the Royal Air Force. Some were now living in semi-exile watching the turn of events and pondering their chances of bettering their political position when the opportunity arose.

It was never easy to answer their constant queries about the prospects of the political future of their people, and as time went on I found their probing ever more embarrassing. At last, after much debate, the appointment of a Kurdish Minister with special power was effected, but when in practice it came to nothing, it was obvious that the Regent and his government were insincere in their expressions of sympathy for the Kurds of northern Iraq and the British were too heavily committed with war against the Axis to spare a thought or time for anything else. The fact that the Kurdish people overlapped into eastern Turkey, Syria and Persia, was more of a disadvantage than a support for their political ambition as all three governments had suppressed the Kurds in their area – the Turks with all the severity of which they were capable. The Kurds, like the Poles, were divided among the adjacent countries and the possibility of uniting them into an eastern Switzerland was remote. I had no brief for encouraging them and as time went on I realized that I was getting tired and stale and that it would be better in every way if I were out of it. The German advance to the Caucasus had by now been checked, the battle of Alamein won and the threat to Iraq removed; so, as I had been six years away from home, when I had news that my father was slowly sinking and had asked for me, I applied for leave on compassionate grounds and was given leave home [early in 1944] on what was labelled 'Consultations with the Foreign Office' ...

[After arriving in England I went to London and] reported to Sir Harold Caccia at the Foreign Office; and while in the building whom should I meet but my old friend Andrews, formerly Vice-Consul at Kirkuk, one of the best officers in the service who has since retired as Sir A. E. Chapman Andrews. He insisted on taking me off to lunch at a nearby eating house where he was well-known, and there over lunch he asked me about all the news from Iraq and about my future plans. I told him that I considered the main part of my mission completed: the Iraqis were now all co-operative; the threat to the oil fields had passed; and as I could not do anything more for the Kurds I felt it would be better to break away. I didn't want to work for the Iraqi government any more nor live in the country any longer than was necessary. At that he suggested my taking up his former post as British Consul at Harar which had been vacant since the Italian invasion of Ethiopia [1936]. The Foreign Office were now looking for a suitable candidate and Mr Howe, the present Minister [in Addis Ababa], was now in leave in London, living with him, and if I agreed he would arrange for an interview. I had no hesitation in closing with such a kindly offer ...

[Before going to Ethiopia I had to return to Iraq.] On arrival at my headquarters I found there had been several changes since I had left. The senior officer to whom I had handed over had been evacuated sick, the three musketeers [the Special Service officers] had been flown off to Yugoslavia, and the war atmosphere had evaporated from the Middle East. The British and Polish Army Corps had been replaced by a token force of Indian State Troops and the bulk of the work was now concerned with plans to avoid a famine in the land which seldom had a surplus and was now very short of food and faced with fast-rising prices.

Mulla Mustafa, the Barzani Chief, impatient in exile, had skipped off to his own country and was now [September 1944] with a well armed company of his followers trailing his coat up and down the mountains in full view of the young King's summer palace, inviting the garrison to come out and have a go. One of my first jobs was to persuade him to be less conspicuous and in this I succeeded, though I knew it wouldn't last long. Other tribal chiefs were likewise getting restless; and as my sympathies were entirely on their side I became ever more conscious of the delicacy of my position. If I couldn't help them I should clear out and I awaited with impatience the official letter offering me the appointment as HM Consul at Harar in Ethiopia, and when it eventually arrived I lost no time in applying for demobilization.

I could not bear to say goodbye for ever to some of my Iraqi and British friends without offending others, so as was my custom, I left without any fuss and was seen off by Judge Pritchard, with whom I stayed my last night in Iraq, in which I had spent the best part of twenty-seven years.[6]

---

6. Edmonds recorded in his diary that he had seen Lyon off on the Nairn Bus on 30 December 1944. 'A great loss.' Edmonds Papers, box 27/3.

Select Bibliography: Iraq 1914–44

Bassam, T., *Arab Nationalism: A Critical Enquiry*, ed. and trans. by M. Farouk-Sluglett and P. Sluglett (London, 1981)

Batutu, H., *The Old Social Classes and Revolutionary Movement of Iraq* (Princeton, NJ, 1978)

Bell, Lady (ed.), *The Letters of Gertrude Bell* (London, 1927)

Boyle, A., *Trenchard* (London, 1962)

Brady, J., *Eastern Encounters. Memoirs of a Decade 1937–1946* (Braunton, Devon, 1992)

Burgoyne, E., *Gertrude Bell: from her Personal Papers 1914–1926* (London, 1961)

Busch, B. C., *Britain, India and the Arabs, 1914–1921* (Berkeley and London, 1971)

Chaliand, G., *The Kurdish Tragedy* (London and New Jersey, 1994)

Cohen, S. A., *British Policy in Mesopotamia 1903–1914* (London, 1976)

Darwin, J., *Britain and the Middle East. Imperial Policy in the Aftermath of War 1918–22* (London, 1981)

— 'An Undeclared Empire. The British in the Middle East, 1918–1939', *Journal of Imperial and Commonwealth History*, vol. 27, no. 2 (1999), pp. 159–76.

Edmonds, C. J., *Kurds, Turks and Arabs* (London, 1957)

Farouk-Sluglett, M., and P. Sluglett, *Iraq since 1958. From Revolution to Dictatorship* (London and New York, 1987)

Graves, P., *The Life of Sir Percy Cox* (London, 1941)

Haj, S., *The Making of Iraq 1900–1963* (Albany, NY, 1997)

Hamilton, A. M., *Road through Kurdistan. The Narrative of an Engineer in Iraq* (London, 1937)

Hay, W. R., *Two Years in Kurdistan. Experiences of a Political Officer, 1918–1920* (London, 1921)

Hourani, A., 'Ottoman Reform and the Policies of Notables', in W. R. Polk and R. Chambers (eds), *Beginnings of Modernization in the Middle East* (Chicago, 1968)

Ireland, P. W., *Iraq. A Study in Political Development* (London, 1937)

Izady, M. R., *The Kurds. A Concise Handbook,* (Washington DC and London, 1992)

Jawad, S., *Iraq and the Kurdish Question 1958–1970* (London, 1981)

Karsh, E. and I., *Empires in the Sand: The Struggle for Mastery in the Middle East, 1789–1923* (Cambridge, Mass., 1999)

Kedourie, E., *England and the Middle East: The Destruction of the Ottoman Empire 1914–1921* (London, 1956)

— *The Chatham House Version and Other Middle-Eastern Studies* (London, 1970)

Kelidar, A. (ed.), *The Integration of Modern Iraq* (London, 1979)

Kent, M., *Oil and the Empire: British Policy and Mesopotamian Oil 1900–1921* (New York, 1976)

— (ed.), *The Great Powers and the End of the Ottoman Empire* (London, 1982)

Khadduri, M., *Independent Iraq 1932–1958. A Study in Iraqi Politics* (London, 1951; 2nd rev. edn, London 1960)

Kirisci, K. and G. M. Winrow, *The Turkish Question and Turkey. An Example of Transstate Ethnic Conflict* (London and Portland, Oregon, 1997)

Kirk-Greene, A., *On Crown Service. A History of HM Colonial and Overseas Civil Services 1837–1997* (London, 1999)

Langley, K. M., *The Industrialization of Iraq* (Cambridge, Mass., 1967)

Longrigg, S. H., *Iraq 1900–1950. A Political, Social and Economic History* (London, 1953)

McDowall, D., *A Modern History of the Kurds* (London and New York, 1997)

Madden, A. F. and J. Darwin, *The Dependent Empire, 1900–1948* (Westport, Conn., 1994)

Marlowe, J., *Late Victorian. The Life of Sir Arnold Talbot Wilson* (London, 1967)

Monroe, E., *Britain's Moment in the Middle East 1914–1956* (London, 1965)

— *Philby of Arabia* (New York and London, 1973)

Nevakivi, J., *Britain, France and the Arab Middle East 1914–1928* (London, 1969)

Olson, R., *The Emergence of Kurdish Nationalism and the Sheikh Said Rebellion, 1880–1925* (Austin, Texas, 1989)

Omissi, D., *Air Power and Colonial Control* (Manchester, 1990)

Pearce, R., *Sir Bernard Bourdillon* (Oxford, 1987)

Rothwell, V. H., 'Mesopotamia in British War Aims 1914–1918', *Historical Journal*, vol. 13, no. 2 (1970), pp. 273–94

— *British War Aims and Peace Diplomacy* (Oxford, 1971)

Sassoon, J., *Economic Policy in Iraq 1932–1958* (London, 1987)

Shikara, A. A. al-Razzafi, *Iraqi Politics 1921–1941* (London, 1987)

Silverfarb, D., *Britain's Informal Empire in the Middle East: A Case Study of Iraq 1929–1941* (New York and London, 1986)

— *The Twilight of British Ascendancy in the Middle East. A Case Study of Iraq, 1941–1958* (New York, 1994)

Sluglett, P., *Britain in Iraq 1914–1932* (London, 1976)

Soane, E. B., *Through Mesopotamia and Kurdistan in Disguise* (London, 1912)

Stark, F., *Dust in the Lion's Paw. Autobiography 1939–1946* (London, 1961)

Storrs, Sir R., *Orientations*, (London, 1937; 2nd edn, London, 1943)

Tarbush, M. A., *The Role of the Military in Politics: A Case Study of Iraq to 1941* (London, 1982)

Tauber, E., *The Formation of Modern Syria and Iraq* (Ilford, Essex and Portland Oregon, 1995)

Warner, G., *Iraq and Syria 1941* (London, 1974)

Wilson, Sir A. T., *Loyalties: Mesopotamia 1914–1917* (London, 1930)

— *Mesopotamia 1917–1920: A Clash of Loyalties* (London, 1931)

Winstone, H. V. F., *Gertrude Bell* (London, 1978)

Index

13th Hussars, 80
15th Sikhs regiment, 119, 120, 121–2
18th Hussars, 156
39th Irregular Light Horse (Lyon's Own), 157, 158
52nd Sikhs Frontier Force, vii, 50, 64, 68, 69
110th Transport Company (Indian Army), 162

Abadan, oil refinery, 2, 16
Abbas-i Mahmud, 109, 120
Abd al-Ilah, Regent, 212, 213
Abdul Hamed, a cook *see* Hamid
Abdulhamid II, Sultan, 36, 188
Abdulla Khan, Jemadar, 69
Abdullah, Amir, 4, 7, 13, 15
Abubeker (Mulla Effendi), 91–2, 142
Acre, 4
Adila Khan, 85, 100, 157, 158
Agidat tribe, 224
Al Ahd al-Iraqi organisation, 6, 7
Ahmad Effendi *see* Usman, Ahmad Effendi
Ahmad Pasha, 103, 131; deportation of, 101–2
Aku tribe, 122
Alamein, Battle of, 227
Aleppo, 3, 5, 6
Alevis, 34
Alexander the Great, 88
Ali Beg, 97, 98, 99
Ali, Tahsin, 41, 178, 179, 180, 181, 182, 183, 184, 185, 186
Alkosh, tomb of prophet Nahum, 65
Allah, Shaikh Ubayd, 36
Allenby, General E.H.H., 6, 71
Allfrey, Major, 190
Altun Kopru, 87, 88, 123, 139, 144, 192, 193
Alwieh Club, 194, 203
Amadiya, 68–9, 96

Amery, L.S., 21
Anders, General, 221
Andrews, Sir A.E. Chapman, 52, 227
Anglo Persian Oil Company (APOC), 84, 92, 100
Anglo-French Declaration, 6, 8, 10, 12, 13
Anglo-Iraqi statement, 39, 40
Anglo-Iraqi treaty (1924), 39, 41, 212
Aniza tribe, 61
Aouchi, Haji Hassan Effendi, 172
Aouchi family, 172
Aqra, 70
Arab Bureau, 71, 94, 95
Arab Legion, 214
Arab rising (1916), 5, 13
Arbil, 41, 42, 44,-45, 84–106, 107–28, 130, 131, 132, 141, 142, 147, 150, 151, 152, 154, 157, 159, 178, 188, 207
Armenians, 36, 65, 81, 181–2, 222; massacres of, 63
al-Askari, Ali Rida, 139
al-Askari, Jafar Pasha, 6, 14, 16, 25, 96, 139, 187
al-Askari, Tahsin, 187–8
Assyrians, 23, 30, 75, 79, 80–3, 88, 111, 113, 119, 190, 225; massacre of, 25, 30, 199; riot against, 209 *see also* levies, Assyrian
Aston, Captain C.C., 194, 211
Ataturk *see* Kemal, Mustafa
Auboire, Octave, 225
Auchinleck, Major C., 70
Avroman tribe, 107
al-Ayyubi, Ali Jawdat, 6
Aziziya, 195, 196, 198

Baba Ali, son of Shaikh Mahmud, 166, 167
Baba Gurgur, 200
Babakr Agha, 109, 153
Baghdad, 2, 4, 12, 13, 17, 20, 21, 24, 25, 27, 32, 35, 36, 41, 44, 80, 83, 92, 94, 108,

117, 125, 128, 138, 139, 146, 148, 153, 170, 187, 211, 213, 214; British command in, 116, 155, 167; government in, 7, 27, 39, 40, 46, 190, 194–201; taking of, 3, 87
Bagzada, 135
Balisan, 124
Bani Banok, 107
Bani Huchaim Confederation, 31
Barke, Colonel, 105
Barlow, Major J.E., 7, 72
Barstowe, Major J.E., 88
Barsum, Dr, 183
Barzan, 25
Barzani, Mulla Mustafa, 35, 42, 47, 190, 191, 227, 228
Barzani, Shaikh Ahmad, 35, 42, 47, 189–90, 192, 227
Barzani family, 190; revolt, 43
Barzinja, Shaikh Mahmud, 32, 35, 36, 43, 46, 47, 84, 99, 107, 110, 111, 112, 117–18, 146, 150, 152, 153, 155, 156, 159–60, 162, 164–9, 227; claim to Kurdish kingship, 70, 166
Barzinja, Shaikh Said, 36
Bashi-Bazooks, 64, 98, 106
Basra, 1, 2, 4, 9, 13–14, 15, 16, 17, 20, 22, 27, 31, 32, 90, 92, 93, 211, 215
Bastura Chai, 79
Bawil, Nuri, 137
Beduin, 206
Beha-ud-Din, Muhammad, 35
Beirut, 3, 210
Bekal Spring, 124
Bell, Gertrude, 5, 9, 10–11, 13, 15, 17, 22, 71, 94, 96
Bill, J.H., 70, 73
Bobery Pack, 162
Bolshevik party, 40
Bond, Captain L.O., 46, 100–1, 107–8, 117, 152
Bonham-Carter, Sir Edgar, 11, 12
Boucher, Captain, 63
Bourdillon, Major B.H. (later Sir), 146, 168
Bowman, 'Beery', 109
Boyce, Lieutenant, 97
Brady, John, 211, 213, 214; detention of, 215–18
Brassneck, master of hounds, 162
British American Tobacco Company (BAT), 49

British and Polish Army Corps, 228
British Yeomanry regiment, 187
Bromilow, Major-General D.G., 50, 62, 72
Burton, Sir Richard, 85

Caccia, Sir Harold, 227
Cairo Conference, 16, 25, 31, 38
Caliphate, 4–5, 8; abolition of, 47
Cameron, Colonel G.G., 152, 157
Cameronians regiment, 119, 120, 123
Campbell, Jock, 120
Capitulations of Ottomans, 19
Carvosso, Captain J.P., 105
Chaldeans, 75, 134, 154, 172, 211
Chaliand, G., 34
Chamchemal, 100, 107, 108, 113, 159, 166, 187, 202
Chapman, Captain A.F., 41, 110, 214
chibbis cultivation, 196
Chittas, 114, 115, 119, 121, 122, 124, 125, 139
Christians, 11, 14, 16, 36, 73, 74, 75, 81, 134, 141, 149, 150, 154, 155, 172, 181, 182; Nestorian, 30, 36 *see also* Chaldeans
Churchill, Winston, 15, 16
Colonial Office, 15, 38; Middle East Department, 38
Committee of Union and Progress (CUP) (Turkey), 36
Congress of Berlin, 36
Cook, Captain J.G., 100, 108
Corner, Dr W., 86, 87, 103, 105
Corner, Mrs, 164
Cornwallis, Sir Kinahan, 21, 40, 41, 48, 51, 52, 95, 96, 141, 144, 185, 211, 213, 225, 226
Council, under Naqib of Basra, 13–14
Cox, Sir Percy Zachariah, 2, 7, 8, 9, 10, 12, 13, 14, 15, 16, 17, 20, 35, 38, 50, 70, 74–5, 80, 84, 94, 96, 127
Crawford, Louise *see* Lyon, Louise *née* Crawford
Curzon, Lord, 12–13, 15, 82

Daghistani, Daud, 198
Damascus, 4, 5; taking of, 5, 6
Daniels, Major A.M., 110
Daud, Haj Pir, 103; deportation of, 101–2
De Bunsen Interdepartmental Committee, 3

Declaration to the Seven, 6
Deir ez-Zor, 7, 12
Deir-al-Zafferan, 182–4
Dera, 132
Desht-i-Harir, 97, 103, 104, 136
Devenish, Lieutenant, 105
Ditchburn, Captain A.H., 194, 203, 211, 224
Diwaniya, 202, 205, 206
Diyarbakir, 37
Dobbin, Brigadier H.T., 119
Dobbs, Sir Henry, 20, 25, 39, 47, 111, 112, 113, 124, 129–40, 146, 147, 155, 168–9
Dobbs, Lady, 168–9
Dohuk, 42, 61–83
Dowson, Sir Ernest, 188, 189
Drower, E.M., 62
Dunkley, George, 208
Duwin Qaleh, 97

Edmonds, Major C.J., 21, 28, 29, 40, 41, 42, 43, 44, 46, 47, 48, 51, 70, 100, 108, 109, 111, 112, 113, 114, 117, 125, 147, 205, 211, 225; *Kurds, Turks and Arabs*, vii, viii, xi, 45
Egypt, 1–2, 5, 10, 11, 18, 28, 30, 36
Enver Pasha, 77
Essex Regiment, 214
Ethiopia, 52, 228; Lyon's attitude to, 52
Exmouth, Viscount of, 215
Exodus Hunt, 162

Faisal, Amir, 5, 6, 7, 12, 15–16, 17–18, 20, 22, 23, 26, 139, 225; as King, 38, 40, 45, 48, 71, 84–106, 107, 166, 176, 178, 184, 187, 203, 206 (deposition of, 12; visit by, 141–53); death of, 24, 199
Faisal the Second, King, 226
al-Fatat organisation, 6
Fattah Pasha, 108
Forbes, Rosita, 185–6
Foreign Office, 11, 12–13, 15, 227
Forward Policy, 167, 168
Fosdick, Captain S., 157
France, 3, 4, 12, 127, 210; Free French, 220, 223
Fraser, Major-General Sir T., 70, 73
Frontier Commission *see* League of Nations, Frontier Commission
Frontiercol, 119
Fuad, King, 86

Gaffuri family, 115
al-Gaud, Nijiris, 79
al-Gaylani, Rashid Ali, 26, 32, 43, 207, 209, 220, 212, 213, 215, 218; revolt, 21, 42, 51
Gaza, 4
Geddes Committee, 18
Gelli Mizurka, 97
Georges-Picot, François, 4
Germany, 2, 22, 32, 206, 207, 210, 212, 214, 215, 216, 220, 221, 222, 227
Ghazi, Prince, 20, 21, 186; as King, 206, 225, 226; death of, 208–9
Girgiri tribe, 73–4
Glubb, Sir John, 214, 224
Godfrey, a civil surveyor, 216
Golden Square, 212, 215
Goldsmith, Major H.A., 99, 107, 108, 109, 110, 204
Gough, Major the Viscount, 106, 107, 108
Gowan, Captain C.H., 41, 62, 80
Grand, Colonel, 222
Graves, P., 15
Greece, 3, 96
Green, Haji, 214
Grobba, Dr, 206, 209
Guides Infantry, 186–7
Gurkhas, 222

H1 Fort, 216
Habbaniyah RAF base, 20, 30, 31–2, 205, 213, 214, 215; attack on, 217, 220
Hafsa Khan, wife of Shaikh Qadir, 110
Haifa, 4, 207
Halabja, 100, 157–8
Haldane, General Sir A., 46
Hama, 5
Hama, a syce, 120
al-Hamada, Ali, 76
Hamawand tribe, 44, 45, 101, 108, 117, 155, 159, 165, 166; revolt of, 36
Hamid, a cook, 117, 126, 127, 136; death of wife, 91
Hamid Beg, 100, 158
Hamidiya Cavalry, 36
Hamilton, A.M., *Road through Kurdistan …*, viii, 132
Hankey, Maurice (later Lord), 3
Hardinge, Lord, 2
Harir, 98–9
Harris, Wing Commander A. (later Sir), 117

Hashemite family, 4, 7, 10, 11, 96
al-Hashimi, Yasin Pasha, 11, 203, 204, 205
Hassech, 199
Hatra, 79
Hawtrey, Air Vice-Marshal J. ('Johnny'), 32
Hay, Major W.R., 33, 44, 45, 87, 88, 89;
  Two Years in Kurdistan ..., viii, 45
Headlam, Colonel, 190, 191, 193
Herki tribe, 89, 113
Highland Light Infantry, 162
Hijri Effendi, 176
Hitler, Adolf, 152, 209
Hogarth, Dr D.G., 5, 71, 94
Holt, Captain Vyvyan, 132, 135, 139, 203–4
Homs, 5
Horrocks, an RAF officer, 115
Household Cavalry, 214
Howaizi, Jemal Agha, 114, 115, 121, 139
Howe, minister in Ethiopia, 228
Howaizi family, 115
Hughes, Colonel 'Spookey', 109
Humphrys, Sir Francis, 20
hunting and fishing, 28, 75, 86, 91, 128, 129, 148, 149, 158, 167, 173, 195, 200, 204, 208
Hurmez, a servant, 191
Husain, Sharif, 4, 5, 8, 10, 15
Hussein Effendi, 67
Hussein, Sayed, 176

Ibn Saud, 10, 15, 24
Ibrahim Jissar, 77–8
India, 4, 14, 29
India Office, 11, 12, 15
Indian Army, vi, 7, 9, 28, 45, 50, 62, 73, 74, 127, 168, 207, 210, 213, 219–28; Lyon retires from, 51
Indian Expeditionary Force (IEF), 2, 3
Iran, 33, 35
Iraq: as British dependency, 1–22; coup and revolution in, 202–18; independence of, and new government in, 12, 14, 20, 21, 29, 84, 92, 125, 204; issues coinage, 192–3; member of League of Nations, 19; summary of history of, 22, 144–53
Iraq Petroleum Company, 83, 170, 200, 201, 208, 213, 215–16
Iraqi Army, 21, 25, 30, 31, 32, 43, 139, 147, 167, 168, 178, 186, 187, 190, 198, 199, 202, 205, 213, 214, 220, 221, 227

Ironside, General, 185
Ishtar, a goddess, 88
Islam, 150, 160–1, 171, 189, 197, 224; land laws, 194 *see also* Shias *and* Sunnis
Ismail Agha (Simko), 81, 110–12
Ismail Beg, 137
Istanbul, 3, 36, 142
Italy, 3, 22, 210, 212
Izady, M.R., 33, 34

Jabal Hamrin, 195, 196
Jabbari tribe, 45
Jackson, Brigadier Sadleir, 103, 106
Jafar Pasha, 187–8, 190–1, 203, 205, 206
Jardine, R.F., 68, 120
Jemil, Haji, 172
Jerusalem, 3, 4, 6
Jewad Pasha, General, 146, 148
Jews, 11, 14, 23, 36, 75, 141, 149, 150, 194, 202, 206, 207, 208
Jibbur tribe, 76, 107, 173
Jissar, Ibrahim, 120
Johnston, Squadron Leader, 214
Jones, Dr Ridge, 125
Jones-Williams, John, 117
Joyce, Colonel P., 95, 96

Kakil Agha, Saiyid, 114
Karagulla, Ibrahim, 78
Kedourie, Elie, 5, 6, 22–3, 26
Kemal, Mustafa (Ataturk), 16, 37, 38, 44, 82, 93, 96, 180, 184
Kerim Khan, 131
Kerim-i Fattah Beg, 45, 108, 117, 152, 165
Kermanshah, 224
Kerr, Sir Archibald Clark, 203
Khadduri, M., 25
Khalhani tribe, 89
Khanaqah, Saiyid Ahmad-i, 35, 172, 220
Khanaqin, 42, 80, 219, 221
Khedive of Egypt, 1, 2
Khidier Beg, 144
Khor Pasha, 130–1
Khorsabad, 77
Khoshnaw tribe, 44, 45, 104, 150
Khurshid Agha, 112
Kidher, son of Haji Pir Daud, 103
Kidher Ilyas monastery, 77
Kifri, 42, 87
Kinaru, 155, 156
Kinch, Alec, 139–40

Index · 235

King's Own Regiment, 155
King, Bob, 49
King, Percy, 155, 156, 164, 178, 185
King, Vera *see* Lyon, Vera *née* King
Kipling, Rudyard, 'Ballad of Bodathone', 108
Kirkuk, 4, 26, 41, 42, 52, 70, 86, 87, 89, 90, 95, 106, 107–28, 139, 141, 146, 147, 152, 154, 159, 161, 164, 165, 170–7, 188, 199, 200, 202–18, 219, 222; description of, 175–6; land settlement in, 194–201; notable families in, 172
Kitchener, Lord, 3, 4, 5
Kitching, G.C., 41
Koi Sanjaq, 44, 45, 46, 89, 108, 109, 110, 113–16, 121, 123, 138–9
Kramers, J.H., 147
Krupp Harvesters, 207
Kurdistan, 33, 34, 36, 39, 43, 45, 46, 85, 131, 159; road through, 152
Kurds, vii, 10, 16, 22, 23, 25, 63, 68, 70, 73, 80, 81, 83, 85, 89, 93, 95, 96, 99, 114, 130, 131, 173, 226, 228; and British over-rule, 33–48; as Muslims, 36; autonomy for, 40; dialects of, 34; dress of, 226; fragmentation of, 39; incident with armed tribesman, 65–6; language of, 39, 41, 150, 159, 176, 226; nationalism among, 42, 95, 97; origins of, 33–4; possibility of nation, 37; rebellion put down, 150; religion of, 39; rights of, 46; state of, 16
Kut-al-Amara, 3; land settlement in, 194–201; siege of, 30, 50, 61–2, 77, 93

land register of Iraq, 188–9
land settlement, 48, 189, 194–201, 203
Land Settlement Commission, 208
Latif, Shaikh, 167
Laurence, Lieutenant Colonel 'Stuffy', 156–7, 158
Lausanne, Treaty of, 38
Lawlor, Private W., 73
Lawrence, T.E., 5, 7, 8, 15, 22, 28, 63, 71, 73, 94, 178, 184; *The Seven Pillars of Wisdom*, 8
Layard, A.H., 75
Leachman, Colonel G.E., 9, 50, 61–7, 70, 178; murder of, 74
League of Nations, 1, 2, 6, 13, 16, 18, 19, 20, 23, 29, 37, 40, 42, 46, 84, 145, 150–1;

Frontier Commission, xi, 30, 47, 141–53, 178–93
Lebanon, 3, 210
Lees, Captain George, 100
Leinsters regiment, 50
Levies, 14, 21, 25, 29–30, 46, 90, 103, 106, 109, 113, 114, 115, 116, 119, 159, 167, 178, 222; Arab, 16, 27, 29, 62; Assyrian, 16, 29, 30, 31, 83, 103, 105, 111, 112, 124, 143, 152, 154–5, 156, 157, 164, 165, 189–90, 214; Kurdish, 29, 125
Levies Brigade, 119, 122, 123–4
Lewis, a young officer, 69
Littledale, Captain Charles, 29, 46, 68, 89, 90, 98, 102, 103, 108, 110, 111, 114, 116, 117, 120, 125, 126, 133, 135, 137, 141, 147, 148
Lloyd George, David, 82, 95
Lloyd, Captain H.I., 164
Lloyd, Mrs, 164
locusts, 173 5
Longrigg, S.H., 8, 23–4, 86, 87; *Iraq, 1900–1950 ...*, xi
Lyon, Wallace: as Administrative Inspector, 19, 26; as British Consul in Harar, 51, 228; as Land Settlement Officer, vii, 21, 29, 48, 189, 194–201; as political advisor, 43, 219–28; attitude to Arabs, 51; birth of, 49; buys house in Cheltenham, 207; career of, 48–52; detention of, 215–18; dies of cancer, 52; education of, 49; linguistic abilities of, 51; offer of contract with Iraqi government, 128; ordered to Sandhurst, 50; recruited as APO, 7; service in Indian Army, 51, 127–8; works for BAT, 50, 61
Lyon, Gordon, 49, 50
Lyon, Louise *née* Crawford, 49
Lyon, Revd Paul, 48–9
Lyon, Roy, 49
Lyon, Sheila, vii, 170
Lyon, Vera *née* King, 164, 167, 169, 189

Macdonald, Captain H., 68
Macdougal, Dr, 62
Mackmur, 89
Madras Sappers and Miners, 122
Mahabad, Kurdish Republic of, 47
Majid Beg, 166
Makant, Captain R.K., 46, 108, 117, 152

Maksoot, an Assyrian commander, 157
malaria, 221–12
Malay States, 1
Mamind Agha, 122
Mandates Committee, 41–2
Mandates: award of, 11–12; British, viii, 1, 2, 8, 13, 18, 26, 84, 152 (end of, 20, 178–93, 200); French, 71
Mansergh, Captain, 190
Mardin, 75, 178–82
Marshall, Major C.C., 86–7, 95, 106, 113
Marshall, General Sir W.R., 145
Marshimun, 30, 80–2, 110
Marshimun, Daud, 225
Mason, Monk, 209
Maxwell, Squadron Leader, 110
McDowall, D., 33, 42
McGregor, Flight Lieutenant, 155–6
McLeod, Dr, 179
McMahon, Sir Henry, 5
Medes, 33
Mejid Agha, 77, 97, 111, 132, 133
Mejid Effendi of Kirkuk, 172
Mesopotamia, vii, 1, 2, 3, 4, 5, 6, 7, 8, 9, 10, 11, 12, 14, 15, 37, 50, 81, 84, 86, 145
al-Midfai, Jamil, 73, 184, 185, 203, 206, 207
Midhat Pasha, 188
Milabel, a slave, 72
Miller, Captain A.F. 'Pa', 86, 87, 106, 126, 139
Minas Effendi, 155
Minchin, Captain H.C., 50, 62, 64
Mirani Abdul Qadir Beg *see* Qadir Beg, Mirani Abdul
Mohammed, a servant, 186, 191
Mohammed, the Prophet, 99
Mohammed Ali, mayor of Ruwandiz, 137–8
Montagu, Edwin, 12, 15
Morocco, 10
Mosul, 4, 7, 8, 9, 12, 22, 24, 27, 28, 30, 31, 32, 36, 37, 38, 41, 44, 47, 50, 61–83, 87, 89, 90, 92, 93, 96, 98, 101, 106, 107, 117, 119, 126, 131, 141, 145, 147, 177, 178–93, 212, 219; arrival of, Frontier Commission in, 146; awarded to Iraq, 20, 29, 40, 46, 47, 102; consulate attacked, 209; Great Mosque, 211; occupation of, 3; prisons in, 63
Mudros, Armistice of, 3, 44

Muhammad, Saiyid, 45
Muhsin Beg, 40
Mulla Effendi, 147
Mullroy, a police officer, 209

Nadhim Pasha, General Husain, 188
Naftchizada family, 172
Nairn brothers, 153
Nalder, Major L.F., 62, 67, 68, 73, 84, 101
Naqib of Baghdad, Saiyid Abdur Rahman, 15, 17, 38, 92, 96
Naqshbandi order, 35
Nazim Beg, Umar, 146, 148, 170–1
Newton, Sir Basil, 213
Nicholson, Dr, 78–9
Noah, Shaikh, 76
Noel, Major E.W., 38, 111, 112, 113
Northcliffe, Lord, 67
Northern Army, 6
Nuri Bawil, Shaikh, 65–7, 137 n.4

Obeid tribe, 107, 120, 173
Obeidulla, Shaikh, 98, 101, 103
O'Connor, Captain, 97, 104
Ottoman Empire, vii, 2, 3, 4, 5, 6, 7, 14, 19, 22, 23, 24, 27, 29, 34, 35–6, 37, 44, 81, 142 *see also* Turkey and Turks

al-Pachachi, Muzahim, 194
Paiforce, vii, 227
Palestine, 6, 8, 202
Pan-Arabism, 23
Paulis, Colonel A., 145, 147
Pearson, Captain A.C., 62, 64–5
Pellew, Edward (later Lord Exmouth), 49
Pelly, Flight Lieutenant, 190
Penjwin, 164, 224; garrison, 164–5
Persia, 227
Petros, Agha, 81
Pett, 'Crasher', 109
Philby, H. St John B., 17, 85, 94–5, 141, 225
Piramerd, Haji, 176
Pizhdar tribe, 44, 109, 110, 120, 125, 153, 156, 167–8, 227
Polish Army, 221
Popham Panel, 114
Pover, Major W.A., 142–3, 152
Pritchard, Judge, 86, 126–7, 214, 228
Pritchard, Major *see* Pritchard, Judge

Qaderok, a sweeper, 91
Qadir, Shaikh, 110, 162
Qadir Beg, Mirani Abdul, 133, 134, 135, 150, 151
Qadir al-Gilani, Shaikh Abdul, 35
Qadiri order, 35, 36
Qala, in Arbil, 88
Qala Diza, 46
Qalian, Bishop, 77
Qirdar family, 172
Quinan, General E.P., 215

Rahman, Saiyid Abdur, 35
Rahman Beg, Abdul, 104
Ramzi Beg, 46, 222
Ranicol, 46, 114, 122
Ranya, 44, 45, 46, 100, 121–3, 159
Raoul, an Assyrian commander, 157
Raqib, Shaikh, 98, 101, 103
Rashid Ali *see* al-Gaylani, Rashid Ali
Rashid Beg, Haji, 69, 135
Redding, Captain John, 178, 186–7
Reza Shah, 220
Richard Coeur de Lion, 130
Rida Beg, Ali, 187–8, 205
Riscoe, an Armenian dragoman, 67
Robinson, General Rowan 'Row Row', 190, 191
Rowlash, 113
Royal Air Force (RAF), 16, 21, 25, 27, 30–1, 42, 44, 46–7, 77, 83, 98–9, 100, 110, 113, 114, 115, 117–19, 123, 125, 135, 151, 152, 155, 161, 162, 167, 178, 185, 191, 192, 205, 207, 209, 211, 213, 214, 215, 227 *see also* Habbaniyah air base
Royal Army Medical Corps (RAMC), 69
Rupert, the pup, 85, 86, 125
Russia, 2, 3, 4, 30, 37, 40, 80, 81, 87, 92, 97, 110, 123, 136, 159, 221
Ruwandiz, viii, 44, 45, 47, 80, 89, 97, 98, 101, 106, 108, 111, 114, 120, 123, 124, 130, 131, 176, 190, 193, 221
Ruwandiz Gorge, 122–3, 124, 143, 152

Sabaeans, 73
Saber, son of Kerim-i Fattah Beg, 165
Said Beg, 73, 78–9
Said, Shaikh, 150, 166
as-Said, Nuri Pasha, 25, 41, 96, 187–8, 203, 204, 205, 210, 212, 215
Salah-ad-Din, 97, 130, 226

Salmon, Captain H., 86
Salmond, Sir John, 47, 113, 116, 118, 119
Samuel, Sir Herbert, 15
San Remo Conference, 6, 8, 9, 37
Scott, Captain K.R., 62, 64, 67, 70
Semak Sherin, 114
Sèvres, Treaty of, 16, 37, 38, 159
Shaiba base of RAF, 31
Shaikh Said rising, 39
Shammar Arabs, 131
Shammar tribe, 131, 179, 196, 224; Shammar Toga, 196, 197, 199
Shaqlawa, 103, 133–4, 138, 150
Shar Bazher district of Sulaimani, 155
Sharif of Mecca, 4
Sharqat, 119, 132
Shefiq, Colonel Ali (Oz Demir), 44, 46, 99, 101, 107
Shepherd, Charles, 102
Shero, Hamo, 61
Shias, 8, 10, 14, 15, 22, 23, 24, 25, 34, 38, 85, 161, 202, 203; rising of, 25
Shikak tribe, 81
Shillash, Shaikh, 76
Sidqi, General Bakr, 25, 205, 206
Sikhs, 109, 121–2, 125; reception for, 90
Silverfarb, D., 32
Simayl, 199
Sisawa, 103, 104
Sisayl, 30
Soane, Major E.B. (later Ghulam Hussein), 70, 85, 99; *Through Kurdistan in Disguise*, 85
Sowar Agha, 122
Spears, General, 224
Stalingrad, 222
Stark, Freya, 32, 185
Storrs, Sir Ronald, 5
Stuart, Lieutenant B., 7, 72
Sudan, 7, 28
Sufi brotherhoods, 35
Sulaimani, 37, 38, 39, 41, 42, 43, 69, 70, 84, 93, 95, 96, 99, 101, 107, 108, 110, 111, 112, 114, 125, 139, 141, 146, 147, 152, 153, 155, 157, 158, 160, 164–9, 170, 177, 178, 202, 224, bombing of, 117–18; under Iraqi rule, 154–63
Sulaimani Vale hunt, 162
Sulayman, Hikmat, 206
Sunnis, 8, 10, 15, 22, 34, 36, 38, 85
Surchi tribe, 44, 45

Surma, Lady, 82
Surridge, Lieutenant R.A., 105
as-Suwaydi, Naji, 41
Sykes, Sir Mark, 3–4, 5
Sykes-Picot Agreement, 4, 5, 6, 37
Syria, 3, 4, 5, 6, 7, 9, 12, 14, 30, 33, 36, 45, 71, 159, 210, 220, 227

Taha, Saiyid, 35, 111–13, 124, 137
Tai, Hatim, 177
Tal Afar, 7, 72, 73; rising, 184
Talabani tribe, 172
Talib Pasha, Saiyid, Naqib of Basra, 13–14, 15, 17, 93, 94
Tall Kayf, 73–4, 211
Taqtaq, 139
Tarbush, M.A., 24, 25
Tauz Malik, 182
taxation, 8, 11, 45, 47, 63, 152, 155, 160, 168, 173, 196, 207
Teagle, Flying Officer, 99
Teleki, Count Paul, 145, 147–52
Tigris river, 195–6
Tillett, Ben, 178
Timur-i Lang, 75, 87
Toynbee, Arnold, 37
Trans-Jordan, 7, 15
Troop, Sapper, 68
Tunisia, 10
Turkomans, 75, 107, 173
Turks and Turkey, viii, 3, 5, 11, 12, 14, 16, 19, 28, 35, 38, 39, 44, 46, 47, 62, 63, 68, 69, 75, 77, 80, 81, 82, 87, 88, 92, 96, 101, 110, 111, 113, 123, 124, 135–6, 141, 145, 146, 148, 149, 150, 159, 166, 176, 180, 181, 188, 203, 206, 227; armistice with, 64; attitude to Arabs, 136; attitude to Christians, 154; campaign against, 107–28; peace treaty with, 102 *see also* Ottoman Empire

al-Umeri, Umjad, 67
Usman, Ahmad Pasha, 85, 100, 157
Usman, Ahmad Effendi, 89, 101, 111, 112, 141, 143, 147, 148, 149, 154

vaccination, 179
Versailles Peace Treaty, 74
Vincent, Brigadier B., 119, 120

Wahab, Abdul, 175
Walker, Captain F.R., 71
Walker, Sergeant A., 73
War Office, 15
White, Captain S., 125, 126
Wigram, Dr, *The Cradle of Mankind*, 80
Wilcox, Sir William, 71
Wild, Major, 106
Wilkins, Captain J.F., 185
Willey, Captain D., 68
Williamson, Dr H., 89, 90
Wilson, Sir A.T., 7, 8, 9, 10, 11, 12, 13, 14, 23, 26, 28, 37, 70, 84, 92; *Mesopotamia 1917–1920*, 13
Wingate, Sir Reginald, 5
Winstone, H.F.V., 17
Wirsén, E. af, 145, 147
Wynter, Colonel, 62

Ya'qubizada family, 172
Yahia Effendi, 156
al-Yawir, Shaikh Ajil, 76, 179
Yezidis, 34, 61, 73, 74, 75, 78, 182; rising of, 25
Yorkshire Regiment, 119, 120, 121, 122, 123, 124
Young, Sir Hilton (later Lord Kennet), 186

Zaid, Amir, 141
Zakho, 42, 65
Zarari tribe, 130